love, death & photo synthesis

Bela Koe-Krompecher

"Things just seem to go away
when you rob everything you see,
Things just seem to throw away,
is there anything to breath in this dead world,
When you're gone,
anything will grow in your place"

JERRY WICK
"LOVE, DEATH & PHOTOSYNTHESIS"

"what's wrong with me/
why am I so moody/
what happened to my family, oh no/
how did I get unhappy/
la-la-la la-la-la/
I'm dying here/
hey look at me I'm dying here"

JENNY MAE
"HO BITCH"

Published by Don Giovanni Records
Printed in the United States of America
First Printing 2021
Edited by Lisa Carver & Cynthia Santiglia
Photos: Jay Brown unless otherwise noted
Book layout by Henry Owings
ISBN: 978-0-9891963-8-3

for:
Saskia & Bruno

praise for love, death & photosynthesis

"*Love, Death, & Photosynthesis* is such a generous text. One that offers both a timeline and a soundtrack of living. One that populates a world with people who could easily be your kind of people, immersed in days and nights that could be your days and nights. I loved this book for how it acts as both an intimate profile of a time and era, and also a mirror through which a reader can see their own history, their own affections, and their own music."

HANIF ABDURRAQIB
AUTHOR OF *THEY CAN'T KILL US UNTIL THEY KILL US*

"Bela Koe-Krompecher's *Love, Death & Photosynthesis* is a remarkable book: an exploration of indie rock, a memoir of drinking and, then, not drinking, and ode to Columbus, Ohio, and most of all an elegy for a handful of musicians—particularly the haunting singer Jenny Mae—who lived hard and bled art and died too young. Koe-Krompecher, a co-founder of Anyway Records, is one of the spindles that keeps the indie-rock world spinning and *Love, Death and Photosynthesis* is a wild, real tender combination of Patti Smith's *Just Kids* and Michael Azzerrad's *Our Band Could Be Your Life*. Hell, *Love, Death & Photosynthesis* isn't even a book—it's a juke box, the wonderous kind that you find in a dive bar and that seems, suddenly, to contain every song you need to hear."

DANIEL A. HOYT
AUTHOR OF *THIS BOOK IS NOT FOR YOU*

"I'm guessing I met both Bela and Jerry on Mudhoney's first stop in Columbus circa 1988, but it's a bit murky. Whenever, it was an instant kinship based on music, records, & booze. Fellow Travelers. I know these people, but if I didn't, I'd feel like I did after reading this. A beautifully vivid, heartbreaking tale of friendships cut far too short."

STEVE TURNER, MUDHONEY

"In *Love, Death & Photosynthesis*, Bela Koe-Krompecher gives us a memoir that arrests, entrances, repulses even as it fascinates, pulls the reader close enough to whisper in the ear, holds at arm's length to assess life's ruins, and explores the sanctuaries we build within and around that wreckage. It's a book born of fresh young Ohio corn fields and autumnal brass marching bands, just as it inhabits barrooms dank with despair yet illuminated by the melodic rings and howling squalls of music—the ever-present, blessed music—that holds it all together. Crushingly sad and defiantly hopeful, it's a paean to Jenny Mae, it's *On the Road* for the Rust Belt, it's a desperate diary of struggling for equilibrium in a wildly spinning life, a broken-bottle bare-knuckled account of the '90s Columbus music scene, and a sober love letter to hope and forgiveness. There's real blood and tears and, yes, laughter in these pages."

MATTHEW CUTTER
AUTHOR OF *CLOSER YOU ARE: THE STORY OF ROBERT POLLARD AND GUIDED BY VOICES*

"Bela so beautifully writes about the connection between love, identity and an underground music scene—if music's been the way you've made sense of the world this book will move you to tears."

MATT SWEENEY
VICE/GUITAR MOVES

"I never sat with Jerry Wick—on a double-date and drunk—through a Mel Brooks double-feature, violently laughing as our disgusted dates dashed out the theater doors. I never woke any morning to find a homeless Jenny Mae sleeping in my car's front seat, torn candy wrapper and broken thorns stuck to her face. Nor did I sit with her as she played her haunting songs on the organ in her parents' basement or have a jailhouse conversation in which she, in a too-rare lucid moment, explained the reasons for her addictions. In fact, I never met either of those underground musicians before they died young due to dissimilar, yet equally sad, circumstances. But I feel like I knew them. Bela Koe-Krompecher's music-memorized and booze-drenched memoir, *Love, Death & Photosynthesis*, introduced us. Then we became friends."

JEFF BURLINGAME
NAACP IMAGE AWARD-WINNING AUTHOR OF
KURT COBAIN: "OH WELL, WHATEVER, NEVERMIND"

"In his candid decades-spanning memoir, Koe-Krompecher's journey through the grayness of Ohio gets entangled in music, love, mental illness, loss, addiction, and death—but he leaves a sliver of hope. It's a tribute to his gone-too-soon friends and musicians Jenny Mae—who "burned brighter than the surface of Mercury" —and Jerry Wick—who "could light up a room with his humor, wit, and songs"—but it's also an insight into the music industry, a hard-knocks upbringing, and battling addiction, sometimes told with hilarious anecdotes. Koe-Krompecher's non-fiction dirty realism is the stuff Raymond Carver would've written if he had lived in Ohio. In the end, it's music—and friendship—that saves us"

GARIN PIRNIA
AUTHOR OF *REBELS AND UNDERDOGS: THE STORY OF OHIO ROCK AND ROLL*

for his three graphic comics:

"Bela Koe-Krompecher delivers a touching eulogy for two doomed, talented friends. The helplessness and frustration he feels witnessing their spiral is heartbreaking, but also strangely uplifting. Bela never gives up on his friends, even as he knows full well that he can't save them. Wonderfully drawn by Andy Bennett, the reader can smell the dust stirring off the sidewalks of Columbus' High St. and feel the sweat of the jostling crowds in the legendary Stache's. The music of Jenny and Jerry lives on and in "Jenny Mae 'n Jerry Wick" Bela gives us the hearts, and the minds, and the tragic flaws, of the people behind the notes."

DERF
EISNER AWARD WINNING CREATOR OF
MY FRIEND DAHMER, TRASHED, PUNK ROCK & TRAILER PARKS
ON JENNY MAE N JERRY WICK GRAPHIC COMIC

"...like reading a chapter from a Jeffrey Brown book or something that Nate Powell or John Porcellino might share with their fans."

ROB McMONIGAL, PANEL PLATTERS
ON "DO YOU REMEMBER ROCK AND RECORD STORES" GRAPHIC COMIC

"fantastic"

TERMINAL BOREDOM
ON "DO YOU REMEMBER ROCK AND ROLL RECORD STORES" GRAPHIC COMIC

"a fascinating look at a true American original"

BLURT
ON "NEGOTIATE NOTHING: JIM SHEPARD" GRAPHIC COMIC

"..like discovering *American Splendor* again"

STATIKNOIZE
ON "JENNY MAE 'N JERRY WICK"

1988.

Jenny didn't have a driver's license. She assumed her main function as a passenger was to count how many words she could push out of her mouth by the mile markers, every word trying to out-funny the word prior. At other times, depending on whether the car had a cassette deck, she would turn on the AM radio and roll the dial between oldies from the '50s, old country, and the soft pop of Bread, Anne Murray, and Neil Sedaka. Everything was an opportunity to crack a joke or to make a skit, turning the real into the surreal.

Driving west on I-70, South Vienna, Ohio was only 40 miles away, but it might as well have been on the other side of the world from "cosmopolitan" Columbus in terms of attitude and lifestyle.

The halfway point was just outside London, a traditional Ohio small town, with a feed store downtown and small shops strewn with banners supporting the local football team, the Red Raiders. A McDonalds lay right off the exit ramp, and Jenny would insist on stopping for a Quarter Pounder with cheese, which she would say through clenched teeth so the "cheese" was drawn out in a spittle-filled lisp.

"Bela, stop I'm hungry," she exclaimed from across the large vinyl front seat.

"We're almost to your mom's house, just wait. I don't have any money."

"Yes, you do, you have 11 dollars in your front pocket, I checked before we left."

"Jenny that is all the money I have, my account is overdrawn, and I don't get paid until next week. Plus, we'll have to get five bucks in gas to get back home." I was annoyed; this happened every trip. Every bill we paid was late and checks bounced weekly. Just purchasing stamps was a stressful endeavor.

"I don't care, I want a Quarter Pounder with cheeeeeeese pleeeease," the lisp even more drawn out for cute effect, dotting the windshield with small pellets of spit.

"Goddamnit, Jenny, for Christ's sake. We. Have. No. Money. And we need to buy beer on the way home. So, no. Forget it." I shook my head in the dark.

"I'll give you a blowjob."

I quickly cut over two lanes and pulled off onto the exit ramp.

As we pulled into the drive-through, Jenny said, "Don't worry— I can get my mom to give us $20 when we leave—so order what you want, as long as it's not over 11 dollars." I looked over at her. We both knew what I would do as I stopped at the small speaker to place our order. In a drawn out redneck voice I shouted, "Yeah, yeah. We'll take a Quarter Pounder with Cheese, err a…hold on." I pulled my head away. "Shut up you fucking brats! You ain't gettin' nothin', you little shits! This here's for your mom and me!" The "me" curved down at the end, almost a burpy-bark.

Jenny chimed in, looking into a backseat that contained nothing but an Army coat, "Listen to your dad, if y'all weren't such godawful kids, maybe you'd get a Happy Meal to split but yer just brats and I can't wait till we get home to teach you some lessons."

Poking my head back outside and with a much calmer voice: "Sorry 'bout that, these kids are ungrateful and just plain rude sometimes. So, yeah, a Quarter Pounder with cheese…shit. Hold on." To the empty back seat: "Ah said, you need to shut yer traps, you got your cereal at home AND yer bag of Cheez-Its, I don't wanna have to come back there!"

Jenny removed one of her shoes and swatted the seat. "That's it! You little shits, you ain't gettin' nothin'! And if you cry it'll be your dad doing the swatting!"

My turn. "Sorry 'bout that ma'am, so me and the missus will have the Quarter Pounder with cheese, a large fry, and I really like them tiny pieces of chicken y'all got, the nuggets—" turning again into the nothing— "*No!* You ain't gettin' my nuggets, I'm hungry. Your Dad is hungry and tired from driving you little shits everywhere. And I think we'll take a large Coke. Thank you."

A crackly voice spoke from the speakers: "Is that everything? A Quarter Pounder with cheese, a large fry, a large Chicken McNuggets and a large Coke? Do you want anything for the kids?"

"Does it sound like they deserve it? No, they are just fine with their cereal."

"OK, please pull around."

We both laughed as we pulled up to the window, tickled by our own stupidity, and five concerned faces of McDonald's workers appeared to see who would treat their children this poorly. It was dark, so they couldn't see in the back seat. Two large bags were extended out the window.

"We put some extra food in for the kids," a short-haired woman our age said as she tried to peer around us.

"Aw, you didn't have to do that."

Jenny spoke to the emptiness behind us: "You hear that kids, this nice lady gave you some food even though you don't deserve it."

"Jenny, is that you?" the worker asked. "Jenny Leffel?"

There was a long hesitation in the car, Jenny looked at me and I looked at her.

"Bela? Jenny?"

Leaning across my lap, Jenny smiled up into the window. "Oh hey, Theresa! How are you and the kids?" She spoke as if nothing had just happened. Theresa Henry had graduated with us. She'd been pregnant our senior year, and had another kid a year or so later.

A billow of laughter came from inside the McDonald's. "Oh geez, you guys are fucking hilarious! We thought you were just the meanest parents." She looked behind her. "This is Jenny Mae Leffel, I went to high school with her—they don't even have kids!" More laughter. "Well, you guys have a ton of food to eat now. My kids are good, are you still up at Ohio State?"

With a French fry hanging out of her mouth Jenny replied, "Yup, love it. Give my best to your mom. See ya! Come on, Bela, let's go."

1991.

When the cap of the aspirin bottle snapped off into my left hand, the motion to my mouth was immediate, there was no thought behind it. The decision to commit suicide was as natural as breathing. The white tablets tumbled down my throat like unchewed Chiclets. Or concert-goers rushing a Who show. My throat welcomed them. "You finally arrived, let's open the gate for you." *This was too easy* was my first thought, followed by a decidedly uneasy feeling of doom. Next came regret, the worst regret there could possibly be, then disbelief, and finally fear. Terror. The scales had been tipped the other way in a matter of seconds. I didn't want to die. I drove to the hospital.

After charcoal and tubes had gotten the death out of my belly, a young psychiatrist determined that despite swallowing at least 50 tablets of aspirin just hours earlier there was no more concern that I was suicidal. No one I called could come get me, not even my mom. There was nothing for me to do but get back in my compact car and drive home, tears streaming down my face.

Throughout the years the thoughts of suicide would ebb and flow, sometimes rising so quietly and subtly, sneaking up into my brain and smiling softly its deathly grin whispering, "hello, it's me, did you think I left?" There were visions of wading into the sea,

love, death & photosynthesis

drifting out into the deep waters and pulling the waves over my head like a blanket. Security comes from the darkest of places, some find it in the very things that kill them, a perverse existential dance to the end, who is fooling who? Solace would be hard to find if the thing that is trying to kill you is your mind, so the trick is in finding how to quiet the mind. There would be women and expectations, and the inevitable failure of disappointment that nudged itself between the relationships, a thorny invisible cloud that drifts in and slays the very thing that tethers someone to someone else, "Cut it at the root," it mutters, as the relationship comes crashing down. "See, I told you," speaks the voice.

Jerry Wick came by that night and took me to the Dube where we drank vast amounts of coffee and he introduced me to wet fries (covered in gravy). "I don't know what the fuck to do, I'm fucking empty." I stared at the fries on my plate, Jerry reached over, picked it up, dipped it in a bowl of brown gravy and popped it in his mouth.

"You know what cures everything? Especially getting over stupid girls?" He grabbed another fry while fumbling to light a cigarette at the same time.

The pain in my chest felt like cement. "Tell me, what?"

Blowing a stream of smoke from the side of his mouth, his toothy grin making him look like a cross between a young Charles Brolin and Snagglepuss, he said, "Masturbate. It solves everything. It's easy to clean up, and it won't break your heart."

The tears I'd been choking back turned to laughter. "You know how old I was when I got glasses? Fifteen. You think there is a coincidence?"

Jerry guffawed. "One time my mom caught me jerking off and she threw me in the bathtub and yelled, 'Maybe that will cool you off, buster!'"

"She called you buster?" I swiped a fry in the gravy.

"Yeah. She never cursed. The devil's language and all that."

I decided that I was not going to drink again. Jerry gave me advice on women, mostly to stay away. I was still a fragile man. Jerry nursed me through this time. Almost nightly, we bounced between the Dube and Stache's; we watched Scrawl, the Afghan Whigs, or Tar. An endless parade of bands traveling across the stages of our lives. We told each other our incredible bizarre stories and we developed best-friends rapport. Soon we were finishing each other's sentences, creating our own inside jokes.

We played records and went dancing. Mostly to the largest gay bar in town called The Garage, known to regulars as The Gay-Rage, where the music on off nights leaned to bouncy Anglophile fare such as the Pet Shop Boys, the Cure, New Order and The Smiths with the token Madonna track thrown in. Jerry and I fused over loving to shake our skinny, almost transparent asses. Music was escape for us, a way to close out the world and tie our emotions to something tangible yet ethereal, a passage to our inner selves that still managed to encapsulate the whole world. Combining the music with movement heightened it. There were rumors that Jerry and I had become lovers, which we only were happy to fuel by publicly kissing each other at Larry's or Stache's. But this was just for show; we got a kick out of other people's assumptions. We thought we were about as punk as anyone could be.

Jerry was quite a good dancer, one who would let his emotions empty out of his body, his pointy teeth poking out of a grin cast towards the heavens, beer in one hand and the other raised high above his head. I loved to dance too, ever since I was 15 and saw Michael Stipe doing the crooked-shimmy in a trench coat at Wittenberg University, I was directly in front of the stage and was mesmerized. Michael Stipe was the first man, besides my crazy Latin-raised uncles, who I saw let himself go dancing. I figured if he can do it, so can I.

At live shows, so many of our friends in the underground rock scene were too self-conscious to dance and would stand in the back, hands in pockets, hesitating. Jerry and I would be in front of the stage at any show. The opportunity to be transported was too precious to waste. We could talk for hours about the historical significance of Pere Ubu or such up and coming bands as Pavement, Bikini Kill or Urge Overkill. It may have looked silly, but it was of great importance to us. Jerry's adolescence was prohibited by the religious fanaticism of his family, who were blue-collar born-again Christians and did not understand their boys' fascination with punk rock and Kiss. He was completely estranged from his family. He had a younger brother but spoke little of him, just, "he is just like my parents." For me the confines of living in a very rural small town during my high school years was excruciating. Heavy metal and Hank Williams Jr. were the only types of music most kids listened to, thus one way to bond was eliminated by a chasm between the macho music they listened to and the kind that was saving me on a daily basis. Both Jerry and I had longed for a way out of the boredom of provincial living—yearning shot through us like a geyser—and music was it.

We were full of self-doubt, which was hidden under a barrage of vocal opinions on music, art, lifestyle, politics, and just about anything else we were confronted with. With little resources to support our own emotional wellbeing and a headful of anxiety when it came to relationships and our own values, music was *the* shelter in our lives, and we took umbrage with anybody who wasn't as enthusiastic or respectful as we were. This may have come off as snobbishness or being overly serious, but we were in essence defending the love of our lives.

If there was a line that people adhered to, we often crossed it, Jerry much more often than I ever did. For Jerry, thumbing his nose was an art form. If you had a balloon Jerry would be obliged to pop it, sometimes with hilarious results, at other times it would go over like a shriveled penis. It is a testament to his charm that he didn't get beat up on a weekly basis. There were times we would go to certain clubs like the Newport, or restaurants where we thought the food was too expensive, and we would go to the restroom together. We would both stand next to each other at the urinals and pull our britches all the way down to the floor so our little bare asses stared out to the waiting masses. Five-year-old pissing style. We would be pelted with a variety of insults such as "you fucking fags" or "grow up you fucking idiots" which just made us cackle louder. Men in suits would shake their heads at us no doubt wondering just what the hell we were doing in a place that was a step below a dress code. We would laugh on the way out and saddle up to the bar, next to our dates who always got a kick out of our adolescent behavior. The angry businessmen no doubt wondering how such beautiful women were in the company of such idiots. We laughed louder, longer, and more heartfelt than anybody in those crusty establishments and we took a certain amount of pride in this.

1998.

Jenny spoke with an almost southern accent; her voice was hard—not just from childhood experience. Western Ohio is hard. A struggle for survival, where scuffed knuckles and the worry of the next paycheck are ever present, and eviction or foreclosure is just around the corner. Though she spoke indelicately, her knowledge of language revealed itself in written form. She was a lovely writer—both in her crafting of short stories and her actual handwriting. In song, Jenny's voice slid from a simple, innocent delivery to a husky pillow drenched in Maker's Mark. Then came the pain she let slip out in an ethereal gasp. Hers was a voice that fit nowhere; she lacked the polish that provided so many female artists an avenue of acceptability in the man's world of indie-rock. She was too pop and sing-song-y to attract the punks, yet too bold and outrageous in personality for those who wanted their female singers to provide solace—to not only sound pretty but to be pretty, to act pretty. On her first tour t-shirt, instead of cities she wanted to list her sexual conquests on the back, with a nod to the Columbus nightclub Stache's motto, "Stache's... I Been There." She wanted to write, "Jenny Mae, You Been There," followed by the name of the lover and the date she slept with him or her. Laughing as she described the shirt, "actually, now that I think of it-it would have to be tour gown to get all the men on there."

She fit not in a sexist and classist world.

Jenny was confounding as an artist, at times brilliant and at others a pathetic mess who would rather smash her equipment and drink beer than practice or play shows out of town. It was as if every time something was planned for her, a collective breath would be held and more times than not the breath would be blown towards the floor as a small community would slowly shake their heads. She sang without misgivings. At times, depending on her alcohol intake, she could go tragically off-key, not unlike Guided by Voices' Bob Pollard, while at other times, her breathy voice would crush, as evident on her song "Ho Bitch," which is one of the greatest songs on living with mental illness that I have ever heard. Which would it be tonight?

The Middle East nightclub, Boston. The club is sold out, it is packed. We get there midafternoon. The night before Jenny played in New York with Neko Case and Amy Rigby in a small club that was overstuffed from front to back. Jenny was featured in *Time-Out New York* and *Paper,* both carrying color photos of her and highlighting the show. While we sipped our drinks in the front bar at the Middle East waiting for her sound-check she told me that "Neko Case is a fabulous kisser. Man, she is hot." Tonight was a big gig. This was Cat Power's first show back in Boston in nearly three years. There are only the two bands that night; the Boston Phoenix has a preview of the show and writes extensively of Jenny's new album, and while the review of the record is the first mediocre one I've seen, it doesn't dampen the mood. Jenny and her band are pumped.

I'm pretty hammered before the show even starts. A black-haired waitress states that my five glasses of wine and two Maker's Mark are a bit much for a meal and cuts me off before the main doors even open. I am incredulous, which doesn't seem to help my cause. I go inside where there is another bar and I don't appear to be as wasted to this bartender. I grab another drink with every intention of pacing myself. A short man approaches me and introduces himself; his name is Joe and he is a writer for *The Boston Phoenix*. He has a mustache. 'Who has a mustache?' I think to myself. I continue to think of the bush above his lip while he's telling me about himself. The small thicket of hair bobs up and down as if it has a mind of its own. 'Let's see... the drummer from Husker Du has a mustache. Lots of bands have goatees. Um, maybe one of the guys from Railroad Jerk.' I can't think of anyone with a regular mustache, let alone one that looks like something out of a cigarette ad from 1974 or a gay porno like Joe's does. Well, there is Tom, the indie-rock customer at Used Kids. Joe keeps talking but I am too baffled by his mustache to hear him. Finally, I find a way to get his having a mustache out of my mind- I just assume he is gay. He tells me how much he loves Jenny's first record, how her new one is different and how important he thinks her music is. I spy her in the background stumbling over her keyboard as she tries to set it up. She's a gag in her own comedy. I ask Joe what he does for a living and he says he just writes. I think he has to do more than write for a weekly arts paper. I ask again, and he smiles "Oh, you know, I'm kinda self-employed also." I don't get it. I ask, "Self-employed, you mean like a carpenter?" "No, you know, um, self-employed. I sell things." The heavens open. "Oh, you sell things. Right." I smile at my intelligence. Joe and I drink some more together.

Jenny played a very good set on this night, which is lucky because usually she is either really good or she is a train wreck. Cat Power is the train wreck tonight. Chan is nervous and she is playing mostly solo. She forgets the words to her songs. A friend joins her and tries to help her sing her own songs. It appears that she cries for a moment and then laughs. Jenny says, "Oh, fuck, man. I feel bad for her. I know what that shit feels like." Mark from the band Kudgel appears after the show to congratulate Jenny. We start our drive back to Columbus and I eat a large pizza in the back seat of the van. Jenny never plays Boston again.

2006.

Cold and wet morning. The air felt as miserable as any mood I'd ever had. I put my jacket on, made a feeble attempt to find my wife's umbrella and went out to my car. I was pretty much soaked at the end of my eight steps to our Volkswagen Golf. It was 7:30, the hour that divides the day workers from the night crawlers. My wife Merijn yells out to me, "make sure you actually use the umbrella and bring it back!" I pulled out, flicked the wipers on and drove the quarter mile to Tim Horton's, where I bought a dozen doughnuts and four large coffees and drove to the Goodwill parking lot. I scanned under the awning and spied a group of people lying in a huddle with a brilliant assortment of multicolored blankets. I pulled up and rolled down the window. An unshaven man wearing a battered Red Sox hat peered out from the global village bedding and asked, "Who's that?" He was familiar. He wandered the streets with his twin brother.

"Is that you Kevin? Or is it Paul?" I asked.

"It's me."

I rolled my eyes to myself. "Which one, Kevin or Paul?"

"Oh, Kevin. Paul's at the other end."

Jenny Mae: Jon Stickley, Jeff Regensberger, Jenny Mae (Leffel)

Just then, a man who looked just like Kevin peered out from the other end of the nine-foot patchwork of blankets and asked, "Who's there?"

Kevin wiped some of the groggy out of his eyes and spoke. "Oh, hey Bela. She ain't here. She slept in the camp." He did a half nod towards the rear of the Goodwill.

The scenic ravine sloping down behind the Goodwill has no trails but if you follow the creek eastward, it opens into a small park complete with a cliff and two picnic tables. A perfect setting for young coeds to steal off into the night and fuck under a covering of stars and trees hidden away in a large city. The ravine is blanketed with woods and in the summer these woods are covered in weeds, brambles and vines dotted with empty liquor bottles, fast food bags, tin cans, tiny plastic bags that used to hold crack cocaine, and 20 or so people sleeping. When the air starts to chill, the people amble out of the woods and

love, death & photosynthesis

construct a camp just to the rear of the Goodwill, separated only by tall chain link fence and weeds. Trashcans burning in the middle of the camp provide warmth, light, and a way to cook hot dogs, beans, or chicken on wide metal grids. Tents are made of found materials: wooden grocery store pallets, blue plastic tarp, and cardboard boxes. They form a half-moon around the fires.

On this morning, I passed several piles of 40 oz beer bottles, one nearly five feet tall. I walked to the edge and noticed a few men middling around one of the trashcans stoking the fire. One of them turned and said "Oh, hey there Bela. Good morning. Hold on, I'll get her." He walked over to the largest tent and brushed the blue tarp. "Hey Jenny! Bela's here." He looked at me, rain bouncing off his grimy face, "She'll be up in a second." I breathed in the smell of burning wood and stale beer. It was raining pretty hard. First the rain ricocheted off my coat, then penetrated it like water in bread.

The tent parted, revealing a familiar face. Jenny smiled and said, "Hold on. I'll be out in a minute." Out popped an umbrella, one side with three of its metal arms poking skyward like tree branches, the other side in perfect working condition. She walked out, stooped but dry. "Hey, I was wondering if you were coming out. It's kinda early huh?"

"Yup, I got you guys some coffee and doughnuts."

Jenny said, "I can't drink coffee with my stomach but maybe I'll try to eat a doughnut. I'm sure Dale will have some coffee." From the bowels of the tent I heard "Hey, Bela. Yeah, thanks."

Dale is Jenny's boyfriend. He is in his forties with boyish features uncommon for a man who has been homeless for the last five years. Dale is a light skinned black man with eyes different shades of blue. The left one is almost translucent. He has been in and out of prison and mental institutions for most of his life. He is gentle when he isn't smoking crack and since he has been with Jenny he has only smoked crack once. She won't tolerate it. Dale told her that he killed a man once when he was a teenager because the man molested him.

The tarp shakes and leans, almost toppling over. Dale is tall, about 6'2". He steps out and says, "Oh, boy it's raining out" to no one in particular, as his hands move up and down his arms, trying to rub some warmth into his body. Jenny, seemingly reading my thoughts says, "Oh, you wouldn't believe how warm it is inside these tents. These fellows know what they're doing." Jenny had been squatting in The Ohio State School of Music building where she could play the piano for hours in the practice rooms at night. Once discovered, she was tossed out and took to the streets sleeping with different men for comfort and care until finding Dale and the small group of homeless men and women he kept with. They provided safety and an affinity to try to stay off cocaine and only use alcohol. After she was kicked out of the School of Music, she came to Used Kids Records, a small yellow and bruised suitcase and a Hefty trash bag full of what was left of her belongings—these were clothes her ex-husband had bought her, Versace, real gold earrings, a diamond necklace. Nobody would have guessed the contents. Tears were streaming down her cheeks when she got kicked out of the School of Music. Not at being once again without shelter, but because now she wouldn't be able to play the piano.

I hand the coffee and doughnuts to Jenny and say, "I need to get back to the house and take Saskia to daycare and drive Merijn to work. Maybe I'll stop by after." Jenny thanks me and says, "We won't be here this afternoon; we have to meet some of the church people. They dropped off a bunch of food last night so we feel obligated to go listen to them preach. I hate that. They should just drop it off and not try to make us feel guilty. It is so boring, all the Jesus stuff and holy this and holy that. They mean well though. We do appreciate it, but that church and singing they do is so ridiculous. Before that we need to get to Bev's because she'll feed most of us after her lunch rush." Bev is a woman who owns a diner up the street. I look into Jenny's eyes, they are awake but dark around the edges. Her pores reek of booze. She bends down and picks up an empty bottle of Mad Dog Wine, it's more wet on the outside than on the inside. She tosses it into an old grocery cart, "I tell the boys here to pick up after themselves, I don't want us all to get kicked out of here plus I'm trying to let them know this is our house, and we gotta keep it clean." A small brown puddle of mud is climbing up around her shoes, they're cracked brown vinyl, and she notices me looking at them, "These aren't too bad, they keep me warm, they are better than what everybody else is wearing here." She nods towards the small tents, water now pouring off of them like a spigot. I spy Dale's shoes. Brown thick boots, worn to the heel and only halfway laced up because the laces have been torn and knotted in several places. "The guys really need shoes, you don't think about it but shoes are vital out here." She wipes the rain from her nose and looks at me, her blue eyes still brilliant but clouded with the remnants of the night before and the night before that and the weeks and years before that. "Thanks for stopping by. I'll talk to you later." I climb back in my car and drive the quarter mile home where I have another cup of coffee with my wife and watch her nurse our baby girl. My mind flows back to the small sea of empty liquor bottles and the yellowed fingers, burnt by the endless supply of cigarettes that the men and Jenny have in their camp. Saskia stares up at her mother, her blue eyes large, wet with newness. She sucks her mother's gaze in along with the milk. She is safe.

love, death & photosynthesis

1985.

As a high schooler, my mother mixed with Beats, philosophy majors, and slunken artist types who burrow under hushed lights, trying to make sense of the world while chasing sex and literature with copious amounts of alcohol. She was a registered communist at an early age, and our stereo had Pete Seeger, Jean Richie, Joan Baez, Woody Guthrie, as well as a steady stream of opera and classical. She protested everything and was active in organizing the rights for migrant workers, she had corresponded with Cesar Chavez. His picture was up in our house, a framed black and white photo of courage hanging on the living room wall. My brother and I were dragged to impeach Nixon rallies in our orange corduroys carrying Colorforms to play with on the sidewalk while my mother held signs in front of county courthouses.

As a grade-schooler, I was awkward, small and prone to bouts of ridiculous laughter. My nickname was "Spazz" and no doubt I would have been given Ritalin if it had been more prevalent back then. My mother changed towns as if they were blouses, never looking back, never settling in long enough to get all the books unpacked. We moved nine times in my first ten years of school.

I was a latchkey kid from 2nd grade on. If the sun wasn't shining, I would get a plate of cookies and a tall glass of Kool-Aid and head to my room. Pulling the box from the closet, sprawling out in front of the closet door—not even making it to the bed, I would read the comics over and over. The slightly mildewed smell of the pages—even the ink had its own smell. This was comfort.

Other times, the four of us pinched into small two-bedroom apartments, my sister sleeping on the couch or with my mother, my brother and I in a metallic bunk-bed that was cold to the touch, only slightly more freezing in the winter months than the pock-marked linoleum floors.

When I was 14 my mother married a newly ordained Methodist minister who was given a parsonage in Catawba. Catawba is a small burp of a town lying in the shadow of Springfield, Ohio, on a few rolling hills with shimmering fields of corn, soybeans, and as if just to make sure, even more corn spreading out around it. It is the kind of place that Hollywood must think Ohio really is. Fields of America's breadbasket, interrupted by small towns filled with churches and general stores— Hollywood only got it partially right. There were no stoplights in town, in fact there were no curbs on the streets, but every yard had a garden filled with plump red tomatoes, green beans, yellowed brawny squash, peppers and rows of cucumbers. Early every morning most folks would hang an American flag off the front-door frame. The population consisted mostly of farmers and blue-collar workers with a wariness of outsiders, which my brother Zoltan and I, by our names alone, decidedly were. Perhaps too, the town was skeptical of the new minister who had remarried a woman with two kids. And not just any two kids. Catholics. I was told that "Catholics aren't real Christians" by one of my classmates one summer afternoon as we awkwardly tried to find something, anything, in common—apparently it was not going to be God.

By the time I was 17, my brother had joined the Army and was stationed in Germany, my sister was living in Florida, and my mother had left her husband the minister (and me) and moved to Columbus. Whereupon my stepfather had a nervous breakdown and was hospitalized, and it was just me for most of my senior year in high school. Me and my books and records.

All I ever wanted to do was listen to music, for temporary deliverance from my surroundings. Witnessing the bludgeoned emotional lives of my parents, music was the balm that allowed a mind to turn off and get lost in the wonder of being. It helped that my parents had long been either gone, or distracted in the morass of their own lives and insanity, so they couldn't pick up on the danger to my forming thinking, potent in the

love, death & photosynthesis

songs of The Ramones or The Smiths. It was my secret. Stereo turned to ten, head bouncing, cracking out-of-tune voice bellowing the words to "Bring on the Dancing Horses," I was fortified for the moment. And when the song ended, it was back to suffering.

Then came the day Jenny Mae spoke to me.

Jenny was a star. She was a member of 4-H, won first place in the State of Ohio Soil Judging Contest as well as the State of Ohio Wool Judging Contest. She was taking all college prep classes and was told by several teachers to be wary of me, due to my mischievous nature and poor grades, and for three years, Jenny heeded their warning, despite having a locker right next to mine for all of those three years. It wasn't hard for her to ignore me: she was always early; I was always late.

One day she arrived at our lockers just as the bell to get to class rang. She was a bundle of energy and decided to address me, explaining her lateness and her outfit to me—a black and white pinstripe jumpsuit: She was on her way to a National Honor Society function. I tried not to notice how the cut of the suit showed off her 17-year-old breasts. She glanced at the very old sandwich at the bottom of my locker—an ongoing biology experiment that I dared not touch—and then her eyes moved to the calendar hanging inside my locker door marking my countdown to freedom (112 days left).

She said, "You really hate this place, don't you?"

Smiling, I replied, "Yup."

She was carrying a box of chocolates and as she grappled with her locker, it spilled to the floor, small chunks of circular and square confections rolling in the dust and grime. "Shit, now I'm really late!" she cried.

I bent down and helped her pick them up. "Here, put the spilled ones on this side of the box and give that part to your friends," I suggested. "They'll never know."

"Good idea. A bit of dirt never hurt anyone." Crouched down over the bits of ruined drugstore candy, we laughed and looked at each other. She stopped my being as she gushed, "You have the most beautiful eyes I have ever seen." It came to me that she must have a boyfriend who gave her the chocolates.

"Er, ah, thank you. I'm late for Mr. Wasserman's class."

"Just tell him that you were helping Jenny Mae. He loves me."

It worked. He didn't count me tardy that day as he usually did. Mr. Wasserman did not love me at all—quite the opposite in fact. But everybody loved Jenny Mae.

A couple nights later, Jenny Mae and a collection of her friends bounded up the parsonage steps to serenade me with Christmas carols. As bits of swirling snow hovered around the small flock of girls, my heart heaved wide and large. I smiled at them, offered them to come in, but they demurred that they had other people they needed to carol for. I closed the door and sighed deeply.

Love was elusive— found, I thought, only in the underground songs I listened to or maybe in a different life in New York City once I cast off the invisible ropes of rural Ohio. Instead, love found me on the front steps of a Catawba parsonage in the gentle and eternal song "Silent Night."

I had no money for a date, no job, and nobody at home to watch what I did, so I invited Jenny to come back to my house to hang out and listen to music, and to my amazement, she thought that was a good idea. I did in fact have about $7, $5 of which I gave to Chris Biester for a six pack of Pabst Blue Ribbon and $2 for gasoline to go pick her up.

We climbed the stairs to my bedroom, six pack in hand, and Jenny gawked at my record and tape collection. She had never seen so much music in anybody's room.

"Who is R.E.M.? Is that short for something? What is The Replacements? Lou Reed, Velvet Underground... I have never heard any of this. Oh, wait, I know who The Rolling Stones are. You listen to them, huh? And I love The Cars." She scanned the wall of records and then the one of tapes, "How did you get so many of these? There must be hundreds." I could have offered that they were purchased with the fruits of loneliness, but in that moment, with her standing with her back to me, gazing at rows and rows of music, I was filled with a profound sense of belonging such as I had never experienced before. So I opened the first beer of the night and explained, "I got to DJ at the Wittenberg radio station for the past few years, so some I taped from there, some are from my friends in Athens. Or from scouring the cutout bins on trips to Columbus. You can play whatever you want to."

We stayed there in my room, listening to music and drinking beer, completing each other's sentences. We laughed at how we had appeared to have known each other since birth but had only tonight really talked. With clumsiness, we discovered each other's bodies, and the anxiety I had felt all my life slipped away, replaced by a confidence that, somehow, this is the way things were supposed to be. She pulled her top off and I saw her emerald green brassiere and later, to my astonishment, matching green panties, which she refused to remove. I felt her lips around me as her head bobbed in sync with Ric Ocasek's cool new wave voice: "Let the Good Times Roll." Afterwards, I staggered out of bed and said I was going to take a shower and, figuring I may as well go for broke, invited her to join me. She did, saying, "I've never taken a shower with somebody before."

It was nearly 10 o'clock when we left the house, and my car was covered in snow. Turning the key in the ignition, it gave a gasp and then a groan. "It had better start," Jenny worried. "My dad would kill me if he knew we came back to your house instead of going out for pizza." The ignition turned again and came to a shuddering start. The exhaust convulsed with black smoke, causing us to laugh nervously, and we roared out of the driveway into the twirling snow. I have never considered what her father must have thought when his daughter came back at 10 pm with wet hair, but he never did seem to take a shine to me in all the years we were involved in one another's lives.

Two days later, we sat on a hard wooden pew while Midnight Christmas Services went on, holding sweating hands and exchanging notes. One said, "Only two days." It had felt like forever, as if past and future were complete in our twitchy arms.

We spent every day together. She used Gloria Vanderbilt perfume and smuggled it into my house so she could spray my pillow, which I snuggled and smelled after I drove her home.

Jenny had her sights on Ohio State University in Columbus; she was going to be the first person in her family to graduate from college. She had scored high on her college entrance exams, as well as winning several Future Farmers of America awards and playing first trumpet in the marching band. The band director said that she was the most talented musician he had ever taught, though she drove him nuts because she couldn't read music. He would frequently contribute trumpets to her cause, many of which would be dinged and left behind in various houses and boats. I decided to switch from Ohio University in Athens where I'd always planned to attend Otterbein College, just north of Columbus. My dependence on Jenny was in full bloom. She made the world brighter, crisper, more relaxed. Someone wanted me.

1989.

I hated Discount Records, a corporate store I worked at. But as I was manager, I got to hire a man I admired, Craig Regala. Craig had about 77 piercings and tattoos, was funny as hell and held our place of employment in the same disregard I did. One of us would crouch below the counter as the other rang up a pain-in-the-ass customer, and we'd pull our penises out and wiggle them around, just out of eyeshot of the customer. Or pull on them as far out as we could until it hurt, like skin-taffy. Craig turned me onto Galaxie 500 and the fact that Mo Tucker of the Velvet Underground was playing Stache's up the street. Later Craig would start Datapanik, the direct inspiration for my record label Anyway. He took interest in the classic country music I had been listening to for several years. He didn't laugh when I tried in vain to grow mutton chops like George Jones. I was living with Jenny and much of the life we knew consisted of drinking 12 packs and making prank calls to pizza joints. Eating at the Wendy's salad bar was a night out. Through Craig, we were introduced to a world where everybody made an impact, where genius really did live next door. Heroes weren't confined to MTV. The fellow selling you a quart of beer or serving you food could also be the one writing songs about your loneliness or your crush on that barmaid down the street. Or she might be the one singing about her secret crush... on you!

Bela Koe-Kromopecher @ Used Kids

"Touch Me I'm Sick" was the first single by Mudhoney, a soiled diamond of a song that for many of us changed everything. Along with "Everything Flows" by Teenage Fanclub and "Smells Like Teen Spirit." The music was ugly, beautiful and comical all at the same time. Lyrically it was brilliant, nobody was singing songs like this—at least to my young ears. It was a stab against the clean bullshit of hair rock and the pastel sounds of candlelit pop.

Punk rock hit me like my first orgasm. It made total sense and a part of me asked, "Why didn't I know about this before?" The world changed, there was no longer a hierarchy to art, no longer a manner in which someone had to dress and music was not to be used to sell anything other than pure emotion, either frustration, anger, joy, or confessional sloppy love (sex).

Ron House

love, death & photosynthesis

Mudhoney: Mark Arm, Steve Turner

This revelation was widened by my lunch breaks spent at Used Kids, a literally underground (located in a basement) hidden record store down the street from Discount. It was started by Dan Dow of The Gibson Brothers and Ron House of Thomas Jefferson Slave Apartments. Dan's motto was "get the music to the people" which meant it should always be affordable. Music may have been a commodity out in the world, but at Used Kids, it was an inherent right. It was tiny, just a cramped shoebox of a store, with thousands of records crammed in every corner. The décor was made up of hundreds of flyers from various punk and indie shows and old LP covers. A great deal of the decorating was done on several spastic afternoons by Jack Taylor (birth name Richard Violet). Richie had plastered the walls and ceiling of Used Kids over two afternoons, using wheat paste and his haphazard manner of symmetry, where one flyer would appear to push out the presence of its neighbor. It was as if Big Black were jostling for attention over Richard Thompson. Then inexplicably he stopped and only 2/3 of the store was covered.

I had been living and breathing whatever music I could find for as long as I could recall. As a child, I would plead with my father in Kroger's that I would happily eat eggs and cereal all week if he just spent the grocery money on records. Entering Used Kids, I was like a fat man walking into an ice cream shop that sold more than just vanilla and chocolate. I didn't want to leave and I wanted to try everything. The dollar bins were bulky, stuffed with an assortment of records such as Breaking Circus or Salem 66. I found my first Guided By Voices record, "Self-Inflicted Aerial Nostalgia," there.

Summer was bleeding Ohio dry in the summer of 1988. The pavement was so hot that the soles of tennis shoes stuck to the sidewalk. Slipping from my air-conditioned corporate record store job everyday day around 3, sweating in my best rumpled dress shirt, brownish off-the-rack pleated pants and a bulky name tag stuck to my chest, I would venture through the shuddering waves of heat to Used Kids, where there was no air conditioner. The best way to cool off was to grab a beer from Dan or Ron, and hope that it wasn't too crowded with damp, sticky men. At Discount, the non-offensive soft sounds of Tracy Chapman, James Taylor, or smooth jazz matched the artificially cooled atmosphere. Ron would put his bottle down on the counter, lay a single on the record player, his left hand wheeling the volume knob as he smiled and nodded, and what came blaring out of the speaker above my head, a fat-squishy and ragged blast of noise, was like fire. The sound was both new and primordial. The singer's voice crackled as if it were in a comic book bubble: "BLARRGHHH!!!" It was the sloppy and crusty sound of a lion bellowing. A drunken, grimy, rabid lion, but a lion nevertheless. And when the chorus hit, something had transformed me.

Touch me I'm sick, indeed.

After a while, the two men at Used Kids gleaned that I knew my stuff, especially when it came to classical music and rock, and soon I was doing short afternoon stints when I got off at Discount. I felt kinship and a great deal of admiration for Ron and Dan. I felt invited into a small community that I was born to find, and now I had. The secret code of life had come in the form of a round vinyl record.

1974.

Long Island was uh, long and enigmatic, when we entered New York City for the first time, driving straight through from the soon-to-be burned out streets and houses of Youngstown, Ohio. I was jostled awake by my mother and siblings, "Wake up we are in New York!", I crawled from the floor of the back seat, no doubt my face filled with red indentations from the plastic floor coverings. I rubbed my eyes and stared straight up out of the window, the highway twisted around high-rises that stood like science-fiction trees, with thousands of lights bursting into the sky— I thought of all the people who lived in them. We lived on the far east end of Long Island, in a small town near East Hampton called Springs. It is best known for being the town where Jackson Pollock lived. Willem DeKooning lived a few houses down from us, but by that time in the mid-seventies, his mind must have been eaten up by dementia, although my mother remembers him talking to her about us, her children.

My memories of Springs are idyllic although we barely spent more than a hiccup there. My step-father at the time, David, had gotten a job working as a scientist near Montauk which lies at the tip of the Island complete with a massive and brilliant lighthouse. His office was just down the road from the lighthouse, and I have vivid memories of walking the beach at Montauk as what appeared to be billions of mussel shells stretched over the sand in crunchy bunches that cracked and split under my shoes. The dense odor of salt and fish is still in my nose nearly forty years later. We lived in a small house that abutted a small thatch of woods to the rear of the house, with a quick shuttle through the woods, nary a spit from our back door, we would be at a small harbor. We spent hours in those woods and on our small wooded street, where I taught myself to ride a bicycle, got bit by a dog and had my first attempt at a sleepover.

There was a community picnic one evening, just off the beach, volley-ball was set up and the older children had taken a group of us fishing. The sky was a whirl of clouds, twisting over the ocean, mimicking the breaking waves, filled with grays, whites and iridescent blues that appeared to be a cauldron that could come and swallow the ocean if the universe would only let it. I held an older boy's hand— the rain would come, I was certain of that— but for now, we were going fishing, and my parents lay just beyond the lump of trees that provided a shimmering barrier between the beach and the grilling of chicken, hamburger, hotdogs, and corn. In hindsight, this must have been the week-end of the fourth of July. There were piers constructed of hunks of blue and black rock that strode bravely into the sea, where one could fish and stare into the vastness of water while contemplating the smallness of oneself. These were slippery rocks and we were instructed not to go to the end of the piers where the water was more dangerous and violent. Only the big kids could go there. A young fattish boy, with a yellow ball-cap helped me bait my hook; I had some experience fishing with my father and told him I could cast the line myself, which I dutifully did. I sat quietly by myself as the bustle of ten and twelve year olds raged on further down the pier, no doubt engaged in primitive games of mascu-linity intended for girls who giggled at their antics, probably because they had no other idea of how to react. The fishing rod pulled gently, a small tug, me knowing instinctively to tug a little back, and suddenly like a shot, whatever was on the other end of the line swallowed hard and must have sensed immediately that the food it had just eaten was not a normal dinner. The hook dug deep in its throat, frantically tearing away from the thin line that twisted in its mouth, "Good God! What the fuck is this?!" it may have thought, if it's possible for a sea creature to hold such a thought. It fled, and in doing so, my little-boy hands, soft from innocence and barely large enough to hold onto the fishing pole, wrapped themselves around the base of the pole, frantically trying to reel the fish in.

My brother was towards the forbidden end of the pier as I struggled, no doubt throwing small chunks of rocks into the sea with the other boys. Someone shouted out

love, death & photosynthesis

behind my slight shoulders, "That kid's got something!" By now my fishing pole was bending into an almost half moon and sweat was pouring from my brow. "I'm sweating!" I thought, "I never sweat." Suddenly the fat boy with the ball cap cupped his hands over mine, "Let me help you," he whispered behind me, "Wow, you got something big here." A small group of children hovered around us, trying not to slip on the wet rocks, "Be careful" somebody hushed to another. The line was taut, and for every spin of the reel, the fish would take another foot of wire deeper into the sea. The struggle of the fish was apparent in the effort we were putting into bringing it ashore. At one point, it became obvious that we were winning, as the pole almost dragged us into the water, and with a couple of yanks and pulls we managed to shore a long, slick black eel, its body twisting out of the water and its sharp teeth clutching tight against the fishing line. "What is that thing!" yelled yellow cap. "It's an eel, they are delicious!" I spoke for the first time, "My dad eats smoked eel." Someone behind me shouted, "That little kid caught an eel!" The realization that I had done something exhilarated me. "Hold on!" I screamed and went yelling towards the picnic. Leaving the group of children with the frightened animal, whose entire world had just been transformed into nightmare absurdity. I ran across the sand, "I caught an eel! I caught an eel!" If I had died then, I knew in my heart that I had accomplished something extraordinary. My gravestone, tall and proud, enscripted with the words: *HE CAUGHT AN EEL* My mother hearing my shrieks had thought my brother had fallen into the sea, "Where is he? Is he ok?" She must have thought I was screaming, "Z fell into the sea!" instead of "I caught an eel!" or something like that. Quickly settling things, my parents and the others ran towards the pier, and upon arriving on the wet rocks, the wind picking up with thick pellets of rain striking our faces, we were informed that the eel had slipped through the rocks and was back out at sea. "Did you get the hook out?" I asked, not wanting it to suffer. "Yeah, I was taking it out when it squirmed away" yellow cap replied. "You are a good fisherman, kid," and he rubbed my head. Zoltan told everybody what happened, how I was fishing by myself and off on my own, and then how I caught the fish. "It smelled real bad!" A part of me was disappointed that the eel had gotten away, but I was also relieved.

1991.

Jerry was setting up the stage; his new band Gaunt was getting ready to play. He is so excited that he drinks a few beers. "Beer?" I asked. "You're drinking?" He wiped his hands on his thin black jeans. "Yeah, you know—sometimes a little bit of booze helps." He laughed nervously and paced around the stage, unplugging and plugging guitar cables from various plastic pedals. This was a real club they were playing, with a stage, a hired soundman, a "professional" doorman and a drink tab. Stache's. They were playing on a Monday night with the New Bomb Turks, who were also psyched about the club, where Sonic Youth, Dinosaur Jr., Scrawl, and The Replacements have played. The stage was small, but big enough to house incredible egos quite comfortably. The television was showing the Simpsons, and the five regulars who are there every day would not leave until The Simpsons was over. Jerry was balanced precariously on a barstool, hanging a sheet across the back of the stage. He'd spray-painted the sign of an asshole on the sheet. It was very large and looked like this: "*". This was the official start of the "Jerry's an Asshole" phase of his life, and he wore it proudly. The soundman, shaking his head, asked Jerry what he was doing. Jerry told him to mind his own business, which I believed was exactly what the soundman was doing. Jerry went to the bar and got another beer.

Gaunt Live: Jerry Wick, Eric Barth

The tag of "Jerry's an Asshole" had been birthed at the same time as his new thirst for beer. Or vice versa. Jerry was always a contrarian, but it was heightened when he drank.

Gaunt was a powder keg live, one moment brilliant but in another a disheveled angry machine if a guitar string popped or the atmosphere wasn't right. Jerry formed Gaunt with Eric Barth, who had played in several excellent Columbus bands, a deft and melodious bass player, and Jeff Regensberger. Jeff was new to the drums but what he may have lacked in drum rolls he brought in an easy-going enthusiasm to the seriousness of Jerry's songs. Jeff was more than capable of banging out a basic—even quick—punk rock beat to the music of Jerry, and he smiled throughout their live sets. He was a lantern of goodwill on stage.

On this night, Gaunt played a hurried set, full of nerves and angst when Jerry interrupted the set to read from *Breakfast of Champions*. He made no sense; the book seemed

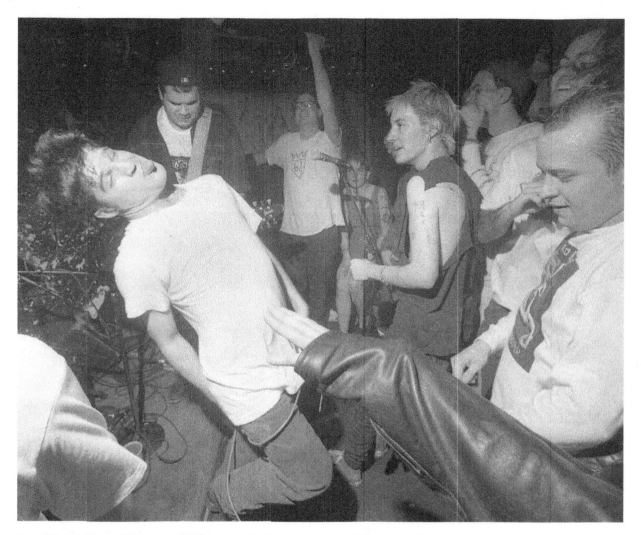

New Bomb Turks (live at Bernie's): l-r Eric Davidson, Jim Weber, and Bela (standing)

to have nothing to do with the music, which is loud, manic and electric. It was as if he was trying to cram every idea of what he ever wanted to do for a rock show onto the small stage that night. The wheels of the thus far excellent show were starting to wobble off. Several of his friends, including me, cringed. Soon enough he picked up his guitar, jumping nearly four feet in the air, hair bouncing wildly as he screamed into the microphone: "Punks don't wear no silly watches…arrghhhhh!" From this point on they were awesome. Jeff smiled towards Jerry and said "All right!" as if recognizing this moment as the reason Gaunt existed.

The Turks played next and they somehow had taken the energy that flew off of Gaunt, mixed it in their drinks, chased it with about five pots of black coffee, and regurgitated it. A final roar and a collective smile from the ten people who came to the show. Their songs were more punk than Gaunt's, and laced with irony, almost as wordy as Elvis Costello songs. Words pushed and crammed against one another as if the entire song had to be forced through a two-minute miniature funnel. Unlike Jerry, these guys didn't drop out of their English Studies majors.

After the show the audience, made up almost exclusively of girlfriends and record store employees, milled around and congratulated each other. I was lit, Jenny was lit. We stumbled around in a protracted electric hum left over from the buzzing amps still plugged in on the stage. Jenny and I were in the midst of a breakup. I spied a blonde at the edge of the bar and thought how beautiful she was. Jenny grabbed my shoulder and said we needed to go.

We stumbled towards home, feeling more alive than ever before. Jenny remarked how mesmerizing Jerry was live. She said, "Fuck, if he keeps that up he may even get laid one day."

1991.

On the walk home from the Gaunt show, Jenny's mood shifted.

"Who were you looking at earlier?" she demanded.

"I dunno, I think she is in Ron's band, her name is Nora."

Jenny sniffed. "Well, quit looking. I don't like you around blondes." Every speck of guilt I had ever accumulated bubbled forth, and then sat in me like stagnant sewage water.

When Jenny had initially confronted me about an also-blonde Monica (my first indiscretion with whom I had an ill-advised, almost slapstick affair with) I was all bumbling and stammering lies, and all I could muster was, "What about Bob? Or Barry or Juan or Salvador or Randy, and who knows who else?" Jenny had answered: "What about them, you have no proof. And anyways I NEVER FUCKED THEM!" She was a professional at the "I'm not guilty-you're guilty" retort. How could I argue with this? She had no proof about Monica either, other than my confession, but Jenny wouldn't confess even if—when—caught red-handed. She tossed me out of the house, which really meant I had to sleep in the other room for a while, or on large piles of brown paper record bags in the back of Used Kids. The cot had finally broken under my weight one night when I could not muster the ability to make it off of High Street after a hard day's drinking.

Jenny had learned the skill of switching the topic from her flaw to someone else's in childhood, from her father. He would get in an angry and brutal mood and come after his children with teeth bared and hands stretched to their maximum for full effect and, when he was done, disappear into the night. By the time he came back, his behavior had morphed into the family's fault.

For three months following the Monica incident, upon meeting anyone new, Jenny would lean over, shake their hand, and say "Hey, glad to meet you I'm Jenny Mae and this is Bela who just cheated on me." So-and-so had no idea what to say, wondering if Jenny was serious or not. I would smile almost as hesitantly at so-and-so and say, "Hey, how are you doing?" Jenny, picking up on the person's nervousness, would add, "It's OK now, we're over it. I'm just still punishing him." I would step back behind her, a beaten man, quiet and smiling in my public humiliation. I had believed this was a normal part of the penitence I had to perform for holding those huge tits of Monica's.

I knew very well who the blonde at the show was, and I suspect Jenny did, too. We both knew it was Nora from The Jefferson Slave Apartments, on whom I had a profound crush and who I would see for a brief period after leaving Jenny. After Jenny and I broke up, she would stop by my apartment and just take one of my little notebooks. She made a song out of a poem she found that was a declaration of love to Nora. But Jenny transfigured it into a dark paranoid paean to obsession that she called "Blazing Saddles." I hoped Nora would never hear it.

1997.

Jerry met Lisa Suckdog when they played a show together at CBGB's in New York. Suckdog was an experimental spastic/performance art troupe led by *Rollerderby* zine founder Lisa Carver and Dame Darcy. Borrowing from the stage antics of GG Allin but injecting sexuality and a vast amount of humor, Suckdog pushed both visual and audio limits. *Rollerderby* was essential reading for anybody associated with the underground scene—extremely well-written, wry, funny, and stacked with sexuality from a woman's perspective. Jerry was stoked, to say the least. Although most of us had some Suckdog records, few of us listened to them, but not Jerry: he played *Onward Suckdog Soldiers* constantly, and in the process he would empty Used Kids.

Jerry and Lisa Suckdog's meeting went well, leading to the nastiest of places, the bathroom stall of CBGB's, and from there he and Lisa took their explosive and difficult love affair from state to state, always meeting and abruptly parting. In direct contradiction to the perambulatory and seedy-glamorous tone of their relations, what Jerry really wanted was to marry Lisa and live on a farm in the country. I said, "Jerry, you can't even drive." Maybe he was thinking he would get around on a cart pulled by a mule.

Jerry always struggled to balance his sense of identity as an outsider bohemian with a belief in the wholesomeness of romantic commitment that bordered on complete fantasy. He developed an instant crush upon meeting my sister, a double divorcee living in the suburbs with her two young daughters and a license plate that read SOCRMOM. I was completely perplexed by this. My sister tried to construct the all-American house-hold: two kids, a cat and a dog; she wore sweaters and loved Rod Stewart. Not the early, gritty stuff, but the spandex, disco, highlighted hair Rod. Jerry became obsessed with my sister and his idea of her life at the same time he had a girlfriend, Jill, who was the complete opposite: underground-sophisticated, cynical. Her roadmap to men, as told to my girlfriend Robin, was: "Just give them a blowjob on the first date and they'll do anything for you." Myths live fast in our hearts, even when the brain tells us something different, the imbalance is sometimes never bridged and the search to meld the present with fairy tales is infinite.

Always trying to meld his incompatible parts to one another created friction that boiled over in to every part of his being. Jerry off and on swore he was celibate. "I don't need sex; it's overrated," he would say between swigs of beer and draws off his cigarette. Yet the idea of romance loomed large, the wanting of a monogamous relationship. Much of this tension came out in his music, the hope and heartbreak found on "Yeah, Me Too" and "Kryptonite." The love was easy, the heartbreak was harder. It crushed our spirits as if they were made of Styrofoam. Jerry would say to me: "Fuck love, I don't need it and you don't need it either. You always get hurt by girls, Bela." In retrospect, I should've said, "No Jerry, I just always hurt."

Jerry's usual advice on women went: "Stay away from her, she's just as crazy as the last one." But I needed a warm body close by just to prove to myself that I was still alive, after the laughter dissipated at last call, and through the next four hours. I marveled at Jerry's ability to get through the night alone. It was as if getting close to someone betrayed some inner promise he'd made. He could be almost monk-like. He braved soli-tude like a bird perched on the highest tree limb.

2001.

I was living in Gainesville, Florida. Jenny was in Miami with her husband David and working as a bartender in a rich man's bar situated amongst the docks of Coconut Grove. My marriage had fallen apart, and I was going insane. I called Jenny and she suggested I drive down and visit her for a long weekend. Since I didn't have a job, I decided it was a good idea—anything to break the humidity of Gainesville and my marriage.

I pulled up to the pier and even though this was Miami, it was January and the wind was brisk. The salty air penetrated the thin clothes I was wearing. A snowbird standing next to the sea. I should have brought a coat. Within a few minutes I spied Jenny and David walking towards me. Jenny gave me a hug and asked me how bad it was. Nearly in tears, I replied, "Bad." I shook David's hand and he said we'd go get a drink. First, we needed to drop my bag off. I looked around for their car but was reminded that they didn't live in a house any longer. No house, no car. We walked down the pier and climbed into a dinghy. It was the seafaring version of a Pinto. I was amazed that the few pieces of board even floated. The engine sputtered and started, water trying to choke it out and I yelled across the buzz of the tiny motor, "Did you pull that off a lawnmower?" Jenny laughed and pulled a pint of vodka from her purse. "Might as well have!" she screamed over the din.

love, death & photosynthesis

Jenny and David moved out of their house so that they wouldn't have to pay rent anymore. They somehow came to the conclusion that their two Labradors and pet bird would enjoy living on a boat. The boat, nearly 40 years old, and at one time must have been gorgeous. It had a finished wood interior kitchen complete with a stove and refrigerator. Jenny told me the bathroom didn't work and showed me a bucket if I had to take a shit. I raised my eyebrows and she told me, "Oh, don't worry about it; we do it all the time. Either that or you can try to lean over and take a shit off the side of the boat. Or wait till we get on land."

We dropped my bag off and I was shown my bed, two waterproof pillows laid out near the rear of the boat. I was in a small alcove that protected me from the rain but allowed the wind to swirl and bite at my scrunched-up body. We climbed back ashore, and Jenny said we were going to first go to the Tigertail, where people did lines of coke off the bar and clutched their beer cans for dear life. Nobody smiled and everybody was jumpy and suspicious. Even the light that clawed its way in when the front door opened was treated with derision. "Shut the fuckin' door!" someone at the bar would holler. It was as if they were bats. Not a real big pick-me-up of a place. I suggested to Jenny maybe we could go somewhere else. She shook her head and said she wanted me to talk to her friend Albert, a non-drinking millionaire who spent most of his days in the Tigertail avoiding an unpleasant marriage by watching people slowly destroy themselves. I had no desire to speak to Albert or anyone else. I wanted to go to sleep and wake up with my life miraculously changed.

We sat at the bar and the bartender was a woman named Noelle, but when she turned her back Jenny mouthed "Snowelle" and held her index finger up to her nose and sniffed. Sensing my discomfort, Jenny told me that we wouldn't stay long. I leaned over and said, "It's spooky in here. I'm just not in the mood." She said we would leave soon. I didn't trust her. Sure enough, we met her hookup and for the rest of the evening Jenny and Dave took turns running to the restroom trying to hide a cocaine addiction that had so far only cost them their house and van. I was wasted, but the alcohol couldn't blunt my disgust.

The next day I realized that there is nothing Jenny and Dave could do to provide the salve for my emotional wound. In fact, I was thoroughly annoyed that I had thought they could help. I climbed back in my car and Jenny asked me where I was going. I told her I needed to drive back to Gainesville. She asked me to drive her downtown, which I reluctantly agreed to do. We ended up arguing. She insisted that I am too serious and that was always my problem and that's why divorce was looming in my future. Years of frustration boiled over onto the baked parking lot of the Esso station. "Fuck this," I spat out. I got in the car and drove off, leaving her alone and cursing in my rearview mirror. We didn't talk for months. On the way back to Gainesville, frustrated with her, my wife, and especially myself, I got stuck in an insane traffic jam in front of a police car and slowly pissed my pants.

1985.

Jenny was showing me some of her photographs in her parents' basement and I noticed an old organ. I asked who played and she told me she did. She then proceeded to play several songs that she had written to sing her young brother Tony to sleep. I was impressed. Looking back the songs were not too unlike some of the songs that Daniel Johnston wrote on his parent's organ. The melodies were buried within the claustrophobic chords of the machine, muffled and blunted but strong nevertheless. The sound moved slowly through the basement, which was half finished, her father in the middle of constructing a small bedroom— bare pale wooden frames waited patiently for drywall to cover their nakedness. Jenny hummed the songs and then sang in a trill-y voice sounding like a singer from a 1940s Disney cartoon. Her voice sounded epic. I was transfixed. Suddenly she stopped, turned her head and smiled. "I have something amazing to show you." She scampered to the other side of the basement, reached under the bed and produced a giant burr-penis. It was made by her and her sister Rachel with about a hundred round prickly burrs they'd found on their farmland. They had constructed a giant penis complete with balls. It measured roughly nine inches not including the nuts. Rachel bounded down the stairs, laughed and said, "No, you aren't showing him the burr-dick are you?" We all laughed and then Jenny's mother Ginger walked in. Ginger was as straight as straight is, a woman for whom the phrase "gosh-darn-it" was an offense. She was thin and wore her hair in a beehive, and expressed many misgivings over television shows. One time she exclaimed that Freddy Kruger was "the trashiest man I have ever seen." Later she would bestow that title onto one of the characters on "Revenge of the Nerds," shaking her head. Then, reconsidering her harshness, "My heavens, well nerds are people, too!" Ginger was horrified to walk in on the burr penis and immediately offered me an apology, saying, "Bela, I'm so sorry you have to see that filth, I told her to get rid of it." Jenny laughed and said "Oh, Mom you know you always loved it!" With that she flipped the sticky burr-dick towards Ginger, where it immediately latched onto her chest. Ginger was horrified and as she tried in vain to flick it off, the burr-dick just seemed to become more entrenched in her blouse. "Oh, Jenny you are horrible!" she cried, and then the absurdity of the situation hit, and even she had to laugh. "Just don't let your dad know you still have this piece of trash."

2008.

After having spent a vast amount of time trying to tear our worlds down night by night, beer by beer, and note by note, I now spent my days trying to rebuild lives, sentence by sentence, listen by listen, and patience by patience as a social worker. My client base all had criminal backgrounds ranging from murder to drug possession to forgery. As I strolled across the lobby, trying my best to let them know I would help them all and I was open to their concerns, my mind busily balanced the different fires each person presented me with. Two might need their bus pass and checks, one a bed at a shelter, one a scheduled therapy appointment, another assistance in filling out a government form. I would get the bus passes and checks, see if the forms could wait an hour, and then counsel the other client.

Out of the corner of my eye I saw Dale slumped in a corner chair with Jenny next to him. They had a brown bag at their feet and his shoes were open at the end, his ruddy socks poking through the open flaps like small animals peering from a cave. He had no shoelaces. Jenny waved at me and I strolled over. She was not my client and I let her know that I couldn't really talk to her here; she needed to speak with her own case manager. She laughed. "Man, they like you here. It's like you're Jesus or something."

I cracked a smile. "Yeah, touch the hem of his garment and a bus pass appears."

She howled with laughter and the laugh was too pressed, too much. My joke was not that funny. A smile lingered on her face, not from my one-liner but from whatever was in the giant Wendy's Biggie cup in the brown bag. I unconsciously frowned at the cup. Jenny shook her head, saying, "We have to hide it in something on the bus."

"Jenny, you aren't fooling anybody."

Still shaking her head she defiantly says, "I'm not trying to."

1995.

Jerry and I double date and see a double feature of Mel Brooks's films, *Blazing Saddles* and *Young Frankenstein*. We were both too young to see them in the theater when they first came out. His girlfriend Jill and my wife, Robin, are close friends and always seems to enjoy talking about how disappointed they are with Jerry and me.

Neither of the women really wanted to spend a Saturday evening in a bar masquerading as a movie theater watching two old Mel Brooks movies with their drunk men. We could not understand why. For us this was the perfect night out. Drinking started around 3 at Used Kids. I went to Larry's at 5 for a few Kamikazes before heading back for the last few hours of work, when the music got louder and the laughter was just as intoxicating as the Black Label beer we were drinking. Jerry and I took turns manning the turntable, alternating between punk rock favorites and George Jones and the Jerky Tapes. We had regulars, just like a bar—customers who could come down and have a few beers while perusing the racks of records and CDs.

We decided we would walk to my house after we closed and meet the girls. Jerry and I never made it there. We stopped at Larry's and slowly strolled up High Street, stopping at Dow's on High, Dick's Den, and then finally The Blue Danube. We had walked right past my street. I phoned Robin who said they had been waiting. Her tone was not conducive to laughter. Jerry was leaning against the bar, chatting with the barmaid. He glowed like a lantern on Hallows Eve, his ass crack sticking out of his black grimy jeans. He never wore underwear. In fact, he came to me one afternoon after a Gaunt tour and said that he had a urinary tract infection. I was stunned. "I thought only women got those?" He lowered his voice and said, "My doctor said I got it cause I don't wear underwear and I only have a few pairs of jeans."

"Jesus Christ, Jerry, buy some fucking underwear!"

"Well, I can't get to the mall and I don't want to buy used undies at the thrift store, that is fucking gross."

"Having sick balls is fucking gross."

"Shut up." And he dug his finger deep into his scrotum, grimacing as he tried to scratch away the infection.

He spied me from the corner of his eye, leaned back, putting the ass crack to bed. "Lemme guess, they are pissed off." The air in my balloon had not been sucked out yet, laughing with familiarity: "Of course they are, what did you expect?" The kinship of disappointment bonded us and guided us, forming a steering wheel that directed our path through our lives.

By the time the two women, who must have been energizing each other's disgust, showed up at The Blue Danube, we did not have any insight into our equilibrium, leaning against one another, preparing ourselves for the laughter that would ensue when the movies started. We grinned at the looks of consternation on their faces; they shook their heads at us. At first, they protested even going to the double feature. It was late, the first movie had started, and besides we promised them dinner. "Just get something to eat here at the bar," we said, "and oh, by the way, we aren't hungry." A meal would only slow the buzz that was building into a Ferris wheel in our brains. This offer turned out to be an insult; apparently, we had promised a real meal, one that entailed a waiter, a tablecloth, and bathrooms that didn't have baby cockroaches climbing up the walls. "Losers" Jill muttered to Robin as Jerry and I ordered beers at the popcorn counter.

We stumbled to the theater, arriving midway through *Blazing Saddles*, which annoyed the women even more. For Jerry and me this was now the most important event of our lives, even if we had missed half the film already. Immediately our girlfriends found us gone beyond annoying—we were laughing too hard; there was no way a movie could be as funny as we thought it was. They left us at the theater. They would never understand

love, death & photosynthesis

us, we said to each other, and no doubt this was the same conversation the women were having as they walked home alone. Jerry and I stayed through half of "Young Frankenstein" before deciding we needed to go dancing. Breathing in the autumn air, we felt invigorated, and managed to squeeze out another round of drinks at another bar, telling each other that the expectations the women placed upon us were too much, too unrealistic, too unreasonable, and that they lacked the ability to enjoy life as we did. By the time we arrived at my house, it was just past midnight. I would have to drive us to the disco and we had gone about 20 minutes since the last drink. I had climbed over the edge of my buzz by that point and had settled into the slow comfort of exhaustion; I had no more desire to go dancing. Besides, Robin was still up—I saw the television flickering in the living room. Jerry said he was going to head for a few more drinks at Dow's or Larry's and go to bed. He swayed off into the streetlights, cigarette in one hand, the other hand buried in his coat pocket, and I went inside and tried to make amends.

1995.

Crazy Mama's heyday was in the mid-'80s; stories of playing and doing drugs with Paul Westerberg at Mr. Browns and then heading for some dancing and more drugs at Crazy Mama's. Klaus Nomi played there once, and the promoter left him hanging so he stayed with some rich guy in the wealthy suburb of Upper Arlington who had Klaus mow his lawn to get airfare money. When we arrived around '91, Crazy Mama's was doing whatever it could to stay alive, switching from new-wave goth to bass heavy techno to punk. One never knew what one might hear when you stumbled up its steep staircase, sitting above a thin slice of a liquor store and an abandoned storefront. On the next corner sat a Wendy's fast food restaurant and across the street sat a row of Greek bars, Mean Mr. Mustards, The Travel Agency and many more that have been torn down to the rubble of history.

At times there would only be a few older patrons, with slashing '80s haircuts and either weighted down or skinny jowls, depending on whether the person chose alcohol, cocaine or heroin. The glamour of Crazy Mama's had faded like a bloated Elvis, but once in a while the club would be packed again, and the sounds of Jesus and Mary Chain and The Cramps would rattle the rafters, like an old pitcher who suddenly finds himself tossing a no-hitter. A huge mirror ball hung down and splashed white-light reflections over the herky-jerky and morose bodies, and the reflections went on into eternity as all the walls were covered with mirrors. On Thursdays the bar closed with the wonderfully gorgeous Felt song "Primitive Painters." I imagine that "Primitive Painters" was written to capture the special feeling that only 2 AM can provide, when one is soaked with sweat, plastered with cigarette smoke and filled with a feeling of absolute freedom, courtesy of alcohol. Jerry adored Felt, as did I. We would swirl across the sticky dance floor under the glow of a disgruntled aging disco ball and, for three minutes, the world would be all right.

Tonight was techno night. The full-on beats and stuttering synthesizers left Jerry, our friend Matt, and me feeling annoyed and empty. We moved to a tiny room to the left of the bar where there was a pinball machine and one of those machines you could blow into to see if you were drunk enough not to drive. A crusted cake of spittle on the end of the nozzle no doubt caused it to always test high. Jerry was an energetic pinball player who practically dry-humped the machine when playing it, thrusting his hips into the game as if pinball was an erotic exercise. As we played Jerry and I started to talk about some of the songs he had been recording with Jenny. He was amazed by her songs and I think he had a crush on her because he mentioned that he couldn't go out with her because of our past history together. Matt chimed in and asked if we were talking about "Crazy Jenny?" Jerry, eyeing the multi-ball, said, "Yup, that's her." Matt exclaimed, "Man, that chick is nuts. We knew her from the dorms, we see her at Larry's sometimes. She writes songs!?" As if he were astounded that such a woman could sit still long enough to actually write something down. But actually, she didn't always have to. She would come to my apartment and steal a book of poetry and make a mishmash of lines from my struggle to make sense out of sex, love, abandonment— basically her. Or she'd put melody to an overheard conversation. She was a true folk artist, of the people, not a rock star poet in love with his own turn of phrase. She listened to everyone, absorbed all around her, and music was a part of her, not a vehicle for ego. A few years later, Matt would play guitar on one of Jenny's best known songs, "Runaway."

Suddenly a moment of ridiculousness arrived. The gothic song "O Fortuna" blared out of the speakers and the dance floor filled with more black clothing than a funeral. We were baffled by the overtly enthusiastic reception the song had. I started pacing the length of the dance floor, and posed like Bela Lugosi with an imaginary cape draped over my face. Jerry and Matt joined me; we were jostled and scowled at, which just made us laugh harder. Eventually we were told to leave the dance floor. Matt went back a week later and half the crowd was doing the vampire dance.

1989.

I **wanted to vacuum the house and surprise Jenny.** The vacuum was new. It caught on the rug, and clogged. Outside the sky was melting into the atmosphere, the house thick with humidity and frustration. We could not afford an air conditioner. I wanted to please her by cleaning. I flipped the machine over and saw nothing. "Fucking piece of shit!" Grabbing the vacuum by the long metal handle, it was chucked out the front door into the yard just as she was walking up. It skidded across the lawn and landed at her feet. She gazed down at it, as if it were a slow-moving hockey puck as it came to rest inches from her feet. "What the fuck, Bela? What is your fucking problem?"

"It's a piece of shit, doesn't work!"

She pulled it inside, took the machine apart, and started giggling.

"What's so funny?" I asked as I drank another beer on the couch.

"You are such an idiot, Jesus." She held up a dangling long white tube sock. "You fucking vacuumed up a sock. And because you destroyed one of my things I'm going to destroy one of yours." She ran upstairs and locked the stairway door behind her.

I ran into the backyard, gazing up at her as she climbed onto the back porch roof, holding the first Galaxie 500 record on the small imprint Aurora. "What the fuck? Don't you destroy that record! It's so hard to find!"

Laughing, she slowly took the black vinyl from the white sleeve and paused. She took a sip of her beer and, as if she were doing a slow striptease, she turned, her sundress billowing in the air, and arced the record onto the steamy roof.

"Hey, this isn't funny anymore!" I pleaded.

"You destroy one of my things, I'll destroy one of yours," she repeated. Tossing her head back, she jumped upon the record and shimmied it into the roof. It was utterly destroyed.

1975.

I **have a photograph of myself, circa nineteen-seventy-six,** standing in the backyard of our new house in Newport News, Virginia. It was our second house in Newport News, in reality it wasn't a house but a condominium, with a "brick" façade hiding the particle board innards as if this apparition of strength could hide the fragile, cheap-as-hell construction of the building. We moved from another part of Newport News with concerns that my brother and I were not fitting into our school. Struggling as a family, perhaps moving into something akin to the suburbs might help quiet the chaos that was chewing up our household. My brother was not adjusting to the moves, and the quiet secrets of our lives were coming out in fits of anger and confusion. The condo-community we moved into was filled with families of Navy personnel and middle-class working-class families. I had a small room I shared with my brother, my sister had a room just next to ours and the bathroom connected the hallway to the master bedroom. The yard was roughly ten feet by ten feet, big enough to catch a lizard in and that was about it.

In the photograph, I am wearing a red and white tee-shirt of the Washington Redskins, although I was already a Steelers fan like my big brother. Perhaps, I was trying to find my

love, death & photosynthesis

own identity as an eight year old; perhaps others were trying to find it for me. The photo is faded as so many photos from the seventies are, instantly dated, as if the picture was taken behind marbled glass, it gives the impression that the whole world was slightly askew and blurred. When looking at photographs from the nineteen thirties and forties, it feels as if the poverty that gripped the thin weathered faces of those who managed to stand upright during the great depression was more severe in black and white— as if the world was never in color. Blurred and fuzzy, I stood in the backyard, knowing that even if this was yet another new house, new school and new friends, no matter what, I would forever be tethered to the feelings of isolation that I felt that moment.

2002-2005.

Jim Williams, a semi-retired businessman who loved to sail, eat, and get drunk, was 15 years older than Jenny. They were living in Miami with his elderly mother, a cantankerous woman who never thought her son had amounted to anything. She would take broad shots at him, causing the giant ape of a man to slump at times into a mass of tears and hiccups. There would be times when I would be talking to Jim on the phone and I could hear his mother's shrill voice in the background, sounding like a villain from an Alfred Hitchcock movie, berating him as he struggled through braced teeth and watery mind to vent his frustrations and ask for advice from me.

The first time I met Jim in person was in a DoubleTree hotel in downtown Columbus in 2002. I had been warned by my friend Tom Shannon, who had met him earlier that year, that Jim was a character even by Jenny's standards. Jim opened the door in his bathrobe; he had a thick thatch of black hair, combed over as if he were a police detective in some '70s movie. He was large, with broad shoulders and a wide face that looked pained and stiff even through his smile. He showed me in, and as he sat down in the large plush chair his penis poked its way out of the robe, just checking on the company. Jenny came bounding out of the bathroom, eyes wide and mouth motoring away. She gave me a big hug and said I looked good. I was in perhaps the best physical shape of my life from running five to seven miles a day and recently giving up alcohol. Regardless of how I felt physically, mentally and socially, I was hesitant to be there. The booze that had weighed me down for years had been put away, replaced by exercise, therapy, an itchy mind and a new-found interest in meditation. Jenny was able to cast most of this aside— or I was, with what I felt of her frenetic presence.

A litany of prescription pill bottles huddled around one another on the table, each one hoping to be the next pill popped. Jim, knowing I didn't drink, asked if I wanted a mineral water, I declined. I actually wanted to get out of there at the earliest opportunity. The claustrophobia pushed against the walls with every word Jenny spoke and every peek of Jim's limp penis from his blue bathrobe. The room smelled of excess, a palpable feeling of uneasiness overtook me. Jenny and Jim glanced at one another, giving each other quiet cues that I was not supposed to understand. We made small talk. It was obvious there was more going on than I could place. Jenny grabbed a Heineken and pulled me into the bathroom. She said, "I don't know what I'm going to do with Jim. He is going to kill himself, or me." I eyed her carefully, looking for signs of physical abuse. Jenny had a propensity for getting the shit knocked out of her by men. "I'm fine," she said, following my eyes. "He hasn't hit me." She peeked through the doors. "No, it's the coke and prostitutes combined with all those medicines he takes." Her hand fluttered towards the other room. It was if she were both waving to the crowd of medication as well as trying to magically make them disappear. Looking for a way to bolt through the door, I twisted my foot, perhaps trying to bore my way through the floor. "I think I love him but things get crazy sometimes. I don't really do the coke, he does almost all of it," she added through tight lips, her voice as pressured as a fire hose.

I was roughly six months removed from my last drink, flailing around emotionally as if a toaster had been dropped into my inner bathtub, and I didn't know what to say. I said "Well, why don't you get your shit together and move back to Columbus?" She regarded me with contempt, "There you go again, trying to run my life. You don't even listen. You are no fun, Mr. High-Horse." I was baffled, I certainly had no idea what had just happened. Was she asking me for help or not? Jim opened the door, now dressed in casual slacks and a collared short-sleeve shirt that had a gold anchor embroidered over his heart. "Everything OK in here?" he asked through clenched teeth. His movements were like Frankenstein's, slow, clumsy, and tense. Jenny nodded. "Yeah, Bela was just saying he had to leave." Jim shook his head. "We wanted to take you out for lunch, wherever you wanted to go. As a gesture for all the help you have given us." Confused, I shook his clammy hand; I noticed he too had opened a beer. I could spot a bottle of beer from 300 feet. I had put down the bottle, but I still had beerdar.

"Jim, nice meeting you. Perhaps we can drive down and see you guys in Miami?" I offered. Jim replied, "I'd love to take you guys out on the Lord Jim and out to dinner." The Lord Jim was his yacht; Jim was a trophy-winning sailor. Jenny flatly stated "Bye." I left, shaking with anger and frustration as the elevator took me down to the lobby. I wanted to call my support persons, but they had all warned me that I wasn't ready to see Jenny.

For the next three years, Jenny and Jim would battle back and forth and the weirdness would get weirder and more bizarre. Jim felt an affinity towards me, he admired me because I had been able to quit drinking and stayed quit and for the fact that I cared deeply for Jenny. Jim was a man of individual and familial wealth. Jenny and Jim traveled a great deal, to the Caribbean and to Colorado where they no doubt got hammered and skied, an unknowing sideshow for the rich and famous as they bungled on the slopes and cleared the bar with hic-cuppy stories of their escapades. Jim told me that he was mentally ill, which didn't take much convincing for me to believe, although he denied that he ever had a substance abuse problem. He compared his use with Jenny's, which is like comparing a head cold to leukemia. Jenny would suffer extreme withdrawal symptoms with tremors, vomiting, and pain in her back when she tried to quit drinking. Jim, on the other hand, would have to deal only with a few days of headaches and crankiness.

In the summer of 2003 I got a call from Jim, they had taken the Lord Jim out into the ocean where they planned to detox themselves. Jenny and/or Jim had smuggled some cocaine onto the boat. Jim was concerned about Jenny; his voice was a whisper. He made no sense. "Bela," he whisper-slurred, "you gotta help us. We're out in the ocean and Jenny is claiming that there are people on the boat making her perform sex acts. Listen, I've searched the boat, we are the only people on here."

"Um, why don't you go back and take her to the hospital?" I offered.

Jim, suspicious as a possum said, "Well, I'd like to but she says they'll come and get us if we go back now. I think we should wait it out."

Taking several deep breaths, I tried to wrap my mind around the conversation. "What the hell is going on, Jim?" I demanded.

"I dunno," he clenched, "but there isn't anybody on this boat with us and she insists there is."

love, death & photosynthesis

I heard Jenny in the background. "Who are you talking to, is that Bela? Put him on." Jenny's voice was animated. "Bela, you gotta call the Coast Guard or somebody, we are out on the boat trying to get clean and there are these…OK, don't laugh, I'm serious here, there are these miniature people here and they are making these pornos and making me participate."

Knowing what I knew about Jim, I found this plausible. 'Fuck,' I thought, 'Jim is making her make midget porn. That fucker.' "What the fuck is he making you do!" I asked out loud.

"Nothing. Jim doesn't know about it, they hide when Jim comes to the front of the boat. It's crazy, they aren't like midgets they're like normal proportioned people just real small. The bald guy is the leader. You gotta help. Jim doesn't know what to do but they are real evil people. They're sneaky as hell."

Jim got back on the phone. "Jim," I offered, "I think you need to take Jenny back to Jackson County Hospital."

Jim's response was measured and thoughtful. "I suppose you're right. Maybe we should, huh? You think she could be imagining all of it?"

1986.

Steve was unlike anyone I had never met, with wispy blond hair cut in layered steps, he was lean but athletic with veiny forearms and biceps that slightly bulged from under his Little Caesar's pizza shirt. He had a trimmed mustache, which wasn't odd since this was 1986 when Magnum PI mustaches weren't ironic. The only thing that brought suspicion was his multiple gold hoops in both ears. He was funny, hysterically funny in fact, cracking jokes while he plied the dough, rolling his eyes at the serious assistant manager who wanted every pizza to contain the exact amount of cheese, sauce and pepperoni; to deviate from using the scale meant a loss of revenue. The fact that the pizza tasted like the cardboard it was served in didn't seem to matter. Having recently left the Navy he was working at the pizza place to get enough money to return to San Diego; it was obvious that he was worldlier than all of Livingstone Avenue in Springfield, Ohio. Awkwardly, I tried to knead dough, weigh the cheese and construct pizza boxes, never ending pallets of pizza-boxes. Shy, keeping to myself, I sang my favorite songs to myself and on my breaks I hid in my car and listened to WOSU, trying to find the strength from college radio to make the next hundred pizza boxes. He asked me what music I listened to and he was familiar with the same, he had also seen R.E.M. a few years ago at the Wittenberg Fieldhouse and he has a certain fondness for the Smiths. He asked me to go party with him and his friends the next time we worked together.

That night, telling Jenny that there was one island of sanity in the Little Caesar's Pizza shop, one person who didn't talk about his truck, niggers, or pussy, Jenny said I should go out with him and his friends that Friday. She was working at a drive-in theater; I could pick her up afterwards. "He sounds like the one lone person in Springfield that isn't a racist asshole, plus he said he likes the Smiths so you guys should go out and pick me up later" she advised as the whirl of the tape deck rolled and we passed a bottle of Boone's Farm Strawberry wine back and forth until we just felt right.

Friday rolled around and I went to work, flush with my first paycheck, all $85 of it. I was ready to hit the bars. I looked older and had a smudged-up I.D. The drinking age was 19 at the time. He asked if I was going out after work. I said, "Sure, but I need to leave at midnight to get my girlfriend."

Eyebrows raised, he said, "Oh you have a girlfriend? I never would have guessed."

"Why not?"

Laughing, he said, "Oh, I just assumed you were gay like me, that's all."

For a moment, the world flip-flopped. 'Gay. He thinks I'm gay, and furthermore, he's gay.' Nauseated, every sort of assumption I held true was in flummox. 'Maybe I'm gay and don't know it.' Fer Christ sakes.

I made an excuse and left early, telling him I would catch him next week. What now? If I'm gay, then I can't be in love with Jenny. Is this why I want to move to Columbus? I had been told as a child that Columbus was "a smorgasbord of homos" and that Lucifer walked the earth, and that he would try to tempt me, most likely in the guise of a gay man—all of this spoken in a very serious tone by my Hungarian father.

After I picked Jenny up, we went back to the parsonage, and I confessed my fears to her that maybe I was queer. Although I could never remember ever being attracted to a man before, and I had a stack of Playboy magazine's next to my bed—that had to mean something. "It's ok, if you're gay," she said, stroking my head, "but I don't think you are." Putting a soft hand on my lap. Afterwards, I couldn't shake the feeling that maybe I was, this man had no gay stereotypes, which was all I had been taught living in rural Ohio, no lisp, he was built like a running back and he liked the same music as me. And I liked him, he made me laugh, made me feel welcome in the shit-hole of fast food pizza. I ran to the toilet, barreling through doors, crouching on the floor I emptied my guts into the toilet bowl. "I want to go to my mom's," I said, tears streaming down my cheeks. The world was asunder.

My mother drove from Galion, where she lived with her boyfriend, and I spent a day contemplating what being a gay man might be. Everything would be different, my relationships, my family, the way I socialized and most importantly, the sex would change. When fed hate and ignorance, you try to reject these ideas, but it's difficult. I was bewildered. I had not the ability to understand that you could have relationships with gay men and not have gay sex. The world was still black and white, unspoken lines separated everybody and it would not be until living in Columbus did I fully understand that the world is only black and white if someone chooses to see it that way.

1991.

At the end of our senior year of high school Jenny and I were voted "best couple" and she was voted "funniest female." Our late teens were filled with a great deal of laughter intermingled with heavy laborious desolation. I accepted her promiscuity and other traits that only years later would I identify as symptoms of mania; I just rode it out. I was ignorant, young, and in love. I also had nobody else to turn to. My brother was living in Germany and I was somewhat estranged from the rest of my family. Jenny and her mother were basically it. We spent our time drinking, listening to music, and playing euchre.

In our early twenties, Jenny started writing songs and short stories and making sculptures out of found objects. She would stay up for days on end, her mind twirling as fast as a window fan on the highest setting. Thoughts and ideas would spin out of her as if her mouth was shuffling cards. As much as she could spit energy into a room she could also ingest the energy and suck it dry, leaving the inhabitants sweaty and uncomfortable. Oblivious, the propulsive interjection of her farfetched and usually hilarious words would continue unabated. It was transfixing. She gathered men in her wake like a sex-infused pied piper. The rest of us would sit and watch. Unbeknownst to me, Jenny had dropped out of college, just a few credits short of graduation.

Jenny pursued laughter like antelopes chase fields of grass; she would chase it at all costs with little care for lions lurking nearby. She would climb aboard whatever make-believe spacecraft she had hovering in her head. "Hey Bela, check it out!" And she would lead me upstairs to a place that used to be our bedroom and was now either a greenhouse or a recording studio. "Where the fuck is our bed?" I'd ask. "Oh, it's in the closet. Don't you like my garden? I think I can grow some tomatoes up here. I bought some grow lamps, we can grow weed as well, but I know you don't care for it. I think you have to hang it out to dry or something" she said, tapping the side of her purple-flowered house dress. Her mind thinking and planning and rocketing forward.

"How the hell did you buy them? With what money?"

"I got paid, dumbass."

"We have to pay fucking rent, what the hell are you thinking?"

"Relax, you get paid this week so we can use that."

"What about food, utilities, car insurance? Are you out of your fucking mind?"

"You know, this is why you will never get fucking laid when I leave you Bela. You are so fucking serious, a fucking drag. It's always money this, politics that. Bullshit. You are no fucking fun. Here I thought you would love to have a garden in the house and you just bitch."

"This *garden* is in the motherfucking attic! Who the fuck grows tomatoes in their fucking attic, in fucking March?! And doesn't pay their rent?!"

"Fuck you, Bela, I'm going to go have fun and *you* are not invited!" With that she would go to my wallet, grab whatever cash I had and leave. Later, after listening to records and having a few drinks I would mosey down to Larry's and meet up with her. She would be surrounded by men, and as I scooted in next to her, glaring at whatever philosophy student was trying to get in her pants, all was forgiven. "Thank God you got here Bela, that guy wouldn't leave me alone."

One night at around 10 I arrived home to find it empty. It was bucket beer night at Mean Mr. Mustard's so I headed over there. I got a beer and brought it out back and there to my disbelief was a group of men gathered around a picnic table chanting as Jenny drank beer being poured down the backside of a greasy workmate of hers named Eric. She didn't flinch when she saw me, bug-eyed and furious. "Hey Be," she tossed over her shoulder, "you gotta try this, it's fucking hilarious. We call it the Australian Butt-Chug." And with that she switched places with Eric, dropped her panties and had beer poured down her backside for Eric to drink. I didn't know whether to be horrified, pissed, or to laugh. I just took a swig of my beer, shook my head and wandered back inside to watch the goths sway like drunken vampires to the Sisters of Mercy.

At this time, I was drinking so much that I had a hard time keeping vertical most nights. My body seemingly cemented in two seconds ago, I would grin in the frozen melting of time as the rest of the world moved by me in real-time. On some of these occasions Jenny would take the opportunity to baffle me by her quick dexterity, tearing all the clothes off my body and pushing me out the front door and locking it, cackling from the window and pointing at my nakedness. I would limp off to the nearest place to hide with a dumb-ass drunken smirk on my face. On one of these occasions I remember being stuck in the prickly bush laughing and begging for someone to get me some clothes. Dan Dougan, who owned Stache's, lived upstairs. He'd shake his head in bewilderment. "Jesus, you guys are fucking nuts." This was everyday behavior for us, we thought nothing of it.

During her down periods she would forget to do laundry or dishes; she would smoke pot and watch *The Guiding Light*. Her keyboard would stay under the couch. We would always drink.

I tried to piece together fragments of what domestic life was supposed to be, culled from prime-time television, after-school specials and Sunday morning services. If one isn't shown how to love, then the dance of love between lovers will be clumsy, performed in fits and starts, full of bliss followed by anger, pain and most likely confusion. Metaphorically, it's like putting together the largest jigsaw puzzle but without a picture to know what you are putting together. Some pieces will slide together, as if by greased by butter while others will struggle under the weight of a thick thumb trying in vain to make that LITTLE FUCKER WORK, GODDAMNIT! But alas, they don't and the pain of this confusion leads inevitably to more pain. We learn from our parents, and as I gaze back over the shoulder of my past, lined with globs of dirt bundled up in the road I have walked, at times there are no foot-prints— only the squished plants and the indentation of my body in the trenches off the road. I get the sense that my parents and caregivers had not one idea how to navigate the surging tides of love and sex in their own lives. I am emotionally clumsy, with trepidation to truly give of myself, a key ingredient of love. To give that part of oneself can be danger-ous, should be dangerous, a great risk worth a great reward. But, if one's self is built upon a foundation of worthlessness, how does one find that worthy of giving? Love is epic, as wide and deep as the sea, and like the sea able to well up in white crested waves that can come crashing down in violence, churning, bending and pulling in every direction.

Drinking alone was becoming a habit, although listening to music can make the exercise an almost spiritual experience. Summer had come and settled over the city like a moist shawl. If Jenny wasn't home by nightfall—which she usually wasn't—I'd bring a six-pack into the living room, sit on the floor with legs outstretched, the sounds of High Street floating through the open window mixed with The Rolling Stones' *Beggars Banquet* while the television flickered a semi-forgotten Steve McQueen movie. Three cans in, flipping the record over, looking at the small plastic clock that ticked past 2 AM, a small fear would clutch my chest—it was hard to breathe as I contemplated the fact that she just might not come home until 5 AM again. Sleeping alone, even briefly, was frightening to me. I'd picture my partner giving head to someone else or moaning in pleasure while I stared at the ceiling, unable to sleep. With every late night excursion she took, a small part of me would harden. The cicadas had landed that year, digging out of their 17-year slumber. With only a day to find a partner before death swept over the mass of them, they sang songs of courtship and filled the air with lovelorn chatter.

The Travel Agency, a bar, where she worked was roughly two blocks from our apartment. As the ache built in my heart with every minute after closing time that she stayed away, I debated walking over and fetching her as if she were school-aged: "Jenny you are missing your supper." But that was a trip I had made before. Walking in on her standing in a circle of people, performing her verbal wit and physical comedy to fireworks of laughter. I would enter unsteadily, unsure of my role, only knowing that I wanted her next to me, the surety that she made my other half whole and I felt naked without her. Every time as I approached, I felt the eyeroll, the invisible needling of an elbow in my ribs, to my heart. "Uh, Jenny it looks like your boyfriend is here," some drunk would mutter. Another would raise eyebrows high, and her boss, Randy, the balding former wrestling coach who had repeatedly professed his love to her many times in my presence would rush from behind the bar and yell, "She's still working, she has to help clean up. You can leave now." Turning, she would offer a shrug. "Well, Bela, yet again you arrived too late to the party, just go home and wait for me." On some occasions, she might be weirded out by some creep and ask me to stick around.

It would take me years to recognize that the waiting I held fast in my chest, the anxious energy that built up within me, the wondering, the visions of awful deeds that would dance in my mind was the same pain and fear that I would cause my future partners as the hold of alcohol gripped me tightly, holding my feet fast to the bottom of the bar stool long after the doors had closed, or sinking me to another woman's bed like a thrown stone to the bottom of a lake.

But back then, that one night waiting for Jenny while the cicadas sang away with their doomsday heartache, the front door did open. Footsteps landed on the creaky lino-leum kitchen floor. "Bela, I'm home. I brought a few drinks with me. Aren't you glad I'm home on time?" She wasn't, but it was better than 4 AM. Plopping down on the floor, she asked, "Why are you watching the television without sound?" "Because it's stupid." I did not turn her way. The enjoyment of drinking alone had elbowed everything else out. After a few moments of silence, she moved to the couch, speaking into the air. Her words landed around me, as if they were discarded plastic army men left on the imagi-nary battlefield of childhood.

1995.

Robin and I drove to the courthouse together, to untie the knot that we had made just months prior. We did the dissolution for the low sum of $500, and since we owned very little, it was easy. We appeared in the courtroom, signed some paperwork, and our marriage was over.

Stepping back out, Robin and I looked at one another, nervous smiles across our faces, trying to figure out the next step. We were emotionally wobbly, it was as if our insides had been on an amusement park ride for the past nine months. On the car ride back home, we stopped for a drink, then another drink, and finally got a 12-pack. Nervous energy bounced off each other. Was it sadness, anger, relief, or shame? Heading to the bedroom, we undressed and engaged in the one activity that lifted all oppressing emotions for at least a little while. Afterwards, she laid her head on my chest. Feeling as if I were standing too close to a campfire, my eyebrows singed, I bolted upright. "I gotta go, now!" Scowling, she replied, "That's just like you, you are such a fucking asshole, God I hate your fucking guts. You've *ruined* my fucking life!" I wrestled on a pair of jeans while fleeing, hopping one legged across her bedroom, trying to twist my foot in, one hand holding both shoes while the trousers seemed like they were perfectly happy on the floor, my little dog Istvan staring up at me, wondering where I was going.

Lurching to Ted Hattemer's place, I picked up another 12-pack. The sun dazzled above, a stark contrast to the gray that filled me. Plopping in front of Ted's stereo, I listened to "Dear You" by Jawbreaker. Jawbreaker expressed so much doubt inherent to relationships between disenfranchised people, but avoided the forlorn victimhood of Morrissey, the wariness of lust and love that The Smiths sang about but infused with anger and frustration. That night, after a quick drunken nap, I decided to go out, as there was nothing else to do. I went to Larry's, quickly made conversation with a dark-haired woman who had tattoos stretching up one arm and down the other. At her place, I learned that the trail of tattoos stretched from her ass to her neck. It seemed in the darkness as if they moved by themselves. I felt distant, as if I were a shadow myself, devoid of a body, just drifting over her walls. Afterwards, her fingers tracing my spine, I heard her saying, "What did you say?"

"Nothing, I didn't think I was even talking. I'm sorry. I'm really sorry." I was apologizing for everything: my failed marriage, the shitty and sloppy sex, the breath I exhaled. I wanted an inner shower.

The next night, I went to Stache's, and ended up at The Blue Danube where I ran into Jerry and two women drinking at the bar. Jerry cracked to the women that I just got a divorce which somehow impressed them. Either they were amazed someone would marry a schlup like me or that I had lived long enough to be married and divorced. We eventually ended up downtown, the four of us, dancing at the Garage, our bodies twisting and flicking sweat onto all the gay men hurtling themselves to heavy techno beats. Lost. I went home with one of those women. The urgency to be held. Waking up the next morning in another strange house alone was unnerving. She had left a note with her name and number on the table along with a coffee, still warm. Walking home I was overcome with an even heavier sense of loss than I had the day before.

The night after that, I found myself at Dow's on High and then at Dick's Den. I ran into a bartender named Jen, with whom I had been flirting for years. She said "good" when I told her I was divorced three days ago. Groggy and wobbly, I asked if she wanted to go back to my house to listen to records, the indie version of asking if one wanted to partake in intercourse. Although, on this night as the Pabst and Maker's Mark gave up on pleasing me and instead dredged up more guilt, listening to records really was all I wanted to do.

The attic of Ted's house had been reconstructed to handle my divorce. It was lined with records, CD's, books and a few barely alive plants. The floor was littered with T-shirts and much of the free area on shelves and the dresser had empty beer bottles stuffed with the ends of tan cigarette butts. The bed that at one time was my grandparents' was huge, as it was constructed to hold my grandmother's enormous girth and the dying body of my grandfather. It filled the bedroom. Sheets twisted across it as if they had been lifted by a mini-tornado and deposited at the other end. Dog hair was thick on the carpet beside the bed, but I changed the sheets regularly although the dogs didn't seem to care one bit; I kept it as clean as I could. I had slept in enough stranger's beds to be aware of how it feels to lie naked on a filthy mattress. "It's clean," I said as I pointed to the bed, "except for all that dog hair. I mean, the dogs are also clean, I bathe them. You know? Those beer bottles are new, smell them. I drank them the past few days, same with the clothes. I mean, I didn't drink the clothes. I wore them, but just the past few days. I'm not dirty." At this point, I started to move my hips ever slow slightly to the rapturous sounds of Les Thugs "I Love You So." She smiled. "I mean," casting a mischievous smile her way, "I'm dirty but not like dirt dirty", thinking drunkenly that this sounded witty. We kissed, I leaned into her, but then I wasn't feeling so dirty any longer. Just sad. So fucking sad.

I stopped kissing, sat on the edge of the bed until "I Love You So" faded into the next song, which wasn't nearly as epic and said "hold on." Putting on the first Bee Gees record, I took a piss and came back, talking ahead of myself at the greatness of the Bee Gees and there she stood, naked, with only her earrings covering a small part of that blond hair and a touch of her neck. 'Shit,' I thought, 'I can't do this.' I hugged her, perched myself back on the corner of the bed. She kissed my neck, placing a hand on my chest, "I can't do this now." "Why? You know we didn't come to your house to listen to records." I looked down, not knowing what to say. "I just got my divorce," I muttered as she pulled my shirt up. I was listless both inside and out. "Yeah…," she purred. I waited a few moments, taking some breaths. What to say? "Ummm, I got my divorce because I'm gay," I croak. She waits, then turns my head, kisses me fully on the lips. Eyeing me, she places her hand around my penis as it grows. She smiles and says, "You are *not* gay." And we follow the drunken playbook into the early morning but the sadness remains.

1984-1988.

The crackle of the needle would instantly lift a sour mood as the grooves of the black spinning vinyl record would magically propel me from the displaced atmosphere churning inside of me into somewhere brighter. It was the simplest escape I knew, it didn't involve medication, money or the awkwardness of sex. I hoarded records; their music offered a sense of protection. I collected these round flattened globs of wax like a child clutches his stuffed animals. Each song was about either setting the mood, matching the mood, or changing it. Music provided an elixir to a feeling of isolation; it helped many of us through the suffering afternoons and evenings of adolescence. An opportunity to escape in our bedrooms or, when we hit 16, in our cars, as bald tires lifted us from the mundane and often cruel existence of high school. An album was a vacation, a chance to step into the life of someone bigger than the confines of our current existence. Our favorite singers told stories that we could relate to but at the same time only dream about. In a record or book I could reassure myself of the existence of a world that was different from the one I was surrounded by: cornfields, inarticulate language and dull flatness. I felt constricted by tight fearful conservative values and male stereotypes.

I read ridiculous musical biographies such as *Up and Down with The Rolling Stones*, *Hammer of the Gods*, and *No One Gets Out Of Here Alive*. I mistrusted the glorification of a drug addled rock star whose sexuality made up for poor poetry. I felt that rock stars should be approachable and the sort of people whom I could have a conversation with. My meeting R.E.M. at the age of 15 bolstered this as Peter Buck and Michael Stipe both asked me to go drinking with them after the Wittenberg concert, my older looks combined with a drinking age of 19 helped a great deal with this invite.

My senior year of high school, I traveled to Cleveland and saw Lou Reed play the Music Hall and waited patiently with arms clutching half of his cutout bin catalog for his signature. "Glad you're a fan," he mumbled as he scrawled his name across "Street Hassle" and "The Bells." Lou was much smaller than I had pictured him in my teenage mind. At that time, Lou was doing advertisements for Honda scooters and with his dark sunglasses he was the epitome of cool. He stood in front of me, shorter than me, peering over his sunglasses as beads of sweat dotted his face, his hands shaking as he held my records. He was in his mid-forties and he was totally human. He glanced at me again. "How old are you?"

"I'm 17. Me and my girlfriend." I nodded towards Jenny, who was beaming. "We drove from the middle of nowhere to see you."

"Middle of nowhere, huh? Seventeen? That's cool," he said more to himself than to anybody else. "Keep cool," he advised, and slipped into his white van.

This encounter made sense and did not diminish my attraction to him. It was the humanness of the Velvet Underground and punk rock that I found solace in. There was no fantasizing about the men and women who had provided me sanctuary; they were as real as my own awkward 17-year-old self.

Jerry, too, mistrusted the excesses of rock stardom, despite in his own way aspiring to be a star. It had to more with being immortal for him than holding riches or beautiful models on his arm; he was too sensitive to regard women that way.

Jerry and I channeled our passion for music in divergent ways. Jerry picked up the guitar while I never had the discipline nor the inclination to be a musician. I desired only to make my mark as a fan. I envisioned myself as a writer who would document the events around myself. Jerry craved attention. At the same time he held it at bay: he insisted that it be on his terms.

Jenny sucked up the music falling like rainwater around me, puddles of notes, the secrets and community that gathered. Unlike me—a fan—she approached music from the inside. Her appreciation was as an artist, although she would be loathe to ever identify herself as such. Not even later, in interviews. Her creativity was a product of the propulsive forces within her, the windmills of mania that rotated like bicycle tires speeding down a hill, she had no time for reflective introspection about what came out of her.

Some people burst quickly, like a living firework, or in small twinkles, the flashing of a firefly. Jenny was both—at first she burned brighter than the surface of Mercury and then later she was transformed into something small, bleak, and feeble. Her light was extinguished by drowning it sip by gulp over the years. Jerry was a lit match, get too close and he would burn your fingertips, but he could light up a room with his humor, wit, and songs.

Jerry wanted to be remembered, to be plastered on some kid's wall, a cigarette dangling from his passive lips, eyes scrunched for the camera—in the 20th Century one way to live forever was through records.

Jenny had no inclination towards fame, she wanted attention but didn't think too long about the package of being her, of being an artist—her mind was too unsettled for contemplation. She wanted to sing, to laugh, and in hindsight, to be a part of. To stave off the inner turmoil that ate her up.

1991-2001.

Ted Hattemer was active in the indie-rock scene long before I ever met him in 1991, he was a bearded long-haired bartender at Bernie's, slinging mugs of imported beer for barflies who would try to travel the world on a barstool without ever leaving the cozy, stinking confines of the underground bagel shop. Ted was involved in all types of bands with ridiculous sounding names during the late '80s such as Cavejacket before finding a home in the moody and lumbering Stupid Fuckin' Hippie for which he played bass.

It was at this juncture that I began to know Ted— he was soft spoken, polite, and articulate, and brought a sense of seriousness to any interaction. Stupid Fuckin' Hippie, in hindsight was not that terrific of a band but they did provide a respite from the more amplified churning of most High Street punk and funk bands that dotted most night-clubs. Stupid Fuckin' Hippie sounded like Monster Magnet's little brother without the sense of junkie-dangerousness that early Monster Magnet brought to the table, SFH did not see the necessity to explore anything harder than what most college undergrad-uates experiment with. For the summer of 1992 or '91, Stupid Fuckin' Hippie was the soundtrack at Bernie's and they appeared to be the house band. As the summer rolled on they vastly improved—with their singer Steve (who bore an uncanny resemblance to Jim Morrison) becoming more comfortable with a guttural growl, they provided a pleasant backdrop to playing the Terminator pinball game and swigging Black Label beer.

Ted worked for Ohio State University; he was basically the only person on the scene who had a real job, one that you had to wash a shirt for or even button up. Although it should be noted that Eric's Trip, an un-melodic psychedelic band whose singer had spooky eyes and blew fire out of his mouth, had a working lawyer in the band. Ted worked on computers for the university and he lived in a large house with several men who would later form the more organic sounding Moviola. At this point, Anyway Records was generating a bit of a buzz, with all five of our first singles selling out immediately upon release. Jerry and I did not think of re-pressing anything, we were too hurried to think backwards so we wanted to get as much out as we could. One would never know when the proverbial other shoe would drop. He and I both had lifetimes of shoes dropping around us, their clatter bearing witness to the utter bafflement of our lives.

Gaunt was in the midst of recording their first full-length and I was bankrolling almost all of Anyway myself. Jerry was supposed to be providing a chunk of money, but simply didn't have it. He was disappointed with my leanings towards more pop friendly choices in bands (Log, Greenhorn and Belreve) while his big project was a single by Monster Truck Five whose squalid sounds would frighten the paint off a witch's house. I ended up paying for over half of the MT005 single including the mastering which took an afternoon to do. The noise of the MT005 tape caused the arm of the lacquer machine to jump off the waxy plate every time the engineer tried to carve the sounds into the lacquer. John Hull, a kindly old man who ran our local pressing plant, turned to me after several hours and asked gently, shaking his head softly, "So, people listen to this?" I nodded. "I suppose." Jerry and I were both too unskilled to resolve our annoyances at one another over the MT005 single and we simply did what we did best— bitch about the other person to anyone who would listen. At times, we both thought the other a complete idiot. Yet we were almost inseparable at this time. I was still nursing my breakup but had started coming out of my shell and was dating again, hesitantly. I came to the realization that alcohol would help with my renewed interest in dating. Jerry started drinking heavily at the same time. His flirtation with just drinking coffee and basically eating cigarettes ended as Gaunt became more of his focus. It's difficult to live in bars at night and not pick up a drink. It's like going to a rainstorm and expecting not to get damp.

Drinking proved the perfect antidote for so much of the unease we both felt being around people. We both soaked in attention as if we were lizards basking in the sun, yet doubted we deserved the attention. The alcohol was fun, we laughed nightly. Everything was absurd to us—paying taxes, having a career, getting married. These were all things to chuckle about. But laughing at life also proves difficult to maintain if one wants to embrace the living. Our arguments started mostly around music and women, with Jerry trying to protect me and at the same time trying to bed some of the same women I was. Deep down I strived for commitment, in spite of having a "normal" relationship being such a bizarre idea to me. In fact, I would usually have such inner doubt when it started happening that the easiest thing to do would be to split. Jerry never got to that point, his entire being was to mock any semblance of relationships, thus dooming most before they could get started. This, of course, made him lovable like a puppy that gets up off someone's lap and takes a shit in the middle of the living room and trots back expecting more cuddles. It caused a rift between us, me wanting normalcy and Jerry mocking me for it.

I was approached by Ted and Wayne Lin of Stupid Fuckin' Hippie during this summer and asked if Anyway would be interested in putting out a SFH single that they would finance. I replied sure. Both men worked as bartenders at one of my favorite places to drink, that was one reason, the other was that I thought their music was interesting. Jerry was not pleased, and by the end of the year he would leave Anyway to me. "You are going to do whatever the fuck you want anyway," he said over a beer one night. "Well, of course," I replied. "It's my fucking money, dipshit."

1990-91.

Craig Dunson was an interesting man. Guitarist for one of Columbus' most popular live bands, Pica Huss, Craig was an ex-marine who wore Roy Orbison styled glasses and had a great ear for melody. His style of playing was sophisticated but never showy. Craig took a shine to Jenny's songs, and soon he started recording her on his portable studio which was a step above Jerry's self-described Cornhole studios. Jerry was a bit miffed when this happened. Jerry wanted Jenny to be his discovery, but she had a knack for attracting multiple gifted musicians to help her.

Jenny and Craig formed Vibralux with Mark Deane on drums and Craig's girlfriend Gaye Conley on bass. One of the first songs they recorded, "Junk," was fragments of a poem I had written for her, wherein I tried to explain my smallness next to her colossal nature. "While your eyes say used, and your lips say I didn't love like I was supposed to, and words tumble out like junk dropped on the floor." Presciently, another line was: "You'll always be the subject for me." She pulled it together around a staggering hook that allowed Craig to soar on guitar. I was playing a rough mix of it one day at the record store when Bill Eichenberger from *The Columbus Dispatch* came in. He stopped in his tracks and asked, "Wow, what is that?" I gave him the tape and a week later Vibralux had a full-color article in *The Dispatch* without even playing a show.

Vibralux: Jenny Mae, Mark Dean, Gaye Cronley, Craig Dunson

Ted had a 9-5 job *and* he was buying a house. Nobody I knew bought a house or a new car. And I trusted his judgment. Ted shortly became the de facto art-director of Anyway, laying out most of the covers for singles, CDs, and vinyl. He helped me find out how to procure a barcode for the label. Ted was a rock of stability in my life, allowing me to move into his house after my first marriage fell apart, lending me his car to drive to see a girl-friend, filling in as a soundman when I forgot to procure sound for a traveling band.

One time Craig played me a space-echoey song called "Wrecking Ball" by a gutter punk band named the Econothugs. I was blown away. It sounded like carnival version of Galaxie 500. Craig explained that the singer from the Econothugs, Jake Housh, was making a new band called Moviola and they would sound like this. Craig had formed a label, Eardrop, that would be putting out their single. There were many new labels sprouting up in Columbus, no doubt fueled by the idea that if two drunk fuckups like Jerry and I could find success, anybody could. What we all may have lacked in business or planning acumen was made up in passion and a giddiness for the absurd. Ted was going to play drums in Moviola.

1992.

For some there is a well of sadness, like the deepest darkest sea lurking under miles of ice. The rustling of life that tramples above stirs the sadness in quiet waves, a slight turn of a phrase by a friend or the leaving of a lover turns into a slow ache that upsets the balance of living, spiraling out in waves. A Chinese water-torture of the psyche. A rustling would build inside, stirring softly, and then explode into reckless behavior that was galvanic, shards of emotion shooting out like shrapnel.

Some of these explosions caused deep wounds in whatever emotionally frailty I had. My hurt was my own fault, Jenny claimed, due to my own stupid expectations about her actions. "You knew what you were getting into and I can't help it if you are so serious," she would pronounce, and tug a mouthful of smoke from her cigarette. After a few years of sleepless nights, and anxiety, there was a point where a person gets used to this sort of treatment; an emotional brawniness had formed within me. Nothing was shocking.

And then one night something did shock me. Spring was breaking through the March icicles; the sun was softening the hardness of the winter and after seeing Jenny at Larry's sitting by herself, we talked for a few hours. The conversation was easy, none of the bitterness that had been seeping into our fragile relationship was present, soon we laughed like we did just a few years ago. She asked me to walk her home, "some guy I made out with has been stalking me" she scanned the room, "he will come over and pound on my door in the middle of the night, but I just hide under the blankets." "Jesus Christ Jenny, you have to get your phone turned back on." She sniffed, "It's o.k., he's harmless, but he's not here. Can you walk me home just to make sure he isn't on my porch?" "Of course," as replied, swallowing the last of my Black Label, and we were soon stepping out the back door of Larry's into the brisk night. Walking home, we were silent as we slipped through alleys and cut through apartment complexes. Jenny suddenly clocked me in the head with her purse filled with beer bottles. We scuffled for a moment and I told her to stay away from me, that she was too scary for me.

The next day she checked herself into the psychiatric unit at Ohio State University. I was told I could not visit her. I don't think she told her parents. She was in there for over two weeks. It was the first of many hospitalizations for Jenny. Her illness and ways of treating it would slowly eat everything in her life that she had held of importance including her marriage, her pets, her house, cars, artwork, and music.

2004.

There was a feeling of normalcy to my life; Merijn and I had just come through a tunnel of self-destruction that was so fraught with personal chaos it appeared for a moment that the world around us had collapsed like a shattered bottle on cracked pavement. There were moments in the preceding years where the skin on my body appeared to be a separate entity, slithering away from inner thoughts that bordered on frenzied imbalance. I had awoken from years of creating a world of the absurd. I found myself with no idea how to move from the strangulated sense of self I'd created in my early twenties across the threshold of my mid-thirties. For a while I was the walking embodiment of "what-the-fuck." We had purchased a beautiful old house between the duplexes of north campus and the middle-class pleasantries of Clintonville. We were giving in to the passiveness of normalcy but not without an air of liberal steadfastness; it was as if we were challenging ourselves to stay rooted in the urban confines of Columbus even if we had to live next to a plasma center.

My wife had moved back to Ohio— we both chased a sober lifestyle built around a need to make up for lost time, not only in our relationship, but also just living as adults. I decided to return to college, an endeavor that had scared me shitless in my twenties. The last time I had been in college was 15 years prior, I had dropped out due to frustration, fear, and eventually finding a community that had a disregard for conventional living. Soon after buying and fixing up our house, she became pregnant with our first child. The fear of a domestic life was slowing ebbing away. Jenny soon arrived from Miami, she and Jim Williams had gotten into another fight and he sent her back to Ohio.

Jenny had a tough time that year in Florida; she had entered treatment for substance abuse and bipolar disorder numerous times. She was picked up by the Miami police multiple times on charges of public intoxication, disturbing the peace and for being a danger to herself. Jenny's life at that time was as if she were a walking drain, with every step she took she was swallowed a little bit by her madness and alcoholism. Swirling around in her daily chaos, it was amazing she could even travel from Florida to Ohio. She was repeatedly taken to the psych ward of Jackson County Hospital where she would spend anywhere from two days to several weeks as the doctors tried in vain to subdue the demons that danced in her head. It was not uncommon for me to receive up to 20 calls a week from Jim about Jenny's behavior. Finally, Jenny was arrested on charges of petty theft; she had stolen a mango shake as a joke and spent 90 days in jail. This was the longest period that she'd been sober since her early teenage years. She would phone me from jail and tell me horror stories of the abuse that went on in the Dade County women's jail. Only her humor got her through. She was beat up several times and was once put in isolation for her own protection. In one completely lucid moment she confessed to me, "I've always drank because I've always been afraid. Even when we lived together, I put our bed in the closet because I was scared people would get me." She elaborated on her ongoing battle with hallucinations. "Bela, you know when I told you about those men in the walls, the ones with the beards who were looking at me? I joked about it but I sometimes think they were real. It doesn't make sense and who would believe me?" When she got out of jail, Jim picked her up and soon enough the jail detox unraveled and they were off to the maniacal races, filled with shouting, bruises and tears wrapped around epic bouts of laughter and lovemaking.

Jenny returned to her mother's in South Vienna. This lasted roughly a week before her mother shipped her back to Columbus where her bridges had been torched by her unbalanced behavior. Her life savers were, by this time, burned to a cinder. She was too unpredictable now for many of the people who had reached out over the years to help. She found refuge in the kindness of Wil Foster who used to play in her band. Wil tried to help her the best he could but soon even a seemingly bottomless friendship finds its basement. Jenny was on the streets.

I awoke one morning to find her asleep in front of my car, a heap of booze-soaked personhood nestled underneath a few articles of clothing and twigs, with a large piece of Little Debbie Snack Cake plastic stuck to the side of her face. "Shit," she said when I roused her. "I didn't have any place to go." She winced as she pulled the plastic and small thorny branches off her face. "What the fuck, I don't even eat this shit." That night, I let her sleep in our garage but told her she couldn't drink in it and couldn't tell Merijn. I found her gone the next morning, the garage door open and an empty bottle of vodka upstairs next to her makeshift bed. She walked in while I stood there, my head trying to shake the disappointment from my shoulders. "Oh, shit, sorry." She tried to explain. I told her to leave and she started screaming at me. "Goddamnit, you're so fucking uptight, I can't believe anybody would live with your ass. You fucking control freak, what the fuck, you are such a son-of-a-bitch. Fine, I'll fucking find my own place, I don't need your fucking help if all you're gonna do is try to control me!" Taking a breath as if it were water, I said, "Jenny, there is some expensive stuff in here. What did I say, this is Merijn's studio." "Fuck you, it's not that, it's that you want to tell me what to do, always!" She continued yelling as I went into the house and called the police. By the time they arrived she was gone.

She was soon residing with another former band mate, Sean Woosley. I went to Sean's house one night to check on her. Jenny didn't open the door and I wasn't sure what to do. I turned the knob and the door opened directly into Sean's bedroom. I could see straight into the living room. The stereo was playing "Bee Thousand" by Guided by Voices. Shouting out Jenny's name, I proceeded with a sense of trepidation and doom. On the floor, surrounded by stacks of CDs was an empty bottle of vodka, going towards the kitchen there were several empty 40-ounce bottles of beer and another half empty bottle of vodka. I yelled her name again, fearing that there would be no answer. A painful groan came from the bathroom, and in the corner was the tattered woman I once knew. She smiled a smile that was broken and carved with twisted decisions and so much suffering. "Hey, baby," she murmured. I called 911. Within a few minutes an ambulance arrived and all I could do was show them what she drank. In a voice slurred with tears, snot and vodka she protested about going to the hospital. "I ain't that fucked up, I've been worse." I nodded with raised eyebrows that this was probably true.

The ambulance had a small window that separated the cab from the rear. I tried to supply helpful information. She doesn't live here, she lives in Miami, she is 34 years old, and she has no money or ID. She has bipolar disorder. She doesn't work. Suddenly Jenny became lucid and started flirting with one of the EMTs. "That is a sexy mustache you have there, young man. You can call me mama." Soon there was laughter from the rear of the ambulance. In another moment Jenny crossed to the other side. "Hey, don't you try to fuck me!" she screamed. I looked back and she was trying to sit up, the mustached EMT looked at me baffled. "Get your fucking hands off my tits!" He instructed his partner to stop the ambulance. "I am warning you to settle down or I will put you in restraints" he said. "What so you can fuck me? Go ahead and try it!" This went on for the next two minutes before we arrived at the hospital.

In the emergency room she was talking, laughing again and then she went back into a slurred stupor. She had a BAC test and the doctor, a small Lebanese man with a gentle disposition shook his head. He said she had a BAC over .40, "I have never seen someone this intoxicated and I can't believe she is even talking let alone alive." She was dehydrated, and I spent the next 14 hours next to her in the emergency room, at times filled with disgust, horror and disbelief. The next day after hours of IVs she was discharged. I went home and she went back to Sean's. She phoned me later that night offering me thanks. Her voice was a bit off.

"Are you drinking?"

She paused. "Um, just a little to tide me over."

1998.

I was listening to Lucinda William's "Car Wheels on Gravel Road" at the record store on one of those afternoons that tasted like perfection, with enough breeze to take the bite out of the sunshine and keep the sweat off the back of one's ankles. I was nursing a Black Label that was stashed under the counter alternating each swig of beer with sips of black coffee. The few clouds in the sky drifted across the day, marking the dead time between lunch and the busy evening hours.

Gaunt had heavier commitments due to signing to Warner Brothers, and since Jerry didn't have a phone, he'd use the store phone to do all his business. He was too focused on what he was doing to care that our credit card machine went through the same phone line.

"Okay, Jerry, get off the phone we have a credit card," Ron would say.

Jerry would toss an incredulous look at Ron. "I'm fucking talking to our booking agent in France, hold on."

"Sorry about that," Ron would say to a bewildered customer. Thirty second pause. "Okay, Jerry get off the phone we have a credit card."

Jerry would huddle over the phone with his back to us, pretending not to hear.

Jerry Wick

bela koe-krompecher

"Jesus Christ, Jerry," I would yell, "you aren't even working today. Get off the phone we need to do this credit card!"

Jerry would hang up, glaring at both of us. "Well, if our European tour falls through, it's your fucking fault!" And he'd march up the stairs, lighting another cigarette even though he still had one burning in the ashtray.

When I had a call, it was another story. I had a good friend who was in one of the first battalions to have troops on the ground on Kuwait, Jon, who called me several times: "Shit, man, I saw a bunch of burned bodies today. It was like something out of a movie; these people were just like charcoal. Some still had guns in their hands, they fucking never knew what was coming." When I'd try to talk to Jerry about it, he'd look at me blankly. "Not my problem dude, your buddy shouldn't have joined the fucking Army!" Then he would turn tail and space out at the back counter. "Goddamnit Jerry, why do you have to be such an asshole?" I'd yell.

Sometimes I had to use the phone to order new records, mostly from small independent distribution companies. Revolver was the best for a variety of reasons. The calls would take some time and I needed to get the order in by late Monday so we were stocked for the weekend. A few years after taking over the ordering from Ron, I realized that sometimes, because of the time differences, the call from our sales rep would bleed into my 5:00 pm beer break at Larry's. Eventually, Bob our salesman just started calling me directly at Larry's to take the record order.

2001.

I woke up to the alarm and local news as usual. "An unnamed bicyclist was killed early this morning by a hit and run driver near the Ohio State Campus. A body was found on the intersection of Hudson and North Fourth Street and the pedestrian was later pronounced dead at The Ohio University Hospital." I blinked open my eyes. 'Wow, that is right at the end of our street. I may know that person,' I thought as I shimmied out of the blankets on my way to shower and drink a pot of coffee to prepare for my shift at Used Kids.

With one look at Ron, I knew something was wrong. His mouth was taut and flat. He said, "Bela, I have terrible news. Jerry was killed last night. The police just left." I stared at him and groaned a little, making some weird sort of animal noise. "Well, that can't be. I saw him last night, we hung out here." Ron shook his head. "I guess he got hit by a car, right by your house." I ran to the back room, buried my head in my hands and wept. The tears falling awkwardly out of my body, I felt the uneasiness of myself all around my being and wanted to be anywhere but where I was. Be anybody but who I was. I picked up the phone and called Merijn. She was sweet, said she would come home. I told her not to bother, I would stay at work. I didn't know what else to do. It was too early to start drinking.

I picked up the phone and called Jenny. She made the same kind of sound I did. "That can't be. Jerry? Are you sure? You get stuff wrong all the time." "Yeah, the cops were here and everything."

I walked back into the store, got another coffee and sat at the back counter, staring straight ahead. Soon, many of Jerry's friends around Columbus were phoning the store and dropping in. Dan Dow came in looking shell-shocked. Jim from the New Bomb Turks came by with Brett Lewis and we soon headed up to BW-3 and started drinking. Ron joined us.

Details began to surface. Jerry had spent most of the previous day at Used Kids with me and Mike Rep. We had started drinking around 5 and he shuffled between the Annex and Used Kids until a little after 8. We were in a pleasant mood, Jerry happy to be working as a cook for a semi-upscale diner in the Short North, and he had started recording again. He was making extra money selling some of his records on the burgeoning eBay market under the moniker of Monkey-Pizza. He had recently purchased a small GI Bill built Cape Cod in a neighborhood just across the freeway from Clintonville. He was patching up his relationship with his parents who were helping him fix up the house. After a few beers at Larry's, Jerry asked me to stay and hang out but I had designed a very strict regimen to help keep my own alcohol consumption in check. I did not drink on certain days, nor did I allow myself to be taken off this schedule. By the time of his offer at 9 PM I had already had five or six beers. I drove home and had a late dinner with my wife. Jerry had spent the rest of the evening between Larry's and BW-3. Some people said they saw him at Bernie's. At any rate, he bought a pizza to bring home.

Jerry never had a driver's license. He walked everywhere and eventually got a bicycle. A punk till the end, he didn't think he needed a light, reflectors, or a helmet. Balancing the pizza on his handlebars, dressed entirely in black, he coasted down the incline of 4th Avenue onto Hudson Street. There he was met by a small compact car, whose driver, after having his windshield smashed by Jerry's upper body, drove off into the night, leaving Jerry paralyzed by the side of the road with a broken neck. The driver would, nearly a week later amid public outcry, turn himself in, explaining to Columbus Police that he thought someone threw a rock at his windshield. Needless to say, a large swath of the community doubted this explanation. The man got off with a minor violation. He later tried to sue both Jerry's family and Used Kids for defamation. A few years later, battling my last fight with alcohol, I sat on a barstool next to a woman I had known for a long time. Placing her arm around my neck she pulled me close to her face. Her breath thick with vodka, she whispered more into my cheek than my ear, "My cousin was the one who killed Jerry. He smashed his car up. He's an asshole and a drunk."

1989.

It was a Wednesday and Jenny and I were celebrating the late afternoon the best way we knew how, in a corner booth with cheap beer, telling each other the stories of the day. Jenny worked in a restaurant with a Chinese woman who spoke very little English, and when an older customer asked about dessert, the Chinese woman stuck her head in the kitchen and asked "Ah, Yinny, what is dessert today?" Jenny, whose wit was quicker than her sense, replied, "We have pecan pie, chocolate pie and hair pie." The woman turned around and answered, "We have ah pecan pie, ah chocolate pie and ah haar pie." Jenny ran to the cooler and hid for the next ten minutes while the manager looked all over for the culprit.

In the table just off our booth a man with an Army backpack laughed along with me, he turned and smiling with crooked teeth said "Goddamn, that's the funniest thing I've heard in forever." He had hair just past his shoulder and smelled of pizza sauce and patchouli. He was drinking coffee. I'd noticed him at Used Kids and at some of the independent rock and punk shows I had started attending over the prior six months. I had seen him with his coffee cup at the basement bar down the street where we would watch local music for free and piss on tip-toes as a way to keep the overflowing toilets from flooding our tennis shoes. He had a notebook in front of him with a page filled with scribbles and a small doodle of a skinny man screaming into a ball of larger scribble. He had on a black T-shirt. The T-shirt said "Mudhoney" above four half naked men, it was a take-off of a Slits album cover. I was impressed. He pulled his chair over just as I was rising to go get a few more drinks. I asked him if he wanted one. He asked if I could get him some more coffee. He was still laughing from Jenny's story. As he handed me his cup I noticed his slightly bent shoulders and thin hands and arms; he was as skinny as a flagpole and his long hair draped over his bony shoulders like spaghetti over a mop handle. His entire being was like caffeine come to life. "Really, if you want a beer I'll get you one," I offered. "No thanks, I don't drink." I was shocked and somewhat suspicious. I didn't know anyone who didn't drink. Jenny said, "Really, are you sick?"

From the moment Jerry and I spoke to one another my entire world opened up ten-fold. My circle would go from two people (me, one, Jenny, the other) to several hundred in a matter of months due to Jerry, who made friends and enemies everywhere he went (friends becoming enemies and vice versa). Jerry told us he worked at the pizza place down the street and had moved to Columbus recently from Kent. He claimed that Kent "grew stale, it's a small college hippie-town filled by pretentious rich kids who wear tie-dyed clothes to hide from their mommies and daddies." I made no mention of his patchouli scent to him. When he spoke of the things he didn't like, his voice rose and his intensity was surgical. His energy was epic in scope. Later, when he started drinking, he would cry in bars, and a funk would settle over the entire area of the bar he was nestled in, his personality so strong that he could change the air pressure.

When we mentioned that Jenny wrote short little songs on a Casio keyboard she had borrowed, he told us he would love to hear them. We said we didn't have any recordings, and he offered to record her on his tiny Tascam. We ended up back at his house. He lived just two blocks from us on Indiana. His room was just a mattress with a bookshelf next to it, crammed with the clothes that weren't scattered on the floor, cassettes and paper-back books by Philip K. Dick, Kurt Vonnegut, and music related tales such as "Please Kill Me." He pulled out a four track recorder, covered in dust and stickers (SST, Sub Pop) and coffee stains, and played us what sounded like the solo from "Down by the River" speeded up and muffled under a pillow. I was amazed. There were no vocals. He said it was him playing a one-string guitar and that he was still working on it.

We wobbled home on liquid legs and twisted grins. When we got in the house I boiled a couple of hot dogs and drank three glasses of water to help stave off the headache. We went to sleep in the closet that Jenny had managed to convert to a bed.

love, death & photosynthesis

ohio.

Ohio lies flat in places, blanketed with fields of soybeans, corn and wheat, with a skyline the size of the Pacific Ocean. There are a few larger towns in Western Ohio, most notably Dayton and Toledo; the rest of this wide, smooth surface is mottled with small towns. Places that are glorified as the small town heartland America, with large brick courthouses in the center of town, several ice cream shops, and a hardware store that has every widget known to man, complete with a kindly old gent who knows every kid's name. There amongst the one traffic light towns, lies a sense of nostalgia for something that never existed, at least not for them. The belief in the American dream, long crushed by the greed of capitalism, still stands strong on Memorial Day and on the Fourth of July. But any weekend drive through these towns reveals a deflated dream of Middle America, from the empty storefronts to the lack of children playing softball, kick-the-can, or doing anything at all outdoors.

Then there is another small town Ohio, with images of Sherwood Anderson, unlocked doors, county fairs filled with cotton candy and first kisses. An idealistic concept that feeds into the idea that a small-town anybody can rise from the corn-fields and hidden glens to climb into space, like Neil Armstrong or John Glenn, the Presidency (seven of them-all mediocre- hail from Ohio), or the silver screen, like Paul Newman and Clark Gable.

In spite of all of this, when one grows up in Ohio, one has the feeling of being the underdog, of someone who always comes up just short. Ohio is seen as an also-ran, an almost did. Instead of an ocean we have a lake. Instead of mountains, foothills. We are defined by our collective losses. Our sports teams are known for despair. Cleveland, losing the World Series with one out to go. Cincinnati, tethered to a football team named the Bengals, but better known as the Bungles. Ohio State Football went 30 years between National Championships. Every down the Buckeyes play is with the soundtrack of a collective gasp from the entire state. We are in our hearts cynical but lovable malcontents.

Musically, Ohio is rich, especially when it comes to punk rock, with an abrasive arty sound, propelled by the ample liberal arts colleges dotting the state. The arts scenes have brought forth the terrific and idiosyncratic Pere Ubu, Devo, and the Dead Boys. Cleveland had Prisonshake, the Mice, Death of Samantha, and my Dad is Dead. Dayton had Guided by Voices, The Breeders, Brianiac and a legion of funk bands. Cincinnati had the Wolverton Brothers whose shambling country-art punk is as twisted as anything from a David Lynch movie, the Ass Ponys, and the Afghan Whigs. Appalachian Death Ride and Geraldine were two sinister bands that would be at least marginally famous if they resided anywhere but Athens, Ohio. In Columbus, we first had Jim Shepard, Scrawl, the Great Plains, the Gibson Brothers, Royal Crescent Mob, and Mike Rep all made up of various odd-balls and characters who would play a huge role in the development of what some regard as a high point in the Columbus underground scene. The specialness of that time was mostly due to the large and fanatical friendships and respect we had for not only one another, but also for the bands who set the stage. Jerry Wick and Jenny Mae would both be beside themselves to share the stage with any Ron House fronted band, and the same can be said for the New Bomb Turks, who would open for any band they respected.

We put stock in our friends. Friends who would carry the torch of loneliness offset by a burning desire to be heard and to hopefully lay next to another congenial soul by 5 AM. Our hopes crashed when things didn't quite pan out as we had planned. We were prepared for it, as it is in an Ohioan's soul to step up to the plate and be called out by the proverbial sinker ball. Three strikes. The Trip. The Fumble. The Drive. Etcetera and so forth. Nobody got famous, nobody ever really made a dent in any product counting mechanism like Billboard magazine or the clanging of cash registers, but we cherished one another as if our lives depended on it, night in and night out. We discovered that success wasn't the prize, the prize was the friendship, and the making of art for fuck's sake. That is what an Ohioan does— not always stylish, but always sincere.

Winters in Ohio are choked with the ashen polluted air of decrepit steel mills and coal mines and a landscape populated with battered hopes and forlorn thoughts. These somehow congeal together to make a gray morass that slowly settles like a pelt over the entire state. It comes creeping in in November, makes itself comfortable in December, and by January has dug its claws into the ground- and into the psyches- of every inhabitant. It was fitting that Jerry died in January.

2001.

Jerry was from Parma, just a stone's throw from the exit ramp off of I-71 and a few miles from the Cleveland International Airport. His last name was created by dropping the last five letters from Wickowski. His father worked in a factory, and Jerry would spend his weekends in Cleveland or in his bedroom dreaming of becoming a rock star while listening to Kiss records and a mix of Cleveland greats such as My Dad is Dead, the Dead Boys, and Death of Samantha.

Jerry's funeral was in Parma Heights. I had driven up with Brett Lewis, our friend Jim, and Merijn. I brought along a bottle of vodka and started getting friendly with a 12 pack on the way. We landed at the motel and I headed out to a small neighborhood dive bar that Jerry no doubt would have inhabited if he chose to stay in Parma. It sat catty-corner to the funeral home. Perfect civil planning. The bar still had Christmas decorations up and the bartender was sympathetic. "You here about that funeral across the street?" she asked as she put my Jim Beam shot and beer in front of me. I nodded as I downed the shot and motioned for another one. "A friend of yours? Was he that musician? That was in the paper up here." "Yup." I downed the second shot and ordered one more. In came Bettina Richards and Elliot Dix, a Columbus native who had become a fixture in the Chicago music scene. We laughed as we told ridiculous Jerry story after ridiculous story. When I walked into the funeral home the next day and saw Jerry lying in the casket I quickly turned heel and returned to the dive bar. I had two doubles of Maker's Mark and returned. I needed to be emboldened by the alcohol before I could face my friend. I was becoming someone I swore I never would, a bitter shadow who ducked from participation in life.

We pushed the memories of broken childhoods away to be replaced by the swagger and commotion of searing guitars, cigarettes and laughter. Now these were being replaced by urns and pine boxes. The funeral was rigid. The pastor didn't try to capture Jerry's audacious sense of humor and was much more focused on the afterlife, offering little semblance of hope to this huddled mass of outcasts. Jerry's shattered friends and bewildered family gazed on as the pastor said a final prayer over the muddy hole that would soon envelope his casket. The skyline of Cleveland heaved masses of smoke into the air, the smokestacks like upturned water faucets gushing into an already overflowing gray bathtub of sky. One could hear the hiss of car wheels spinning over the asphalt of I-71.

It was my first time meeting his father, mother, and younger brother. I tried to let them know the joy their son had brought to our world. How Jerry's music touched people far and wide, and most importantly how he'd been able to grant those who knew and loved him so much inspiration for merriment and copious amounts of late-night laughter. I don't know if I came close to succeeding.

Jerry said he wanted to be famous, but what I think he meant was that he wanted to be immortal, a part of something greater than himself: music. And this came true more than he could have ever imagined. The sheer force of his personality permeated through the four chords and rudimentary drums right into his music, sculpting his very being into this simple pop music, embroidered with brawny yet sophisticated guitar licks that amped up his songs just like all the laughter he created. The scars he left on the world were the records that spun his music into the vastness of the listener's soul— this was his way of marking himself upon us all. His grin was fleeting, his laughter has fallen into the crackling husks of the past, but his songs are just a shelf away. He is immortal.

That year, the dinky little label that Jerry and I started just a few years prior would release four full-length records. The promise that Jerry had bellowed in my ear that we would be self-sustaining appeared to be happening, even if by utter accident.

Jerry wanted to matter, to be remembered like his heroes Peter Laughner, Townes van Zandt and Johnny Thunders are. One of the best songwriters we both knew up close and personal was Ron House. Jerry craved his acknowledgement as if he were the coach's son. Since we all lived in a world built on not revealing too much of ourselves, our praise came in the form of backhanded compliments, or maybe a nod of appreciation. We dared not let someone know they moved us. Many of us didn't get the opportunity to say how much Jerry mattered to us musically until after he died, and then suddenly in 2003, Rough Trade records in the U.K. assembled a compilation of their greatest rock and roll songs post 1977. Gaunt was included on the compilation, right up there with The Stooges, Mudhoney, Rocket from The Crypt, The Pixies, and Suicide. *The Columbus Alive* posthumously voted Gaunt's "Kryptonite" the best Columbus record of the past 30 years.

Jerry's family had no idea the impact he had on other's lives or that his music was recognized nationally and internationally. It took his death and the unearthing of boxes of magazines, fanzines and video for his parents to understand. In appreciation for that part of him that they hadn't really known, Jerry's parents had a beautiful gravestone made, with a guitar carved into the granite surface.

1996.

Jeff Graham was a different sort of musician than I was used to; he had short hair that was slightly gelled, good teeth, no tattoos, and he drove a Land Rover. Therefore, I was skeptical of him when Jenny started working with him, due to my biases towards anyone outside of our insular DIY world. Jeff owned a small basement studio called Diamond Mine on the outskirts of what can only be referred to as the hood in the Linden area of Columbus. Used to crappy cassette 4-track setups on cases of Black Label beer with shitty Radio Shack microphones duct-taped to broken mic-stands, I was shocked when he led me down the stairs. His soundboard had different colored lights and looked like it could have come from the set of Star Trek. It was huge and looked very expensive. He played me some of the new songs Jenny was recording with him, Dan Spurgeon, and Sean Woosley. The sound for the album that would become *Don't Wait Up for Me* was rich, deep and sophisticated; I could not believe my ears. I had no idea that Jenny could sing so well. I knew the loveliness that lay behind the crass in Jenny. But to hear, over Jeff's massive speakers, Jenny's coarse voice transform into a blanket of such beauty was both disconcerting and hopeful.

I had started dating Merijn, and I would drag her to the studio and we would huddle around the large console drinking beer and doing shots as Jeff played back the songs. My future wife must have thought that my life was much more exotic than it was.

As the songs started to evolve I sent a few off to my friend James Hunter who was a freelance writer and worked as a scout for several record companies. James is a thin man, whose family provided him with an impeccable taste in music, fashion and the arts, his tastes run to the far end of sophistication, but he is discerning enough to understand the loveliness of a Patty Loveless or Pet Shop Boys song over the annoyance of standard pop fare. I had met James several years prior when he introduced himself to me at Used Kids, he would venture up from West Virginia periodically to the bright lights of Columbus— as it is often said in Kentucky and West Virginia: "readin, writin, and route 23". Many from the southern border states would make the exodus up Route 23 to the hopeful jobs of Franklin County. Jim and I hit it off, he was an early supporter of Guided by Voices and he later interviewed me for a story on the underground scene for the New York Times. We both had a fondness for classic pop and country music, with our ears perking up to the refined sounds of country stars such as Dwight Yoakam and Merle Haggard to mutual appreciation of the euro-beat sounds of Erasure and New Order to the epic vocalizing of Scott Walker and Dusty Springfield.

Upon receiving the tape I sent him, James called me almost immediately, with a voice full of excitement and rush he exclaimed, "This is the best demo I have heard since Basehead and Matthew Sweet." He could not wrap his mind around the fact that this was Jenny singing, he had met her a few times at some of the shows we attended. With her western-southern Ohio drawl and a propensity for saying whatever pops into her gin-soaked brain, Jenny did not always make the best first or even fourth impression. She was liable to snicker in your face with an inside joke that she barely understood herself. That it could be off-putting is an understatement. But here she was on tape, summoning dredged up forlorn darkness now bathed in a perfect light, crafted into three-minute pop songs.

James was working closely with EMI records at the time, with Davitt Sigerson, a long-time music producer who had guided both mainstream and alternative acts. He had just taken over the failing American branch of EMI Records. He asked me to send a few of the tracks Jenny was recording to Davitt and in a few weeks Davitt asked if Jenny could come and play New York. Jenny and her band had not yet played out, in fact she had no stable backing band. Davitt was also advising Deborah Harry on what would then become a Blondie comeback attempt. One of the songs Deborah Harry considered was Jenny's

"Hey Baby." Davitt seemed serious. He must have thought I was more experienced than I was, having run a label for nearly half a decade and working with so many labels and bands. But I was in over my head. I had been from the day I was birthed.

In the mid-'90s, the underground scene became an above ground commodity. Major labels realized that there was something happening that they did not quite understand, and the business model they were used to was shifting under the weight of Nirvana, Pavement, The Smashing Pumpkins and Helmet. There followed shotgun marriages of authentically independent labels such as Matador with Atlantic, then with Capital, Caroline with Virgin, Amphetamine Reptile with Atlantic—they were on the constant hunt for the next independent cash-cow. A ready-made band for the masses to swallow without much work or planning. This very rarely succeeded and when it did, the results usually ended in disaster, ending the musical careers of countless vital bands. In Ohio failed experiments could be found in every town: Gaunt, Scrawl, Thomas Jefferson Slave Apartments, and V-3 (Columbus), Ass Ponys (Cincinnati), Snapdragons (Athens).

Moviola were starting to record their follow-up to "The Year You Were Born" and were interested in recording in a studio that was shoehorned into a closet—they started to record a few songs with James at Diamond Mine. This was not a good marriage, but it did garner the interest of Davitt who became interested in signing Anyway to EMI with Jenny Mae and Moviola the two flagship artists. Much of this would hinge on the New York show. With a handful of practices, we left for New York. I had been able to secure a show at Brownies, which had a history of welcoming Columbus bands.

Arriving early, we headed to a western-themed bar just down the block I'd frequented on previous trips and met up with my friend Ron who also ran a small label. His lawyer was a bartender at the bar. Everybody we knew was a bartender, a record store employee, or a musician. Jenny walked in and stumbled out after an hour. After an eight-hour car ride chased by two hours in a Manhattan country bar, unshaven in a threadbare SST t-shirt and frayed jeans, I met the President of EMI records. Davitt was a large man, and he smoked a cigar the size of my wrist. James was there; he appeared a bit nervous. I was quite content with the way my world was functioning. The prospect of teaming up with EMI did not move me either way. I would have been relieved if the larger label wanted to take Jenny and Moviola and leave me to lurk in a record store abode, content as a cat in a sunbeam.

Davitt and James sat at table off to the side of the stage, while I huddled at the bar, not knowing what to say to the ambassador of music professionalism. It was not apathy that enveloped my life, it was more being completely unskilled in any sort of communication outside of the familiar. Choosing the underbelly of life is a pragmatic choice, one made in increments. Dropping a class followed by dropping out of school. Staying out too late on a Tuesday night, then adding Wednesday and Thursday nights. Choosing a job that allows extremely casual clothes and schedules that are congruent with weeknight drinking and dancing. When one world is as welcoming as an impassioned lover, the disdain for the other grows. I yearned for Jenny and Moviola to have large-scale success, but I was happy to just be a conduit to it; I did not necessarily want a piece of it.

The club was half filled when Jenny played, a few fans were there, James McNew from Yo La Tengo and Lisa Carver were present. Jenny played a ragged set, the band was dressed in suits and this was their first live show together, she was visibly drunk. Any sophistication that was evident on the recordings was displaced by too many glasses of Dewar's and Iron Horse beer. After the show, Jenny stumbled up and met Davitt. She offered him a drink; he declined. She asked again and again he declined. Suddenly she leaned over, clutched his large belly, and told him to "lighten up have a drink!" He was horrified. That sealed the deal: He was no longer interested. Deborah Harry recording one her songs went out the window with one ill-fated grab of the stomach of the President of EMI. Jenny would continue to record "Don't Wait Up For Me" not concerned about the brief flirtation with a major label, chalking it up to a night of free booze in the city and the pleasure of seeing old friends.

2001.

Jerry was the fourth friend I had lost in 16 months. His death followed those of Jack Taylor and Chris Wilson of Monster Truck 005 and Jim Shepard. Jerry had brought me back from the brink of death. He had the same cynical humor as me and the same profound love of music. He pushed every boundary and yet was the gentlest soul I ever knew. He was gone.

I was in shock. I stumbled through days as if I were a cloud bumping into the sky. I stopped promoting shows and putting out music. I attended a fraction of the shows I used to go to. I would lurch towards High Street with the purpose of seeing live music either at Little Brothers or Bernie's but I usually only made it as far as Larry's. The allure of the bottom of the bottle was too great for me to push myself away from the barstool into a night filled with the dramatic crescendos of 4/4 drum beats and ringing guitars. Yet drinking wasn't getting the results it once did, and over the years it had become a glaring issue between Merijn and I. I hesitated every time I ordered a drink and was unsure of myself, not knowing if at the bottom of this glass lay more cheating and lying.

A line had been crossed somewhere along the meandering path that we collectively took. Music had been our map, alcohol and sex our compass. We drifted in and out of one another's lives like the thoughts that raced in our minds, bouncing off each other, collecting the pain of our partners and then sharing a few moments of relief from that pain. But the redundancy of the chase of the epic night, the promise that had once fueled our lives, now left us—those of us still alive—tired, spent and vacant. Cynicism was setting in, shaking away the confidence we'd beamed from barstools and at the front of cramped wooden stages. The glow was flickering out as we sat stiffly, night after night.

It wasn't working anymore. While the edginess that seemed to scrape the inside of my skin would be calmed by a night in Larry's or the subtle hush of a needle using electricity to transform my mood, it was growing and no matter what I did there was nothing to assuage the soft undertone of being imperfect. Every. Single. Minute. Outwardly, things were good. Working in a large record store for over ten years and running a small but respected record label had its perks— being able to stroll into my favorite bar and have a drink placed in front of me before even finding a seat provided a deep sense of security. My girlfriend was beautiful, stunningly so in fact, and at times I doubted what she saw in me, and with my increasingly risky behavior there is no doubt she questioned it herself. We shared a house, near campus, just a mile walk to work with several close bars that I could easily find my way home from, just a stumble to the stoop. Yet nothing could placate the rising uncertainty within me. My life had turned into a slow boil, burbling and rising into the air into nothingness. It happened unbeknownst, like the slow disintegration of a snowman in the late March sunshine—a series of poor personal choices as my drinking escalated and left me bereft inside. I had discovered that it was quite easy to fall into sexual encounters even while in a committed relationship.

Merijn graduated from Ohio State with a Masters in Fine Arts and worried that her U.S. visa might expire. We'd been together for nearly five years and engaged for two, but I was gun-shy about the next step. Merijn came home one day as I sat on our blue couch and she said, "My parents are coming next month and we are getting married." Looking up from my *New York Review of Books*, I replied, "Um, OK. What do I need to do?" She shook her head, smiled and said, "Nothing. Just be there." She'd been applying for teaching jobs, and on our wedding day she accepted a job at the University of Florida. I did not go with her. The idea of relocation was larger than my overstuffed brain could handle: I had everything I needed in Ohio.

The next few months were restless, I was trying to maintain my relationship with my new wife over the phone, get a handle on my drinking, and deal with the death of Jerry,

love, death & photosynthesis

all while living with one foot in dishonesty and the other in righteous anger, much of it from what I perceived to be great injustice in the world. I was 31 and I felt like 50.

One night in August, I left the record store and travelled to Larry's and Dick's Den and made it home by midnight. The minute I walked in the door, the phone rang. "Dude, Jim Stone is having a hot-tub party behind his house." Jim Stone was a campus figure, manning the bar at Bernie's and Dow's on High. Jim's girth was superseded by his easy-going nature; a permanent grin on his face. "I'm there," I slurred into the phone.

The hot tub sat behind the North Campus Taco Bell on the edge of a sordid alley, I arrived and quickly peeled off my clothes. Somehow the hot tub wasn't quite as bubbly as it should have been. Apparently, the party was on its fourth day as the hot tub was rented Friday night. Being Monday, even the water in the tub was tuckered out. The bubbles had lost their bubbliness. It was a cool evening, almost frigid in fact and I ignored the thin layer of human grease and grime that shrouded the surface of the muddied water.

As I slipped into the tub, I took a gander at my bath-mates, Jim Stone was next to me, naked with the exception of a cowboy hat. Next to him were a couple of female bartenders who had definitely enjoyed the better part of the extended weekend. To my right was a nice enough fellow who was the lead singer for an operatic rock band. I had never seen him without a hat, and discovered he had a startling resemblance to Riff-Raff from "The Rocky Horror Picture Show." His long hair drooped past his shoulders and his completely bald head acted like a shimmering dance floor for the moonbeams that sauntered around it. There was a younger man who I didn't know. I felt completely pathetic.

After a few beers, the water was feeling cooler and the shame within me rose higher. I contemplated my wife waiting for me in the suffocating sun of Gainesville and the fact that here I was naked in an alley behind Taco Bell on a Monday night while the rest of the world was in bed. I left the tub, shaking the water off of me, and got in my car to drive home. 'What the fuck am I doing?' I thought as I drove, the shame deep enough to peel my skin. I resolved to do something different. As I put the key in my front door I looked down to notice that I was only wearing a white T-shirt. Just a poof of pubic hair jutting out from the edges of shirt as the August night dipped into the 40s. 'Fuck,' I thought. I climbed back into the car and drove back to the party to retrieve my clothes. (Failing to run inside my house to put some shorts or pants on first.) I listened to the catcalls from the tub: "Bela, you idiot, you forgot to put your pants on."

"I know," I muttered to the ground. "I know."

2002.

I didn't even know my roommate when I moved to Gainesville. This roommate was in fact my wife. For the past six months we had lived separate lives both physically and emotionally. We were strangers not only to each other but to ourselves.

I felt defeated. I tried to muster up the energy to decide that my life did not have to play out in the manner of my dear dead and insane friends. I could not quit drinking by my own volition, no matter how hard I tried. Once a drink was in my hand, my head would not rest until I had my fill. A drunkard's fill is as bottomless as his loneliness. It had turned into a terrible discomforting existence. I could hide it in the cozy confines of my neighborhood bars back in Columbus. Upon my arrival in Florida, stripped to the naked reality of my own madness, I suffered through the days, trying to mend wounds with my wife, who I adored and who had an unstoppable faith in me. I wandered. Clueless. I was a weeble-wobble that kept falling down.

The woman doing the intake was younger than me, 25 at most. She spoke rapidly. Scripted words to convince me that I was, in fact, an alcoholic. I didn't really need one more person to tell me.

"Tell me, Bela, how much do you drink a night?"

"I don't know," I said guardedly. "I mean, right now I'm not drinking that much because I want to stop. Maybe three beers every other night?"

She looked at me side-eyed, "Are you sure about that?"

"I mean, when I want to really drink, usually at least nine drinks. But it could easily be 15 or so. But I don't do that every night." I watch her write down 15 a night. "Listen, I know I have a problem with it. But I'm not drinking very much the past few weeks, because, basically, I feel scared."

She kept writing. "Scared? Of what?"

"That I might hurt myself? I don't know. Everything is a mess."

"Are you suicidal now?" Her voice was clipped and cold.

The certainties in my life had been the love of my wife, music, alcohol, and friendship. Only drinking remained. But… "No, I'm not suicidal. That's why I'm here. I want help."

The woman laid pencil down, it rolled and stopped at a Snoopy pen holder. On the wall above her desk was a framed embroidered sign: "You Are Not Alone" in pink yarn, cursive. I rolled my inside eyes. "OK, I'm going to lay this on the line. We checked with your insurance and we can admit you right now, we have a bed available. I wouldn't feel good if you left, what do you say?"

I felt as if my feet had flown away and I was dangling in the air. "Don't you have something where I just come talk to someone? I have a writing assignment to turn in, the deadline is tomorrow. I can come back tomorrow. I just need a few hours to finish it."

"A writing project is more important than your life?" Her voice sharp, her eyebrows all scrunchy.

"Assignment. It's an assignment for a magazine, and yes it's important that I turn it in."

Leaning over her desk she glared at me. "We may not have a bed tomorrow and I think if you walk out that door you won't come back. You should stay."

"Let me check with my wife."

"Mr. Koe-Krompecher, you are making the biggest mistake of your life."

Thinking of the litany of giant potholes I stepped in over the years, the barrage of idiocy I had lived my life by, this was *not* the biggest mistake of my life.

On the drive home, my cell phone rang. It was my psychiatrist. "I thought we agreed you would get treatment, Bela. I won't see you unless you get help with your drinking. I heard you just left against the advice of the intake coordinator."

Annoyance sat in my throat. "I have a job I need to finish tonight. I will go back in the morning. I promise."

On March 8, 2002, as I walked through the front doors of the Shands treatment center, it felt as if I had entered the army. The smell of antiseptic filled the hallways, which were aglow with a polished sheen. I hugged Merijn goodbye and wiped the tears from her eyes. She spoke softly in my ear, "I'm proud of you," but the last vestiges of pride had slunk away when I drank Natural Light the night before. A nurse unlocked some doors and led me to my room with two beds. "You have a roommate, Mr. Deacon," she said. "He's in the group right now. You'll meet him after lunch." The room was dark, shades pulled down, both beds made. I placed my small carry-on luggage on the bed.

"Is that all you brought?" the nurse asked.

"Yeah, why? I figured I would be out of here on Monday."

"Mhmmm." Raised eyebrows.

She took my blood pressure, temperature, drew some blood, and left. I sat on the bed, the desire to leave swelling like a giant balloon. On the pillow was a small blue bible-like book. "What the fuck is this shit? What the fuck are these people doing?" Nothing made sense, being rushed into this hospital-like place, being treated as if I was lying to everyone here and then left alone with a bible-ly book. Clients shuffled by in bunches. One of them turned and saw me watching, said, "Hey New Guy, I'm Willie. We're going to get our lunch if you wanna join us." He held out a hand for me to shake. It was limp as a sandwich bag.

Willie was yellow. Waves of Hepatitis C had whittled small chips from his complexion over the years, until finally the paleness in his face just gave up and said "fuck this, I'm out" and the yellow moved in. His belly was distended and his shoulders moved in tandem with his legs, as if he were a bear imitating a person, stripped of fur, laid naked to the world. Next to Willie was a white woman, early twenties. Sandy. She was nearly six feet tall. Her legs reaching towards the ceiling, she looked as if she might crumble like a sandcastle. "Hey Bela, what the hell kind of name is that? I mean, it's cool but is that really your name? Why are you here? I'm here because my mom said I need to—this or jail. I hate this fucking place. This is my third fucking time here. Do you smoke? Do you have cigarettes?" Sandy had sunken eyes, hollowed at the edges, her high cheekbones tried to reach her forehead. Her hair, long and brown, hung past emaciated shoulders. She was a fragile beauty, almost broken—her face so brittle that if there were a loud sound, it might crack into a thousand pieces. Willie held his cigarette carefully between two fingers. Long crevices spiderwebbed across his face when he inhaled, transforming him from 45 years old to 70.

Lunch consisted of limp salad laid out in a large plastic bowl, burgers that smelled as if they were bussed in from an elementary school, wobbly red Jello, tasteless pudding, and a

love, death & photosynthesis

variety of fruit juices. After lunch, people moved slowly, mired in invisible molasses, to the atrium. Scattered plastic plants and vinyl couches made it resemble the sitting area of a shopping mall. Eyelids half-open; people were turning their necks as if they were beached seals. I had a strong feeling that I was in the wrong place. A man in a suit and starched shirt came in. He was handsome, held a pen in his hand forcefully, chewed gum. I hated him. "Ok everyone, time for group!" He led us to a large room with plastic chairs, hard enough to make one sit up straight, arranged in a circle. Everybody was a mess, bodies sucked dry of health, bellies grown large one beer at a time, spindly arms and legs, thinning hair, splotchy skin. I looked down at myself. Years of running several miles every morning with hangovers had helped me but inside I was devoid of everything but fear.

Willie was ousting a newcomer who'd taken "his" seat. The man claimed anyone could sit anywhere. "Fuck you man, these seats are fixed!' Willie retorted, and the old man shook his head and heaved himself up and sat down again next to me. "Can you believe this asshole?" he asked me, nodding toward Willie, who had somehow grown even more yellow since his last cigarette. "I dunno," I murmured.

The meeting began. "Hi, my name is Sandy, I'm an addict and my drug of choice is meth." "Hi, my name is Stan and my drug of choice is crack cocaine." "Hi, my name is Willie and my drug of choice is what-ever-you-got." Then the man next to me, "Hi, my name is Jim and my drug of choice is Coors." Then me. I looked around the room. There was a pause. The leader instructed, "Bela, go ahead and tell us who you are and what your drug of choice is now." "Um, my name is Bela and I guess my drug of choice is alcohol?" Big Mistake. Everybody chimed in, "You guess?!" "Dude, you must be in denial, why do you think you are even here if you don't know?"

Sandy talked about Jesus and miracles and trusting the unknown. People clapped. She appeared sincere, but this was the same woman who just told me she "fucking hated this place." Afterwards, I walked out with Willie. "What is this higher power stuff? I didn't realize we had to do work in here."

"Haven't you heard of the 12-Steps? You'll get it. I've been going to AA for 20 years." Willie needed a liver. He had just burned through his second one, and he was back in treatment so he could prove he could be clean long enough to earn a new one. "If I don't get a liver soon, then I'm Willie-toast. I've been on dope since the mid-70's," he told me, "although I was clean when I got my last liver. I had four years and then I hurt my back and couldn't drive a truck. I started using heroin again, then crack, and drinking. Alcohol's always a good standby. I'm addicted to anything that makes me feel different."

Willie wanted a new liver. Sandy wanted to avoid jail. What did I want from rehab? When I left the house, I locked up my dogs in their little doggie room. They may stare at the doorknob but they never would figure it out. They only knew when it turned they were free. That's what I wanted: for the knob to turn. I didn't care how.

Jenny was in Miami. I had called her the day before and she wished me luck. "Bela you do tend to fuck everything up, but I hope you don't fuck this up." I thought of Jerry, whose response would be to tilt his head back, squint his eyes tightly, and blow a powerful string of smoke into the air. Jerry had been dead just over a year.

Jerry was in the center of it all, he blew through my life as if he were a sudden downpour that soaks everything in its path; nothing was prepared for it. Jerry would enter a person's life and open-up like a cloudburst. One could only have two responses to Jerry: anger or laughter. There was no shelter from Jerry, he just was, and once he made a mark on a person, it was for life. He was for me the revelation of a different sort of life that could happen for me. He was dead now, his mold was never to be broken. He died young, he died drunk, and he died alone. He lay to the north, cold in the ground outside of Parma, Ohio. I wanted him to have tasted from the well I had just took a swig from—hope, clarity, and trust. The thought of sharing that with him helped fuel me through my first year of sobriety. There was never a day that I didn't think of Jerry. I felt I could taste the trueness of reality for both of us, no matter how frightening, fragile and delicate it appeared.

love, death & photosynthesis

1993.

I first heard the Ramones in 1981 in the movie *Rock and Roll High School*. By the time I was 15 I owned their first four records. Used Kids, as with hundreds of other small mom and pop stores across the county, became a destination point. Partly because of its proximity to Stache's and the Newport, it was quite easy to chat up John Cale, Maureen Tucker, Pere Ubu, and Alex Chilton, whose early work helped shape our world.

The Ramones had turned into a punk-rock Grateful Dead at this point. They made their money by nonstop touring and releasing semi-pedestrian records every so often that were facsimiles of their braver, younger selves. Still, The Ramones were giants in our eyes, pillars of our musical and philosophical foundation. They played Columbus yearly, and would inevitably stop at the Used Kids Annex to see Captain and peruse the shelves for hours. Johnny was the bigger collector and he would be escorted to the dingy, damp back room to rifle through boxes of hard-to-find '60s garage and surf records. Truly, still a boy at heart.

We had two English gents working at Used Kids, Colin Harris and Keith Hayward (who is now a noted scholar). Keith was blond, handsome with a winsome personality, while Colin wore the dark morbidity of a centuries old island. As I was standing up, slurping down a cold Black Label beer one Saturday afternoon, Keith came barging in the front door of Used Kids. "Mate, you won't fuckin' believe it," he excitedly exclaimed, "but Joey FUCKING Ramone just walked in the Annex!" In my been-there, seen-that voice, I replied, "Yeah, he comes in every year." I had met so many of my idols that I realized that people are the same everywhere. My larger concern was how I was going to drink for the night.

"Holy shite!" Keith exclaimed and shook his head. "I had no idea."

I asked him if anybody was manning the counter next door. "Um, no but give me a beer," he said. I handed him a beer and he disappeared.

A few hours later he reappeared. "You won't fucking believe this, mate, but fucking Johnny Ramone just walked in." I told him to show him the stuff in the back and gave him a few more beers to settle his nerves. I went back there during a lull in the action. Johnny asked about Captain, who left early on Saturdays, and bought a stack of records including a "Wild Angels" soundtrack, which he accidentally left on the counter. He told Keith and me to come around the back of the Newport that night and he would have some passes for us, as it was already 7 o'clock, too late to put us on their guest list.

The Newport was a large concert hall on High Street. The last time I'd been there, several bouncers had dragged me out by my neck, my feet dangling under me as if I were a chicken being carried across the barnyard. As I was being flung onto the sidewalk, I saw Bob Pollard was in line to get in. "Hey Bela, do you need help?" Upon noticing the thick-necked beefy men escorting me out, he rescinded his offer: "Uh, never mind!" I explained to Keith that my name would probably be crossed off the guest list for my past behavior despite Johnny Ramone having put us on there. But that didn't register with Keith, who was excitedly repeating, "The fucking Ramones. Wow, can you believe it? The fucking Ramones, they know my name."

After closing up shop Keith and I ambled up to Larry's to procure a few more drinks so the buzz wouldn't peter out before heading to the Newport. The back of the Newport bordered Pearl Alley and a large tour bus with a Western sunset motif was painted along the side was parked next to the club. A small line of young women stood outside the backstage door that sat atop the fire escape. With beer and whiskey breath we stood on the crunchy gravel, keeping our distance from the chattering, nervous young women waiting to meet the elder statesmen of American punk rock. Suddenly, the Ramones tour manager, a dark-haired man wearing mandatory Ray-Ban sunglasses and chewing gum appeared to be arguing with several staff members of the Newport. A clean-cut man in a brown suit and holding a walkie-talkie appeared. He yelled above the burgeoning din, "You guys have been selling your passes to these girls all night. The show is sold out and none of your passes are good anymore!"

Mr. Ray-Ban yelled back, "That's bullshit! You can't do that! Show me the proof!"

Keith and I looked at each other. How odd this all seemed. Abruptly, Joey was on the scene, with his thin, angular frame in a T-shirt. He pointed towards Keith and me standing in the parking lot, giggling to ourselves. "Hey, I don't know about all these girls but those two guys get passes."

Mr. Brown-Suit looked down upon us, "I don't care who it is, nobody else is getting in!"

Joey scoffed, "They don't get in, we don't play!"

I looked over at Keith. "This is fucking crazy."

"Yup."

It went back and forth for a few minutes, then Joey came down the stairs with Mr. Ray-Bans. "Hey, someone in our crew was selling our backstage passes and now they won't let you in. Why don't you guys come up to Detroit tomorrow and we'll get you in then?" The next day was a Sunday. I said, "I can't. I have some family stuff going on." In reality, I knew a full-on hangover would impede driving the three hours to Detroit, and getting drunk again and driving back didn't sound all that appealing.

"How about Cincy," Joey offered. "We'll be there in two days." This worked and we agreed to see them in Cincinnati.

Keith and I looked at each other as if we were being filmed for a sitcom. "Did Joey Ramone just say they wouldn't play unless we were allowed in?" I asked him.

Keith nodded. "Yeah. He said if the two record store guys don't get it we don't play. Well, now what?"

"Well, we're already on South Campus; let's go to Crazy Mama's."

"Yup, sounds cool. Might as well dance."

As we started walking away, a bespectacled man with a beard right out of a King Crimson gatefold record cover yelled after us, "Hey guys, hold up. The fellas feel terrible that you couldn't see the show, so I wanna help you out a little." He explained he was one of the roadies and drove their bus, a huge concert bus with a western motif airbrushed on the side, a perfect cover for one of the most essential punk rock bands in history. He led us to the bus, telling us he was from Poland, Ohio, and had been with the Ramones for nearly ten years. "The best band you could hope to work for. Total class guys. Salt of the earth." As he was talking he pulled a baggie of marijuana out of his worn, green satchel. "Hey, this is for you guys, for your trouble." He tossed it to me.

I said, "Man, we don't need this. I don't even smoke—I only drink."

He smiled. "Hey, it'll come in handy sometime."

Keith grabbed it. "Shite, I know some girls who smoke." He tucked it into his pants. We thanked the bus driver and assured him we would be in Cincinnati in a few days, and then trudged off to get our dancing shoes on.

The night was strange, with an eerie energy that was raised higher by our intake of Jim Beam and Black Label throughout the afternoon and evening. "Let's take the alleyway," I suggested. "That way we don't have to deal with the bullshit of High Street."

"Good call, man."

We stopped at UDF to share a 40 ounce in the alley as we needed to feed the buzz lest it be too diminished before we completed the three-block walk to Crazy Mama's. Pulling swallows from the bottle, we finished it by the time we got to Crazy Mama's, dumping the empty bottle in a dumpster. I tut-tutted to Keith: "It's amazing that these dumbasses can't seem to do that. Here we are drunker than shit and we know enough to throw our bottle away."

Crazy Mama's had steep stairs and as we climbed them we could feel the sweat inside the room. Bauhaus was playing. "I dunno, Keith, they're playing gothic shit tonight, maybe we should just go back to Larry's."

"We're already here. Besides, some gothic chicks are sexy."

It was packed, with a whole slew of folks we hadn't seen, a lot of punks from out of town, and a group of skinheads lurking on one side of the dance floor. "I don't have a good feeling about this," I murmured to Keith. I hated crowds. Especially drunk crowds. With skinheads. Suddenly "Beat on the Brat" exploded over the bar, and I said, "Cool, we'll stay." I grabbed three beers, two for me and one for Keith.

I sat at a table with my two beers, milking the bubbles spiraling from the dark bottles. Before twisting myself about on the dance floor, I needed to collect my wits. The sparkles of bursting white lights that flecked onto pulsating bodies in a projection of phosphorescence made every person go aquiver in the haze of smoke. My discomposure was amplified by the guitars blaring from the speakers, the room shaking with the energy of stripling sexuality fueled by the eagerness that alcohol imbues. I gazed at my shoes, cracked black leather, a fantastical thrift store find that were discarded once and needed to be again. My jeans were frayed at the knee, one hairy knee poking out like a guarded rodent looking for a moment to cut free. I swallowed the last of my beer and walked out onto the dance floor. Spinning onto it in a swirl, I skirted across the floor, my worn leather soles gliding in the spilt beer. I was in the moment where guitar combines with dance to shut the rest of the world out. The next song was "One Last Caress" by the Misfits, the most beautiful ode to murder and rape ever written. Barely over a minute and a half, enough time to dig into the subconscious isolation that the best punk rock brings to live action. Perhaps sensing the tension in the room, the DJ then blended into "Bring On The Dancing Horses" by Echo and the Bunnymen. The whole room swayed to the words of disintegrating love. As the song petered out, I headed to the bar to fetch another drink or two. I stepped around two of the skinheads who were discussing the "fuckin' pussy music." Back at my table, I listened to the DJ play the heartstrings of the mirror people, and Julian Cope instructed the world to shut its mouth. Keith came and sat down and said, "Mate, those fuckin' skinheads are fuckin' with me." I looked over his shoulder at several glaring skinheads. They wore the uniform of intimidation: ankle high boots with white shoelaces pulled tight, white T-shirts and gray suspenders making a perfect "X" across broad backs. They looked menacing. There were roughly seven of them, unless I was so drunk I was seeing double. They smiled at us.

"Um, those skinheads over there?" I asked as if there were skinheads in every pocket of the club.

"Yeah, especially the big fucker." Keith was short in stature, handsome, with long curly golden locks. The big fucker was nearly a head taller than me, and he wore a crooked grin. I walked over and, with guts full of alcohol and a temperament that was as shaky as North Korean foreign policy, put my beers down on the table next to him.

Keith came up next to me, smiling. Perhaps the friction of violence energized him or perhaps he didn't really think there would be violence. With a history of barroom brawls and frequent ass beatings by my older brother while growing up, I wasn't scared to take a punch. I don't believe that Keith had ever taken a punch let alone thrown one. I leaned up toward the big skinhead's face, stared into his eyes and said, "Hey, are you fucking with my friend here?"

Several of the smaller skinheads had gathered around him. He smiled more broadly and said, "What the fuck is it to you?" When he glanced toward his skinhead buddies for support, I hit him in the chest and he toppled over like a drunken man is prone to do. Immediately, regret rained over me as several other of his team plowed into me as if I was a tackling dummy. I could take *a* punch, but I'd forgotten that skinheads fight in packs. Flipping over a table with our momentum, I yelled to Keith as I felt big-leather skinhead boots kicking against my ribs and the back of my head. I got scared. Being a twisty sort, I had maneuvered the practice of escaping from the years of fleeing from my brother. I held onto one guy's leg and turned into it when he fell over, and managed to scramble away and down the stairs. Keith was nowhere to be found.

I ran into Pearl Alley, which runs parallel with High Street, cut through another small alley and kept running all the way to Larry's where I knew I would be safe. I felt some blood dripping down my neck but it didn't seem too bad.

Bursting through the doors of Larry's I went up to the bar, I asked, "Has Keith shown up?" Becky, the tall bartender, looked aghast. "No, what happened? Your head is bleeding!"

"We got jumped by some fucking skinheads at Crazy Mama's," I explained, and she handed me a drink. Roughly an hour later, Keith sauntered into the bar, flashing his white teeth in a grin. "Oh, thank God you're OK, mate. They chased me all the way to 15th Avenue. I didn't know where to go, so I ran into the party and they were going to kick me out until I pulled out that bag of weed!"

Two days later we arrived in Cincinnati to meet up with the Ramones. We saw the show from the wings of the stage, drinking Heinekens. Afterwards, backstage, Keith pulled out his camera and I suggested he take a photo of the costume cabinets, one of those huge big black leather cabinets found backstage at Broadway shows. On the side written in white spray paint was "Ramones" and inside on hangers were four leather jackets. Joey said they waited until five because they wanted to take us out to eat but couldn't wait any longer. The band had changed into normal casual t-shirts and I don't recall them drinking any alcohol. They truly were salt of the earth. Johnny asked if I had brought his copy of the *Wild Angels* soundtrack. I said I forgot it and he said, "Well, next year I'll pick it up." There never was a next year; they never returned to Columbus and broke up a little over a year later. I still have Johnny's copy of *Wild Angels*.

1992.

Saturdays at Used Kids was an event. At times I stopped at Bernie's before opening the store to pick up a Bloody Mary to help me over the 10 AM hump. I might have sent Jerry down to Larry's to get a cold six pack of Black Label at 2 PM to get an early start on a long evening.

Some Saturdays I would leave work early and stop and get a six-pack or a few 40-ounce beers for the hour-and-a-half drive to Athens, Ohio. By the time I would arrive, I would be half drunk, the sun usually still shining. Things moved slower in Athens, shows didn't start until 11 and didn't end until 3. Athens had a pretty healthy music scene, a bit more ragged, freakish and organic than the hardened punkish and ironic sounds of Columbus. And unlike the standard arms-folded-across-the-chest pose of so many self-conscious independent rockers in Columbus, folks were more prone to dancing in Athens. Even to the more bizarre hardness of some of the Amphetamine Reptile bands such as The Cows and Surgery who played there often. The most popular bands in Athens were the majestic Appalachian Death Ride and Torque. Torque branded itself as hate rock, with a large good-looking singer-guitarist named Pat Brown whose girth was offset by his glinting blue eyes and good-natured laugh. He never wanted for a woman. Appalachian Death

Bela Koe-Krompecher @ Stache's

love, death & photosynthesis

Ride, led by my childhood friend Chris Biester, were basically the house band of the Union, an old biker bar in the 1970s that was now home to the counterculture scene in Athens. A diverse scene made up of filmmakers, artists, dropouts and hate rock purveyors with names such as God and Texas.

Jenny wrote the song "Leprechaun" off her first album from a time she accompanied me to Athens on Halloween, took a hit of LSD and witnessed a man dressed as a shamrock getting squished in the Court Street mob. Jerry too, would go with me on several of these trips even though he stated that he loathed Athens. He always enjoyed getting away from Columbus. Jerry couldn't drive, he never had a license, so it was always me who did the reckless drive to Athens. We would smoke cigarettes and drink cheap beer and talk about girls and music. It was a magical time when one could leave behind any responsibilities for 24 hours and not be frightened of the consequences.

I helped book several shows at The Union, as I was by this time getting my feet and wallet soaked promoting shows in Columbus at Bernie's and Stache's. For every money-making venture of Love Battery, Sebadoh, and Pavement there was a money-gulping show like Moonshake, Eleventh Dream Day, the Grifters, and the incredible Thinking Fellers Union Local 282. I have no idea what shows I helped put on at The Union as I was in the cusp of my baffling, hysterical, frenzied, alcoholic being. I was in a constant elevated state fueled by Jim Beam and long-neck beers and copious amounts of coffee, which brought about tears of laughter as I was a stand-up comic in my own head. The faces of the onlookers were bewildered. Some got my joke: the joke was me. The embarrassment of my situation passed way over my head. I had no impulse control.

1991.

Chris Lombardi phoned Used Kids one day and asked Ron to order the first full-length records on the new label he had started with Gerard Cosloy (who had previously run Ron's old label Homestead). The label was Matador and the records were Teenage Fanclub's *A Catholic Education* and Superchunk's *Self-Titled* debut. We were blown away.

I handled most of the ordering, from Scat in Cleveland, Dischord in Washington DC, Ajax in Chicago, Siltbreeze in Philadelphia, Sub Pop in Seattle and Revolver in San Francisco. Soon I was booking shows at Stache's and Bernie's.

It started when Dan Dougan asked me if I thought he should book Nirvana with Urge Overkill. He had hosted Nirvana earlier in the year and they didn't have a big draw, and now they were asking for $2,000. I had an advance copy of *Nevermind* and told him, "Dan, this thing is going to be huge. Even my brother is going to love it. It will destroy all the stupid hair metal forever." It worked out and, despite the humiliating shenanigans of mine he'd witnessed as my upstairs neighbor, he came to trust me to book shows for Stache's.

The first show I ever booked was Love Battery from Seattle. They were long-haired, heavy, and on Sub Pop. The band had released a superb EP the year before called "Straight

love, death & photosynthesis

Dan Dougan at Stache's

Between The Eyes" full of reverb and a call-and-response chorus that was the soundtrack of many Black Labels pouring down my gullet. Dan asked me what they were asking for and he was shocked at their rate. I didn't think $300 was a lot for a band who had a few records out but at that point I knew nothing about booking. I plastered High Street with flyers and sure enough about 200 people crammed into the small club. Greenhorn and Appalachian Death Ride opened, which meant that there were probably more electric guitars and Marshall stacks on the tiny cramped stage of Stache's than any ZZ Top or Eric Clapton concert. Dan laughed and said, "Well, you know something I don't; I can't get a gauge on any of these fucking bands. First, I lose money on Nirvana and then make money on Screaming Trees, then lose money on The Fluid and now Nirvana is everywhere. I have no fucking idea. Keep doing it." A compliment from Dan was akin to snow in May, one would hear that it had happened in the past, but it was just a legend. But, sure enough, I next booked Thinking Fellers Union Local 282 with the Sun City Girls, again with the asking price of $300. Thinking Fellers would evolve into one of the best live shows of the '90s—a carnival of sorts with men wearing dresses, a Captain Beefheart chugging sense of melody and all the earnestness of a five year old. When the Thinking Fellers played, the band wore their smiles broadly as if there were nothing greater than creating a racket, and it was the aural equivalent of going down a Slip-N-Slide in the nude. They were breathtaking. Gaunt, who drove straight back from New York after playing a Saturday night CMJ gig opened up the show. Roughly 20 people attended and I lost at least $300 as I had to pay the sound guy as well as the rider. It should have been a wakeup call, but I worked on a different value than profit. Music is best experienced live, with the sound vibrating the entire body instead of just entering via small holes at the side of the head, and Stache's and Bernie's were as comfortable as my home. Near the front or just to the side was where we stood, to feel the blast of the guitar and to witness the interplay of the bands, smiling at one another, laughing at inside jokes and singing along. Full-blast.

Bands and label employees knew they could find an ear and a couch in Columbus, and Columbus became a main stop for touring bands. I had two couches: one thread-bare, a relic from the early '70s that my grandmother had given me after my grandfather passed away; the other an orange vinyl sort that was deathly cold in the winter but was easy to wipe off in case any visiting musician leaked onto it.

I discovered that every town had someone like me who was all too willing to shell out meager guarantees to musicians who were escaping their own mundane jobs for two weeks to eat greasy eggs and falafels and snuggle up to a stranger's dog. My own enthusiasm was never exhausted. Music was more important than anything. More important than sex because a record can't reject you, more important than a job because songs don't foist responsibilities onto you, and more important than family because music can't leave you.

Even the stage of Stache's allowed a person to feel not only the music but also the people making the music—to feel their sweat, to see the lines on their faces as the music transformed their bodies—giving themselves wholly to something greater than whatever they were feeling— and to converse with them. The hierarchy between art and spectator was eliminated by sound waves, something was felt and shared together. The ability to bring this to quite literally the end of my street was a blessing, and Dan Dougan encouraged this. There was nothing complicated in the process, just phone calls and building the trust of the booking agents and club owners was all it took. Dan

Nirvana (live): Jenny Mae on top of the speaker

was relieved because he didn't always have to guess if a band would be a hit, and for the small scene we had, it provided an opportunity to experience something momentous even if the show had a small attendance.

Pavement released a ten-inch record on Chicago's Drag City, "Perfect Sound Forever". It was a peek into the future with a glance at the past; the songs were short and filled with a static-y gravel that perfectly captured the exhilarating anxiety a slice of our generation embodied. The joy the band found in music came through in these broken sounds that then brought out the joy for many of us. Some perceived this small indie-scene as an elitist club, that there was a secret in these muffled sounds of indie bands, but the opposite was true. The unpretentious charm of this music was in direct contrast to what we were being told we should like and consume.

bela koe-krompecher

Pavement live: Bela with glasses, some guy, Jenny Mae, Jeff Regensburger, Steve Malkmus

Jenny had called me up, "You're going to let me see Pavement right? And I'm taking Jeff as well." This was not an ask but an order, she was seeing Jeff Regensberger and Gaunt was the opener on Pavement's first show in Columbus. That night 300 people scooted in close to one another, huddled together, the sweat and smells mixing with the pure glee of the band on stage, and so began a long line of nights where everything was truly perfect— even when nothing was— one set at a time.

Over a lifetime, we hoard and discard, playing a mathematical game of emotion versus materialism. I spent a third of my life quitting—quitting drinking, quitting screwing around on my wife, quitting shitty food, quitting expecting myself to be someone I may have been once, but could no longer be. Watching the destruction of longing and attachment eat up the people I love the most has left bare spaces of loss in my psyche that I try to fill up with a new life with young children and of course, music. At times, I play a mental game of revisiting myself as a younger man, wading into a scene I was once very much a part of. Now, I hover somewhere outside the lines, learning— not so grace-fully— to be a sort of bystander, observing, taking it in rather than getting lost in it. Me with my graying hair sticking out like a thorny bush, a slight paunch not from alcohol but from exhaustion, and daily stubble that resembles tiny bits of confetti scattered around my mouth as if there were a small parade for the losers splattered on my wrinkly face. Pockets of age mark the years as if my face were the rings of a tree. I would be a mess in a matter of hours, pining for my old self, a life now rent asunder by alcoholism and mental illness and death. I climb into bed early now, and the band plays loudly and passionately to another young man bobbing his head at the front of the stage.

1996.

The mystery and wisdom of the ocean has held sway over me ever since I spent a year and a half on Long Island in childhood. Since then I've taken every rare opportunity I get to fall into the sea. I breathe in the salt and feel the hard pebbles of the craggly sand under my toes, swim into the calm waves, and let the water ride over me as if I were floating in space, my soul trying to swallow the sea instead of it swallowing me, and I am transformed back into a child, gazing at the wonder of the North Atlantic.

The Netherlands derives its name from being below sea level. The Dutch have managed to carve into the sea, by means of a complex series of dykes and canals, and it's one of the great mysteries of the world. And they did this without earth moving machines! The ocean is ever-present in the minds of the Dutch. It provides life and income; the Dutch made their mark as a hub of international trade since the 1300's. Yet it is in constant peril in terms of rising waters, storms, and global warming. Not able to afford mistakes, the Dutch are surgical in terms of practicality and efficiency. The rows of trees that dot the landscape in Holland display the Dutch sense of order and design; even the wilderness has symmetry. They do not tolerate fools lightly. Which makes it all the more amazing that my wife fell for me.

I met her at Used Kids. She possessed the characteristics of most Dutch women; staggeringly beautiful, deliberate in her communication, confident in who she is, and blunt. Close-cropped blonde hair, stark blue eyes, and a hushed voice that is a cross between Marilyn Monroe and Ingmar Bergman. She was prone to blushing whenever I cracked a joke. She came into the shop roughly three days a week. I flirted shamelessly with her. My coworkers shook their heads at me, and never failed to mention that she was out of my league. In fact, she was out of everybody's league in Columbus. But I was recently divorced and in a phase of total sluthood. And I knew that a way to a woman's secrets is through her laughter. Determination to make her mine set in. I said to my friend Candace, "I think I'm in love with this foreign woman."

Candace smiled. "Is she tall and blonde? She likes you. I'm in class with her, and she said there is this guy at the record store who is very handsome and funny and she keeps going back."

I eyed Candace carefully. "Are you sure that's me?"

After the initial trepidation of new lovers, where one explores the history of lovers, wondering if we match up against the past, I found out that the tall curly haired gentleman who frequently accompanied her was a Dutch friend of hers who was also going to graduate school at Ohio State. A gentle man he was in fact, almost childlike in his amazement of the world. He would let out a moderate laugh at the baffling ways of Americans who could be so quick to do the absurd and choose the illogical avenue that is so contrary to the philosophy of a Dutchman.

Edo Visser was a student of Paul Nini's, the leader of Log whose Kiwi sounding brand of indie-rock I adored and whose members looked as if they all owned homes and made regular car payments, which they all did. Paul taught design at Ohio State and Edo was blown away when I showed him the CD of Log that came out on Anyway. In a sense this helped Edo understand that everything in the world is local, everything is interconnected. Soon, he was accompanying me and my new Dutch girlfriend to shows and being exposed to the world of underground music.

Edo was fascinated with the life I lived, the bands, the art. And he was interested in the fact that I, and so many of my acquaintances had dropped out of college yet were well read; we wrote and created and evolved in our own ways. He was taken aback by the amount of alcohol we consumed—he had never had a drink of alcohol in his life nor did he eat meat or talk derisively of others. He would sit in the corner booth of BW-3 with Ron House, Jerry and myself as 5 o'clock rolled around. While we maintained a buzz, Edo would sip Coke. It was as if we were bugs in a glass jar for him and his eyes would grow big as he ventured into our world. He came into the store at least once a week, usually spending about an hour combing through the $3 CD bin, as he could only afford cheap CDs on his meager grad-student salary. He would pick out music by looking at the cover art; he was interested not only in how things sounded but also how they were presented.

The Dutch are emotionally reserved, as if plunging into a relationship is a violation of ethical concerns. While it can be frustrating, upon deeper reflection it makes sense, as one must keep a sense about oneself when living below sea-level and being dependent on the trading of goods for survival. Edo never spoke of his family, with the exception of his sister whom he appeared to adore. He said, "I don't drink, people in my family did and that was enough for me." There was never a judgment from him about my own intake of alcohol. And when, in a burst of emotional turmoil, my voice would rise towards some dissatisfaction with Merijn, Edo would turn heel and leave.

Edo adored Jenny; he was alarmed that someone whose life was in such chaos could make such touching and delicate music. In her presence he was respectful, hesitant, and curious about her outspoken ramshackle manners. She could easily crack a joke about blowjobs and stinky balls and in the next breath play a song that wrenched your heart. One night, we traveled over to Jenny's whose tiny greenhouse sat directly behind two bars in the middle of a gravel parking lot. Her house was hidden from the neighborhood, as if erected only for an outsider, parked in an alley with only tiny stones and broken glass for a yard. She had decided to have a party. In its own way, every night was a party for her. There would be times where she would invite Merijn and I over, saying she was having a party, and it would only be us and her husband. "Where's the party Jenny?" I would ask, annoyed that we dropped our plans for her "party." "Oh, I forgot to tell anyone" she would say nonchalantly taking a pull from a wine bottle. One night we brought Edo. The house was half full. The Shannon brothers were there (Tom and Dave) who made up 2/3 of the Cheater Slicks, and Jerry, Ted and his future wife Julie, some of Jenny's band mates, and Ron House brought his old friend Mark Eitzel. Jenny was dressed in a thrift store evening gown, with long costume diamonds and pearls. Her husband Dave wore a black suit. In her living room there was a small waterfall that she had dragged from a dumpster, and her walls were adorned with black and white photos she had ripped from old Life magazines and her own paintings of odd looking women with large heads and thin bodies. Edo was impressed. He turned to me and said, "Wow, she is really some artist type person. I always got the impression she was just a drunkard." Later she turned on her fog machine and smoke rolled from her basement practice space and the cocaine lit a fire in her belly and the drunken absurdist Jenny took over. All the while her new record blared from the speakers. I asked Edo that night if he would do the artwork for the record.

Edo took his design work seriously; he was smart and deliberate in his work. He was careful and respectful of Jenny's idea for the cover of *Don't Wait up For Me*. He did a wonderful job. I then asked him to do the artwork for a record I had been trying to assemble for nearly six years. *I Stayed up All Night Listening to Records* was conceived as a way to capture songwriters in their own element, with no assistance from others. The guidelines were that the song, the instruments and recording had to be all done by the performers themselves. I asked a lot of the musicians I greatly admired to participate, most from Columbus. I wanted the artwork to pay homage to the Folkways records I had grown up with as a child. This would be hard to do as it was only going to come out on compact disc; Revolver was not going to splurge for a double LP of mostly Midwestern songwriters. I gave Edo copies of of *Dust Bowl Ballads* by Woody Guthrie, *Music Time with Charity Bailey*, and *Songs to Grow On*. He came back a few weeks later with a beautiful and humble cover for the record that was the perfect complement to the simple four-track recordings that made up the music.

He planned a trip down the west coast by locomotive, just him and the rails in pursuit of the all-American sense of adventure that could only be found in the imagination of a European boy. Taking a sip out of my "Proud to be a Democrat" cup, I asked, "You going by yourself?"

Sipping his herbal tea, he spied me over the steaming cup and said, "Of course." He pulled a map from his worn leather bag, "See, I will fly to Chicago and take a train to Seattle and then travel down to San Francisco and then I will fly home, and then fly home again." One life in Columbus and one in Holland.

I was surprised and impressed that one would choose to travel alone without a reassuring touch available. I had not spent more than a few nights of my adult life alone. Perhaps Edo had no one to go with. He had mentioned a lady friend in Holland—an older, married woman, but in the States he had no romantic partner. In a sense, his years in the Midwest had transformed him into a man without a land to call home. The exposure to American ways of life had mutated his sense of society and was a watershed in that he realized the rigidity of the Dutch as contrasted with Americans. But there was a fine line between knowing too much and not enough. Edo went home a visitor and stayed that way.

Over the next few years, we visited Edo. He had worked for one of the best-known graphic designers in Amsterdam, but quit, explaining that he couldn't handle the egos that bounded around the office. "They seem to lose the sense of art when they do high profile projects. It's all about themselves and the boss. I am not that type." He was growing in reverse, diving into himself.

Edo moved to a small island off the coast of the Netherlands, working as a designer for a boating magazine, seeking solace in the sea as waves of turmoil crashed in his head. When I had to travel to Holland as part of a research class, I contacted Edo, making arrangements to meet up in Amsterdam. But he didn't show up, and he never responded to my emails again. Sometime in August, Edo cleaned up his small apartment, making sure his belongings were in place and headed towards the seashore. He walked into the ocean. What does a person think as the water swallows him whole? Did he fight the current in the end or simply let it carry him away? His sister emailed my wife to tell us his body was found washed ashore nearly four weeks after he had disappeared.

1992.

Exiting the teenage years felt like being propelled from a gun; full of explosions, excitements and smoke, we rocketed into our twenties not only with a desire to escape our families but also with the very real possibility of reinventing ourselves on our own terms. The first person who I ever knew to do this was Jack Taylor, who grew up Richie Violet in the small Ohio town of Urbana. Why Richie chose the John Doe-ish name of Jack Taylor, which screams "average," is unknown to me. Jerry Wick recast himself for a short period as "Jheri Curl." He shed that name along with his patchouli oil shortly after we met, and Gaunt was formed.

The first Gaunt single was a split with the New Bomb Turks, released on Craig Regala's Datapanik label. The funds were cobbled together from the band members, Ron House, Craig and myself. Furious and fast, part Saints, Husker Du, Pagans, and the rest all Midwestern, it was an immediate collector's item. The Turks side got the most attention. While Gaunt could be breathtaking at times, the Turks were a combine harvester compared to the diesel engine of early Gaunt, and they quickly got a deal with Crypt Records, who at the time were the quintessential garage label and the home of Jon Spencer. Jerry felt left behind.

New Bomb Turks standing (l-r): Bill Randt, Matt Reber, Jim Weber and Eric Davidson

Realizing Gaunt needed something more, Jerry asked Jovan Karcic to play second guitar. Jovan was a perfect foil for Jerry's manic energy with his reserved demeanor, and the smart, humorous licks of his guitar balanced Jerry's almost psychotic playing. Jovan served as a tether for the speedball frenzy of Jerry, barely breaking a smile except when looking at Jerry's theatrics. He was the grounding Gaunt needed.

It was time for Gaunt to step out on their own. My ex-girlfriend Sharon was a woman with certain needs. I had thought a credit card would help with these needs, but shortly after I fell deeply in love with her she broke up with me. I was devastated. But now I had some extra money and with this meager sum I suggested to Jerry that we put a Gaunt single out. Jerry pounced on the idea; we decided to form a partnership and call it Anyway after a word I seemed to use with frequency. Jerry spoke grand, with a plan to have the label supporting itself within a year. He was frantic, as if he were plugged into an electrical outlet. Jerry had an outlook on life that was epic in scale; this was with everything that he did, whether it had to do with friendships, music, or now, a label. For him, the thought of not making a mark in the world was unfathomable. Animated by chemicals and passion, only pure exhaustion could shut him up. I was more pragmatic, knowing that I barely made $12,000 a year at Used Kids and Jerry made less between filling in part-time at Used Kids and the pizza joint. I just wanted to get that first single out.

"Jim Motherfucker" was a ferocious piece of music with an almost marching hypnotic beat punctuated by Jerry snarling "Jim! Jim! Jim!" with guitarist Jim Weber from the Turks shouting "Motherfucker!" between each "Jim!" Both musicians were frightened that their mothers would hear it. The covers were made with Xeroxed colored paper from Kinko's. We assembled them by hand, the labels rubber stamped "Anyway Stuff." I called the distributors that Used Kids ordered from: Scat, Twin Cities, Matador, Revolver, Caroline, Get Hip and Comm 4. The single sold out within days.

An undercurrent of support was coming from New York, from Matt Sweeney, Paul Sommerstein and others, whose passion for music was on or above the level of ours. Matt, Paul and some of the folks at Matador were stunned by the amount of good music coming from Ohio, and would pass the singles and dubbed cassettes to critics and other labels to help spread the word. This underground river of music sharing helped immensely in the careers of not only Gaunt, and the New Bomb Turks but also led to the discovery of Guided by Voices, who was championed early on by Sweeney, Cosloy and Sommerstein.

There were several goals most any band had, the first being to press a 7" record, followed by getting a review (not necessarily a kind review) in any fanzine, and finally to play shows out of town. One day Steve Turner from Mudhoney called the store. He and his girlfriend were driving through Ohio looking for rare records. He wanted to know if they could come by the store and grab a few beers afterward. A few hours later, huddled over a table full of beers, Jerry, Ron and I giggled with Steve and Caryn, as Steve shared a story of Mudhoney going to the White House with Pearl Jam. While Eddie Vedder and company got up close and personal with President Clinton, Mudhoney was deemed too insufficient to meet the President. Instead they had coffee with the Secret Service who regaled them with stories of would be assassins whose exploits bordered on Inspector Clouseau proportions. At one point Ron commented that Steve should feel a bit put off by the popularity of Pearl Jam. Ron at one time heckled Steve's old band Green River (who would split into Pearl Jam and Mudhoney, respectively), from across High Street as "the new Bad

Mudhoney: Mark Arm. (Craig Regala-seated, some dude and Richie "Jack Taylor" Violet-standing)

Company"—which was a fairly egregious insult in our smallish world. Steve's reply was something like, "Doesn't matter—trust me, we are very happy to be Mudhoney." Steve was a big fan of Gaunt, and Mudhoney asked Gaunt to open a series of shows for them. A byproduct of this wonderful indie-world was the idea of no hierarchy. It was common for well-known bands to pick local bands to open for them or to tour with. Pavement had the Ass Ponys open for them several times, Superchunk toured with Gaunt a few times, Billy Childish asked the New Bomb Turks to play with him, and the list goes on.

1993.

Kudgel was a band from Boston who dubbed the genre of music they played "lard rock" due to the hefty girth of the band members. They had one stupendous song called "The Alphabet Song" and a new record called *Chimp Rock* and though they were from Boston, they lacked the brainy pop eagerness of other Northeast bands and were more akin to the sludgy sounds of Minneapolis and the Amphetamine Reptile label. Hate rock, but in a goofy way, as half the band dressed in skirts and moo-moos. The shared a bill with the Bassholes and the Cheater Slicks, also from Boston, whose immense guitar sounded as if they were belched from the bowels of the Atlantic during one of those fabled Nor'easters.

I was smashed after the epic three-band set at Bernie's, my ears still ringing from Dave Shannon's squalling guitar sounds as I set Kudgel up to sleep at my house. I laughed as I fetched blankets and a trusty brown plastic bucket that I kept bed-side and showed the gentlemen from Boston the various beds in the house.

"Hey Bela, what's with the bucket?"

Looking down as it swung from my left hand, I said, "Oh, this? I'm gonna puke in about fifteen minutes, this is so I don't have to go to the bathroom. It's OK, I do it all the time."

bela koe-krompecher

Mark Erody, the singer, picked up a medical enema. "And what the hell is this?!" he laughed. "Oh, shit, I gotta be at the urologist in four hours. I have to give myself an enema."

"An enema?"

I had some issues with my bodily plumbing. I had gotten an STD and had to go to the health department as I was too ashamed to go to good old Dr. Brown, he with the Mickey Mouse earring. There was no possible way I could have this kindly family doctor with his earring, bushy mustache and photos of his family on the walls of his office look me in the eye while sticking an 8" cotton swab down the shaft of my penis. But while taking the antibiotics, I was supposed to refrain from alcohol for ten days. I couldn't even go two. When the symptoms returned, I needed to go back. This time I saw a slightly familiar man around my age in the waiting room. That night, Jenny phoned. "Hey, you got the clap again, huh?"

"Shut up, if I got anything it was from you and that vagina that serves as an incubator for disease."

She laughed. "My new boyfriend saw you there. Hahaha, I told him you give everybody the clap!"

Properly taking antibiotics while engaging in active alcoholism is about as easy as eating one potato chip. Finally, I got tired of going back to the clinic and resigned myself to seeing the wholesome Dr. Brown. I figured a shot of penicillin might do the trick. In Dr. Brown's office, I was surrounded by *Highlights for Children* and *Ranger Rick* magazines, my dick itching as if an ant had crawled up it and was making periodic trips down the shaft bringing various crumbs back into its new found home. But at least I wouldn't meet any of Jenny's boyfriends in there. Dr. Brown had been treating me and my variety of drunken escapades for a few years and he laughed when informed of my trips to the VD clinic. He said, "You probably don't even have a venereal disease." He asked me to drop my pants so he could check my prostate. Leaning over, I was startled to hear kindly Dr. Brown shout out, "Good heavens, son, no wonder you are so uncomfortable! Your prostate is huge! Christ, it feels like you're 65 years old."

Pulling up my trousers, trying to look dignified with an aging prostate and jelly all over my ass, I asked, "So, that means I don't have a STD right? That's good?"

Dr. Brown's brow furrowed and he shook his head. "No, it is not good for a 22-year-old man to have a prostate that large. It can only mean two things: it is severely infected or you have cancer."

I was dumbfounded. Cancer? On my fuel injector? Dr. Brown made an appointment for a specialist. I would only have to wait two weeks. Needless to say, there was a great deal of alcohol consumption those next two weeks. I lost at everything. I knew I would never be a cancer survivor.

Which brings us to Kudgel's visit. The next morning, still drunk, struggling to decipher the small print of the instructions of the enema as I laid on all fours, bare ass sticking towards the heavens, I had no idea what to do. My head throbbed, my hands were shaky, but I figured how hard could it be to stick something up one's ass? Apparently, very. The first attempt caused a small bloody cut where I had never believed a cut possible, and I wondered what it would feel like when I took a shit. Standing up, I had half a mind to go ask one of the gentlemen from Kudgel to assist me. Thinking better of it, I plunged the small tube in.

Checking in an hour later at the doctor's, I was informed my appointment wasn't for another week. The men from Kudgel thought it was hilarious when I returned and explained how I gave myself an enema for nothing.

Seven days later I arrived again at the urologist's office, two weeks of heavy drinking and worries stacked up leaving me a mess. The urologist was an old shaky man who asked me to bend over while he checked out the canyon-sized prostate that sat inside of me. I was still drunk from the night before, and dehydrated to the point that a lizard would have felt quite at home amongst my innards. I felt the old man struggling to get to that prostate. 'Fuck,' I thought. 'What the hell is he doing back there?' He asked me to turn around and, taking my sheepish penis in his hands, he checked to see if there was any discharge coming out. He looked me in the eye and said, "You smell of alcohol. This may take a little longer." Leaning again across the table, I felt him try to push something out of the wasteland that was my insides. Soon, my knees grew weak. I felt stars dancing around my head. "Uhh, I don't feel too good," I groaned, and rolled off the tiny urologist bed. The old man caught me and slid a chair under me. He produced a small packet of smelling salts. Waking from the faint, I looked down to see him grabbing my pathetic droopy penis to wrestle a smidgen of moisture out of it as if he were squeezing the last drop of toothpaste from the tube. "That should do it. Before you leave the nurse will give you something to put your ejaculate in." Pulling up the trousers that had sunk like a cordless flag at my feet in utter defeat, I murmured, "Thank you." I felt the damp gel he had used soak into my underwear. Walking through the waiting room, two thoughts came to mind. First, if I'd heard the old doctor correctly, I would have to dispense sperm this morning after the ordeal I just went through. Second, where exactly I would accomplish this feat? I asked the small mousy woman, who combed her bangs forward with enough hairspray to look as if she may be auditioning for a part in a John Hughes movie. She smiled. "Oh, he must want a stool sample." Somehow, the situation had gotten more absurd. I leaned forward. "Hmm, no," I whispered. "He wants something else."

Her face crinkled, eyebrows arched. "I wonder what that could be." Swiveling around her chair, she bellowed to a nurse who was in some mysterious backroom that all doctor's offices seem to have. "Missy?! What else did the doctor want for Mr. Koe-Krompecher?"

A head poked around a doorway in the back, "Oh, he needs a sperm sample!" the nurse brayed.

I turned around, hopeful that none of the grandmothers sitting next to the grandfathers who littered the waiting room like cows staring blankly in a field would have heard. I was met with a flock of curious smiles.

"Oh, that's easy to do," the mousy woman with the bangs was saying. "I'll have to get you a sample cup for you to put your ejaculate in." I stared up at the ceiling while I waited, attempting invisibility. She reappeared and handed me a small plastic cup. I grinned flatly, rocked back up on my heels, and stared at her. She smiled back and nodded. I smiled and nodded. "Er, mmmm, so?" I said finally. Red bloomed across her cheeks, as if a curtain had closed over her face. "Ohhhhhh," she mouthed. "No, you bring it back in sometime in the coming week."

"Great, thanks." And with that I left.

After procuring and returning my sample and awaiting the results, fear was my constant companion. Finally, the day of doom arrived. The elderly doctor entered the same room as before, asked me how I was, and then startled me with his next question. "Young man, how much alcohol do you drink every week?" He leaned towards me, clipboard held tightly to his chest as if he were protecting his chest from the arrows of denial. "Oh, a few beers here and there," I answered innocently.

"Well, maybe, but it appears as if your prostate is infected, and may be sensitive to alcohol and maybe caffeine. When the prostate is infected, we call that prostatitis, and you appear to have a severe case, and alcohol and caffeine exacerbates the situation. My advice to you is to give up drinking alcohol or slow down or you will continue to have these problems."

'That's it?' I thought. 'No cancer, but I have to quit drinking?' I didn't know which was worse. Making sure I'd heard right, I looked up at him and asked, "So you're saying I don't have cancer?"

"You don't. You drink too much. You need to stop."

"I see. Will it kill me? I mean the prostate thing, if I don't quit drinking?"

"No, it won't kill you in and of itself. You are at risk for developing cancer, but in the meantime you will just continue to be uncomfortable if you keep it up. You should quit drinking." And with that he left the room. With a great deal of relief, I left his office, smiling. It would take me another 12 years to decide to quit.

2005.

I received a voice mail from Jenny. Jim Williams was dead and she was back in Columbus, at least temporarily, and she was drunk. Incoherent. Her voice was brittle and frayed. If it were a photograph, it would be faded, eyes staring towards the lens with all the effort of a dustbowl victim. She sounded small, huddled into herself. "I don't know what to do, I'm borrowing some girl's phone, she must think I'm nuts. What can I do without him?! I need help." Click. I had no idea what time she had called, nor was I sure where she was. She had been in Columbus for nearly two months, having tried to find a place to live in Miami with friends. Soon they tired of her— her way of living crowded out everything around her. She went from living in Coconut Grove in Jim's apartment to being on the streets in a matter of months. When she landed back in Columbus it was the same routine she had in Miami, she just burned through her days like a human torch, scorching everything in her path, including herself.

I had been rebuilding myself for a few years at this point. Living back in Columbus, working at Used Kids, and plunging headlong into various volunteer work helping other drinkers, I was ill-prepared to offer solace— or any money— to Jenny. I was a novice at helping people at this point in my life, scraping together ideas I was learning from 12-Step groups and Buddhism as well as struggling to be an adult in the wake of my twenties. The horror of Jenny's life bruised me. It was like watching a prize-fighter get pummeled every round in a never-ending fight, but the ref is sitting at the edge of the ring, smoking a cigarette and chatting with the audience in the front row. She was a terrorist in her own fucking life. Land-mining her own sidewalk, she fell into every hole on her path like an all-too-real Wile E. Coyote cartoon but with real blood. With furrowed brow, I took to the stairs of Used Kids and headed for Bernie's where I assumed she'd borrowed a phone from some future barfly. I poked my head in and the bartender glanced at me. "She left about three hours ago, and she was a mess, yelling at Nate about some craziness. She's off her fucking rocker. I told her not to come back for a while, she's scaring some of the customers." I glanced at a customer with bits of egg in his beard, four inches of stretched belly hanging out over a belt longing to be put to sleep. His T-shirt was blanched and threadbare, splattered with pizza stains, and pocketed with small stretchy holes that barely contained his daily beer-drinker's girth. He raised one eyebrow, hoisted a Pabst Blue-Ribbon tall-boy and slowly nodded his head in agreement. I gazed at another man, decked in faded leather jacket, chain wallet dangling. He looked up from his drink and said, "Bela, that chick is nuts."

Crossing High Street, I entered the OSU Music Building, climbing the stairs to the top floor where the university kept the practice pianos. I crept in quietly and listened. I heard the vague plinking of the Beach Boys "Surfer Girl." Opening the door, I found Jenny, filthy, matted hair clinging to her skull and shoulders, a thin dress drenched in sweat sticking to her arms and back as if it were wallpapered onto her. She gazed up at me, tears streaming down her cheeks, a bottle of vodka stashed between her legs and the odor of sweat and booze blanketing the air.

"Oh, Bela what am I gonna do?" She turned and tried to play "Lady Madonna" but only made it through the first several lines before switching course and attempting "Maybe I'm Amazed." She croaked, "That was his favorite, he loved Paul McCartney. I would play it over and over." Of this, I had no doubt as she once told me they once spent $275 playing "Jet" over and over on a hotel bar jukebox while on a two-day coke-binge. "You know," she slurred, "we saw Paul McCartney five times, we flew across the country to see him. Jim was like that—once he became obsessed with something he did it to death." Even life, I thought to myself. He did that to death as well.

Taking a pull off the warm vodka bottle, she said, to no one in particular, "You know, they threw out all my stuff when he died. His brother and that bitch sister-in-law. They went to the boat I lived on and dumped it all. Even my pink records." The pink records would be the Guided By Voices split single she did, the one that was reviewed in Spin magazine, where Charles Aaron called her "astonishing, one of the best bohemian song-writers alive." She had created hundreds of doilies in manic bursts, painted spindly thin-limbed characters holding glasses of wine or playing skinnier pianos. She also liked to work with coconut shells, decorating them in deranged baubles and gold chains, the hair of the shells combed down to make them glamorous "sea models." She was making "a whole platoon of these things," she said to me once. "I wanna string them around the whole yard, so when it's nighttime, the moonlight can bounce off their jewelry. I have about 40 of them done already." She had them clinking and clanking in the wind, miniature brown hairy painted heads hanging from the roof of the patio along with lobster-shaped garden lights. Now, this artwork in all its ruffled glory had been tossed unceremoniously into the trash heap.

Frozen, I simply said, "I'm sorry." I was angry, upset that anybody would discard somebody's life's possessions with such impudence. Sweat dripped down my back; this room was an oven. "Jenny why don't you go somewhere and get some help?"

Plinking on the piano, she whispered, "You can't help. You never wanted to help, you just want to tell me what to do. Leave me alone."

I left. I felt as powerless as air.

1993.

For a brief period of time, Jerry sparkled like a sliver of glass in the sunshine, beaming radiance until it cut him underfoot. Jerry stood tall in his own eyes, in terms of his future, but in his day-to-day existence much of what he thought of himself was predicated on how he perceived he was viewed.

Jerry and Gaunt were busy prepping their first full-length record on Thrill Jockey, *I Can See Your Mom From Here*, a frantic rush of guitar squall. The first song, "I Don't Care" perfectly summed up the snotty brattiness of Jerry at his finest. The band recorded it with Steve Albini, whose own acerbic view of the world and the music business was legendary, and whose unflinching ideals bonded perfectly with Jerry's.

I Can See Your Mom From Here was finished in the spring and would be released late summer or early fall. Jerry played the test pressing but took it home at the end of his shift. He didn't want Ron House to hear it until it came out. He craved Ron's approval and any sort of perceived negative feedback from Ron would turn Jerry dark and gloomy.

Jerry was anxious. Well, more anxious than anxious: his anxiety had anxiety. His mood would swing from lugubrious to teeth-rattling giddy in a matter of seconds. Sauntering into the store to work his shift, his back would be slightly stooped under the weight of

Gaunt - Jim Weber, Jerry Wick, Eric Barth, Jeff Regensberger

being Jerry Wick. Jerry's wardrobe consisted of tattered shorts cut at the knees, black T-shirts, black Converse Chuck Taylors, no socks and usually no underwear.

His only regular exercise was to pull a Camel out of his rumpled pocket, light it, inhale the entire cigarette in several deep sucks, and then repeat. Stopping only to eat slimy fast food, and to drink coffee and beer. Setting his ratty, stained handbag behind the back counter, he would hurriedly rifle through the shelf below the front counter for any type of reading material that might mention Gaunt. The two gold chalices of print would be SPIN and the *College Music Journal*, although any mention in some of the other highly respected zines would do. *Your Flesh*, *Forced Exposure*, *Superdope*, *Rollerderby*, *Popmatters*, and *Chemical Imbalance* boasted writers and self-publishers who were not only quality and often hilarious reads, but these guys (and gals) pretty much nailed it musically. Jerry would flip through the pages of the zine, frantically scanning for any mention of Gaunt or the New Bomb Turks, and if he didn't find one, he would amble to the front of the store, oblivious to customers who were shopping, stealing, or buying, and cram the periodical back under the counter and either sulk at the back counter for an hour or so or maybe he would slip next door to see if Captain could lighten his mood. If by chance there was a mention of Gaunt, he would keep the article nearby for the rest of the day, stealing occasional glances at the print as if that would magically add a boost in confidence to an already permanently bruised ego. We were all like this for the most part—foraging for any evidence that would placate the sense of displacement many of us grew up with. With Jerry, it was the equivalent of continuously googling his own name but doing it to a single copy of *Your Flesh* fanzine.

He would be extra anxious on the days Gaunt was to play at night, his nervousness combining with his over-caffeinated and nicotine-addled brain making him unbearable. "Yeah, just leave," I'd say after the 14th fucking time he'd mention that his band was playing that night. "I can handle the last hour by myself." Relief would flood him in a flash. "Thanks, dude, I'll see you tonight," he'd yowl on his rush out the door. Closing up by myself these nights, I would go to the back counter and see a litter of cigarettes scattered on the floor. Talismans to his inner jitters. His commitment was only to himself and his music, everything else was brushed aside. I was the same way. Our focus was on what we knew—security was rarely present and if it came, it would only be fleeting a wisp of comfort.

1993.

The small wooden house in the shape of an "L" sat just off the curb of Patterson Avenue. An old woman who had lived and passed on in the house had planted a garden whose perennial flowers jutted up through stone cracks and raised flowerbeds every spring. It was brilliant, especially in contrast to the flaking paint of the house, bits of white and brown rolling in oblong tunnels as the summer and winters of Ohio did their damage. It was as if the mums, tulips, and roses had their own steely resolve, and sprouted up in defiance of the house crumbling beside them.

I lived with one roommate, Tom, for most of my time in the Patterson house and his bedroom was smaller than mine, really just enough to hold his bed and a tiny dresser. My bedroom had a row of bookshelves and a wooden desk given to me by my uncle Pablo who'd pulled it from a pile of rubbish in the '60s and refinished it. I had a typewriter on which I wrote a great deal of poetry and made some stabs at fiction. It was the bedroom of a drunkard: I rarely washed the sheets which were covered in dog hair, sweat, various types of body fluid, and the stale scent of alcohol. The kitchen was a thin hallway, one side had a counter and the other the sink, stovetop and refrigerator, and a small back room separated the kitchen from my bedroom. I had moved into the house after living

love, death & photosynthesis

Gaunt: Eric Barth, Jeff Regensberger, Jerry Wick, Jovan Karcic

with two women the previous year, and it provided a safe place for me to finally begin to call a home for myself.

Drinking was a way to connect, not just to others, but to myself. Alcohol allowed the laughter to flow. The validation of laughter is one of the finest feelings a person can have, a small jolt of pleasure in the desert of the mundane. Jerry, Jenny, and I were all gifted with the ability to wriggle smiles out of others. Jenny and Jerry, in spite of the darkness that crept around their edges, were two of the funniest people I have ever encountered. They had an ability to see the preposterousness of life, to cultivate the absurd and bring it into focus.

After I started drinking again in 1991, it seemed there was no turning back. At first I was hesitant and fearful of the drink, as if I were going to receive an electric shock from picking up the bottle, but after nursing a few Jim Beams and water, the fear dispersed. It was pleasurable and comfortable for a great deal of the time, as if my mind were sinking into an ethereal La-Z-Boy recliner, with the sweet scent of whiskey, water, and tobacco serving as a soft throw-blanket over my being. Other times, the ugliness rose up, nights where I was frightened to go home alone. I would wait at the bar as the bartender slowly cleaned up, rising from the stool only when I knew I was damaged enough to be only minutes from slumber. I had the drunken timing of a professional.

More importantly, the fear of going home alone gripped nearly everyone, man and woman alike at 2:30 AM. Nobody was spared the trepidation of lying in bed alone while the bar emptied out onto the gray and shivering sidewalks of Columbus. Having the warm body of a lover would not only provide carnal sensations but more importantly the secrets of acceptance that only lovemaking can bring. By the same degree, though, came the fear the next morning, the lurching headaches, the awkward nervousness of shaky good mornings and the speeding thoughts of the coming responsibilities of the day.

I had a lover with red hair, a nose-ring, and a slender build. We were wary of one another. Usually she would come over in the early evening, we would make love and she would leave. She had no interest in seeing me get drunk and was one of the first women to tell me this. She said I acted "silly" when I drank, which annoyed me to no end, as I always thought that the word "silly" is itself silly. And stupid. Only on a handful of occasions did we spend an entire night together, and this was fine for both of us, really: we had very little in common with the exception that we enjoyed each other's bodies and we hated being alone. The first time she came into my room, she glanced down at my hairy bed, with sheets that held countless drunken stories between the faded and frayed white fabric. Over to the side of the bed, next to a stack of books that I would never be able to digest because of my inebriated nights, sat my brown bucket. "What is that?" she asked, staring at me with eyebrows askew.

"My bucket, in case I vomit. It's kind of like a gross, rubber teddy-bear, I find myself hugging it at night."

"Why?"

"Well, I sometimes get sick at night—from the drinking but really, it's ok-I'm used to it and I have never done it in my bed…or anyone else's." I was trying not to scare her away.

In her mind she was slowly clicking off the pros and cons of sleeping with me, on the con side there was the bucket, the dog hair, and the constant joking. The pro side had the constant joking. She decided to stay for a while.

love, death & photosynthesis

Cosmic Psychos (Bela, Jerry Wick, Robbie "Rocket" Watts)

Sometimes I woke up on the roof of that small decrepit house. It was over the mud room; all it took to get up there was to stand on the small rusted fence and pull yourself up. It was like stepping onto another level of life. Somehow the largeness of the heavens would calm the rattling of my mind and soothe the civil war in my stomach. A secret hope of mine was to venture into the celestial sphere when I pass on, to taste the violent beauty of space. I would think about this at 4 AM and my inner world would calm. For a while, I continued to live a blessed life. One that allowed me many opportunities to explore the world in which I cared so much about: music, people, and more music.

1994.

I was retreating. Classical music was a refuge, especially Pergolesi's "Stabat Mater." In some way, the soft epic reinforced the mysterious relationship I had always silently offered to my father, unbeknownst to him. I read *City of God* by Saint Augustine, *The Lives of the Saints*, and of course the Bible.

Used Kids opened at 10 AM, and in the late '80s, early '90s, nary a person would come in before 11—perhaps the UPS driver delivering a box of Beat Happening, the Vaselines, and Yo La Tengo. The person who opened the shop had the place to himself for an hour. This was a time for meditation, indie-rock style, which meant coffee, an open front door and the warm grooves of whatever record we used to commune with our inner thoughts. The playlist at this hour for myself consisted of either classical (Dvorak or the choral music of Shultz or Byrd), Townes Van Zandt, Van Morrison, Phil Ochs, or Gram Parsons. The search for the perfect music to dampen a hangover was ever present. Sipping the bitter coffee of Buckeye Donuts, and slowly pricing out records was my way of carrying water, chopping wood, and washing dishes.

Although Jerry and I never really spoke of spiritual matters, he was conscious enough to know my mass schedule, at times volunteering to meet me afterwards. Jenny was dismissive

love, death & photosynthesis

of my longing for quiet. It was as if the barrage of noise in her head could not comprehend—and was in fact threatened by—my having an itch that only silence could scratch.

I started attending mass twice a week, after shifts at Used Kids. For a campus church, Holy Name was not the norm; there were no long-haired glad-handers, no "rock-and-roll" guitar songs proclaiming the happiness of Christ. Parts of the mass were in Latin. The hymns were sung a cappella and tended to be slow, as if the way to salvation consisted of miniscule movements of breath rather than the frantic pace of the ringing strings of acoustic guitars. The congregation was older, and at times barely existed—just a few gray-hairs and myself, huddled alone in the back pew as I resisted the urge to leave and grab a drink to wash away the persecution of unknowing. Tall columns lined the chapel, built of marble and thick chunks of stone. This was a building for the stoic who silently yearned for safety.

Next to the vast stone entrance of the church was a small walkway that led through a wrought-iron fence, around a statue of Christ, arms extended outwards, welcoming the repentant sinner on through to a small side chapel with five rows of pews. There, underneath the shiny polished wooden beams, I would sit in silence waiting for some sort of answer. I sat here when the hangovers were too bold and the alcohol dripped out of my pores as if I were a pungent flower, emanating the sweetest yet sickliest odor. Listening through the small door that led into the main chapel, hoping that I could catch redemption through osmosis, truly I wanted to hear nothing. Not the drumming of my thoughts, the screaming fear of being alone. I would cobble together a prayer, feeling the awkwardness of solitary unskilled appeal. Finally, I would slink away sheepishly as if I were a gawky lover who had left his partner unfulfilled. 'Nothing is good enough,' I would think about myself.

When my daughter was five, she asked me who God was and how do people believe in God. I said that I didn't know. I said I thought we should try to be helpful to those who are suffering, ease their lives. I told her that I thought God was an action and nothing more.

2011.

My son was three; beautiful with soft curly blond hair, almost transparent blue eyes, a giggling machine. He awoke early, after my wife at around 6 AM, while I slumbered away, a middle-aged man still wanting to spend the day in bed. He would run free through the house, every new discovery a sweet surprise, from the falling of the snow to being told it's the weekend. He'd say things like "yeah!" and "yippee" upon hearing that we were having pizza or going to the playground. His charms could blow a bad mood asunder. Thinking back to a time in my life when it was not uncommon for me to wake up pant-less in the bushes, or on a pillow of vomit, making desperate 4 AM phone calls to someone, anyone, I could not foresee what would become my life. It was different in so many ways, so much better and yet…the strains of being a father, the effort of being a husband and keeping my addictions at bay, was a challenge. Hiding in the bottle or in the arms of soft new flesh was not. And the family I came from had secrets, some still untold even here, but they lived on, generation to generation. Bits of anger trickle through the blood in my veins, clumping up within me, festering, until I would snap and the house would go silent. The children would slink away and only my wife and I would be left, in a room that had become a chilly cauldron. "Fucking dishes stacked up," I would spit out. "Jesus Fucking Christ, why are the fucking shoes in here, holy fucking hell!"

But I hid the anger from Bruno. He eyed me with benevolence; a full surrender of himself to what he thought was the vessel of all knowledge, his father, who, unbeknownst to him, was struggling to not scream at his mother, "I just want to sleep! That is all I want, for everything to be quiet!" He is an exquisite hugger, one of the best I have ever known. One time he rolled over and held my head tight in his arms, my ear pressed securely to his chest. It made me wonder who was fathering whom.

He'd talk in his sleep, yelling out to his mother, or at times giggling, which was a most wonderful sound. I'd stare at him sleeping, my wife next to him, and then listen to them breathe as I turned on my side and drifted off to sleep.

Bruno, sitting on my lap, would tell me in his fractured vocabulary what happened that day at school, everything painted by his imagination and innocent emotions. His favorite word was "spooky," and in his world everything was spooky, from the cover of a book on gorillas to the sound of a hemorrhaging muffler croaking by our house. His fears were of things he couldn't see, didn't know. Mine were the opposite: what I had seen, real memories suffocating me into a feeling of powerlessness.

I once had a dream I had to beat the devil, literally. He was completely black, like a shadow but also shiny and metallic. He had no features, just sold mass of slick black nothingness, a moving hole of darkness. I felt him hunting me down, I felt his presence, and in the dream the hairs on my arms stood at attention and the pleasure of rising fear surrounded me until I was almost connected to the devil, just inches away. The realization arose that I would be consumed by the devil if I could not think of how to beat him. He slithered around me, tall, thin and wispy as if he were a cloak, the evil flecking off him as if he were an active volcano. There was only one way to conquer him, but how? Knowing the devil communicates in riddles, I had to think quick, let the answer come to me, and I knew it had to be obvious because evil is never that complicated. So, I thought of my young daughter and all the love I had for her. I leaned in and hugged the devil, and with that, the action of love, the evil from the devil melted away. I had beaten the devil.

2011.

If **Jenny called in the morning, she was usually** lucid and able to showcase some of her caustic wit. We laughed hard at these times, enough to send tears streaming down my cheeks. She had the memory of an elephant, at moments able to conjure a piece of the past that, even if I were there, I would doubt that it could have happened. "I was thinking of that one time we had that New Year's Eve party in that hotel in Springfield with your brother and all his fucked-up friends. Remember?" she said, and I searched the moldiest canals of my mind to 27 years ago in vain. "You and I went and fucked in that broom closet and then went back to the party," she continued. "We paid that security guard twenty bucks to pretend he was arresting Donny Acuff, and then the guy got fired and ended up back at the parsonage partying with us all night. And what's-her-face killed Russ, your goldfish? Boy, you told that bitch off. That shit was funny."

But on this morning, her voice was hoarse, tired, cracked like piece of plastic that has been sitting on hot asphalt the entire summer. Faded at the edges, brittle, but still with the essence of itself. "I'm in the hospital again," she croaked. "Shit is crazy over here."

"Which one?" I asked, annoyed. Annoyed that it is ten till 6 and I have to pick up my two children from school or pay a fine. Annoyed that the motherfucker with the inappropriate large-ass 4X4 truck has no idea how to drive in a downtown city of 1.4 million people. Annoyed that I didn't finish all the work I needed to do. Annoyed at yet another phone call asking me for help.

"Hold on," she said. "I'm downtown. Grant. That's it. I'm at Grant. I've been here for about three days but I only felt well enough to call now. They took me by squad again. They should just park one in our parking lot because of me and Dale." I pictured her in the bed, with tubes stretching out from her arms, a tray of half eaten Salisbury steak and applesauce in front of her.

I maneuvered through outbound traffic, checking the time on the dashboard. I asked her what room number, and she answered, "I dunno, it's Grant. I'm at Grant. The hospital." This was a familiar verbal tennis match that she always won as her obliviousness was far superior to my impatience. I repeated my question, and she said, "Oh, I thought you asked hospital. The hospital is Grant, I don't know what room I'm in, but I'm pretty sick. It's my liver, my pancreas, and something with my intestines, they don't know what. I was puking for about two weeks." I can hear her struggling with the equipment that is dug into her arms, I can almost see her wince. "Ahhhhh, fuck," she mumbles, "I ain't doing good."

"OK, I'll try to come by tomorrow." I started to hang up the phone, as I had arrived at the children's school, with two minutes before the fine would kick in. "Wait! Wait!" I heard her screeching. Closing my eyes, I snapped, "What? I have to get my kids!" Jenny shifted herself in bed. I could hear the phone slipping, her voice getting small for a moment, as if she is laying at the bottom of the bed and crawling towards the receiver. "Hold it, hold it," she said. "OK, I had to tell you one more thing, so hold on, just hold on. Sorry." Pulling open the door to the school, I shook the snow off my shoes, saying, "OK, go on." The hallways were strung with construction paper artifacts of volcanoes erupting, dinosaurs and handsome colorful gardens punctuated by glitter. Kids lugged backpacks larger than they were, they looked like ants carrying giant morsels of food. A few parents smiled at me as I passed. I wanly smiled back as Jenny told me how Dale and her little brother smuggled a bottle of vodka into the hospital earlier in the day, a stunt that had the Columbus Police searching her room. "You wouldn't believe it, I woke up and I had this bottle of vodka in my lap, under the covers and the cops start looking around asking questions. I mean I feel like fuckin' death. I can't believe they did that, I mean my brother and Dale." My first thought was to ask her, "Well did you drink it?" Instead I said, "Well, you sound very sick, just do what the doctors tell you to. If they want to call me they can."

"So, where are you?" she croaked. "At the kid's school, I'm picking them up." Pause, and with a faraway voice she said, "They must be getting big."

With that my daughter ran into my arms. "Daddy, Daddy, guess what? We got our Daisy forms to sell cookies, can we sell some this weekend, can we call Grandma?"

"Of course." I kissed her blonde hair, pulling her small shoulders into my arms.

1985.

A large farm abutted the thin chunk of yard where a tiny ranch house stood, a house that resembled one of millions in America, this one set right of the old National Highway. Three small bedrooms and a closet-sized bathroom for a family of seven. Jenny and her younger sister slept in the unfinished basement, a piece of 1970s frayed green carpet kept bare teenage feet from slapping against the concrete. This was the third house the family had lived in over the past four years. Being poor is not easy, especially in America where people tend to be shuttled between bureaucratic paths that resemble something between a Kafka story and the story of the little girl who fell down the well.

The farm behind them was abandoned, the silo standing as a white beacon of failure to every passerby. This was the mid-'80s when the scorched-earth policies of Reagan cindered many a family farm, policies cloaked in the feel-good speech of an old actor who, while robbing the heartland blind, made us all feel a little safer. Jenny and her siblings each raised a lamb for the annual Clark County Fair. They realized the fragile lesson of life, death, and hardship. The sheep would be slaughtered after the fair, and the money each child made from the sale of the animal would be saved towards college, a car, or to help the family out.

After school, Jenny and I would climb into my tarnished Ford Mustang, with bucket seats that sat so low to the ground you could swear you could feel the heat of the asphalt under your ass. She would run the sheep, who by nature are not the brightest animals, trying to get them in shape to tone the muscles that would soon be ripped from bone and consumed. The animals would stare at her dumbfounded as if she were an alien. They had no reason to run in circles. They were probably thinking, "It's hot and we're wearing wool for Christ's sakes!" I would laugh at her efforts, drinking sun-tea her mother had made. "It looks silly," her mother would remark, "but she wins every year."

Jenny and I tried in vain to get into the barn—the massive wooden doors were shackled together with a rusty thick chain—for the purpose of unhinging our teenage lust in the shadows and moistness of the mildewed hay that we were sure waited for us behind the tethered doors. We would walk the abandoned farm in the cold and in the warmth of spring, traipsing over withered husks of corn, clumps of dirt that remained unmoved season to season. The raspy corn would crunch beneath our shoes; the wind would sail across the unproductive patch of earth that surrounded us. Holding hands, we entertained the questions of our adolescent minds. Jenny would explain things to me as we stepped over forgotten plants, why certain crops could grow in Ohio and how crop rotation works. This was all new to me. I had assumed through my lens of persecution that farming just involved listening to Hank Williams Jr. while riding on a tractor and telling racist jokes. The lump of distaste and protection I had accumulated over four years in living in rural Ohio slowly melted, and an understanding of the wisdom, care and struggles of my classmates and neighbors came into focus.

Nestled in the dirt roughly 200 yards back from the farm, her own house a dot in the distance, we found the carcass of a cow—almost complete, its bones, weathered white and picked clean by birds, rodents, bugs and seasons— we crouched down in awe. "How does this happen?" I asked. "This was someone's cow." I examined a hipbone half-buried in the dirt, resembling a conch shell in the middle of Ohio. She pulled it out, clumps of dirt sticking to its side. "It's weird, huh?" I took a few steps back, resting on my haunches, keeping my balance with my left hand I felt something in the dirt. There was another carcass. Soon we counted four or five cow skeletons. It was if we had walked into a cave, and slowly brushed a beetle off our arm, then noticed that there were thousands crawling around us. "Christ, look at all these fucking bones." The sky was gray, with soft rolling clouds hanging above the earth as if they were licking their collective lips readying themselves to unleash a torrent of cold

love, death & photosynthesis

rain. A splash of lightning shattered in the distance. I looked at Jenny and she stared at me. Large thick raindrops exploded between us. Wind gurgled in our ears. Jenny tried to put the hip bone back where it had submerged, as if it were never disturbed. "I don't know why anyone would let these poor animals die out here and never collect them," she said.

2006.

Jenny's coat wrapped around her body as if it were beaten into her. The rain fell between the cracked plastic and settled into the rotting poly-cotton stuffing that peeked through, making baby faces to the outside world. She huddled into herself, shivering on my porch as the rain whipped at her from behind. At the end of our walkway, Dale waved shyly, his blue eyes a stark contrast to his brown skin. I stepped out onto the porch making sure that none of the cold could slip into our warm house. My wife stood in the kitchen, wondering who would be knocking at our door in this weather. We didn't have too many unannounced visitors, and we preferred it this way. As sobriety surrounded us, the clamoring for social affirmation diminished and we simply kept to ourselves.

Jenny was swaying, to the vibrations of the house, the wind, or some internal song churning in her ears. It had been a long time since she swiped makeup over her face, put a line of lipstick around her lips, or wore a necklace. The skin on her face was taut, tan, and as weathered as the paint peeling off the side of our house. She had been through a lot this past year, from living in South Beach in the mansion of a millionaire to the streets and jails of Miami then to Lisa Carver's house in New Hampshire for six weeks recording a new album with Chris Squire, then back to South Beach only to have almost everything she owned put out on the sidewalk. And now finally on the streets of Columbus. I had been given her trumpet and a small suitcase that held a few of her CDs and records, but the rest was gone.

"Hey, Bela," she was saying, "I know you're busy, but we need to use your bathroom real quick. The Tim Horton's power went out and Dale has to take a shit and we don't have anything in the tent. In case you didn't notice, it's kinda raining out." She grinned. Dale waved in the background as if waving to the President in a motorcade.

I smiled back weakly, turned and said, more to my wife than Jenny, "Sure, come on in. But be quiet—the baby is asleep."

Dale started stomping and rattling the rain off of his soggy body as he trudged in. Jenny with her arms folded refused to go farther than the front entrance.

"Jenny come into the kitchen, do you want some water?" my wife asked.

"No, I'm cool, I'll just hang here, I don't want to wake the baby and I'm real wet, if you can't tell." The smell of alcohol shrouded her.

Dale hovered, beaming. Knowing he was prone to over-thanking us, I nodded towards him and casually cut him off with, "Anytime we can help."

"I'm sorry to come over here," Jenny said to me privately. "Especially when we've been drinking, We have to get a little bit in the morning, you know, I don't want Merijn to see me like this." She paused. "It's embarrassing." Silence hung heavy, and then was interrupted by Dale unloading in the other room. We laughed, "I swear to God, I'm going to kill him. Jesus, his ass is going to wake the baby," she muttered. Jenny's blue eyes held droplets of water, and for a moment the whole room was illuminated in the water goblets in her eyes, for a brief few moments she looked young again, much younger than her thirty-eight years. Outside the powerlines were bending in the wind, blankets of water were hurtling into the pavement, the sound of the storm was just a hair away from being unsettling. We both eyed the window and I wanted to ask her to stay. I could see Merijn in the kitchen, putting away dishes, and going about her business. She stepped into the dining room, "Jenny are you sure you don't want anything, I can make you coffee. It's really nasty out, where are you going after this?" Casting a smile as wide as a trampoline, and as flat as Iowa, Jenny replied, "Oh we are just going back to the camp, we have some food to eat back there, the twins brought some food back from the Resource Center—I told them we would be back to eat with them. They get really proud when they can feed Dale and I. Usually it's us feeding them." The pause was pregnant with twins, then I spoke, "It's ok if you guys stay for a cup of coffee until the storm calms down.' Once Merijn offered I knew it was ok to ask them to stick around. Upstairs the baby started to let us know she was awake, the soft muffled sounds of wakening quickly turned into a bray. "Excuse me" Merijn said as she wiped her hands on a small tea towel and disappeared upstairs. Jenny walked into the kitchen, "Hurry up Dale, the twins are waiting, our cold food will get colder," her laugh punctuating her sentence. Dale stepped through the kitchen doorway. "Thanks Bela, that was a close call. I'm ready Jenny." I watched as they stepped off the porch and into the downpour, Dale holding his hands over his head, as if it were going to make a difference. Merijn came up beside me, holding the baby close to her. "They decided to leave huh?" "Yup."

2012.

"Dale just died, about five minutes ago." It was Jenny. "The nursing home called, he just died. I'm so sad. He died."

"Oh Jenny, I'm so sorry."

"Well, we knew it was going to happen. Shit, his eyes weren't even straight anymore. He didn't know what the fuck was going on. But it still fucking hurts, I'm not going to see my Dale anymore. I'm not going to fuck up, though. I got my paperwork together for my state hearing tomorrow to get my Medicaid turned back on. Thank God I did it last night." In the travesty that is the American safety net, populated by regulations that are constructed predominantly by men who have never seen poverty up close, Jenny had managed to lose her medical insurance because she missed an appointment. She missed it because she was in the same nursing home that had applied for her. She spent nearly three weeks in intensive care and then transferred to the nursing home. Even with the intervention of her case manager and my direct contact, we were unable to get it reinstated.

"Listen, I'm late to work and I have two meetings, but I'll leave early and see you."

She sniffled and said, "Really, you don't have to do anything. Nothing can be done. He's dead, they called me from the nursing home."

Dale Chandler, Jr. grew up in West Virginia. Although Jenny later found that he did indeed graduate college, there was little evidence in his slow-mannered speech. He would search for words that would start with a trail of mumbles and finally end with a gasp and a smile. Tall, and gentle—to a point. He protected Jenny like a lioness over her cub. Being homeless is a difficult existence, especially if you are a woman.

Brian Hall was another tall, thin man who spent time in prison. He wore the violence of the past on his face and arms, thick bumpy scars across his arms and down his right cheek. Jenny was terrified of him. "That motherfucker wants to kill me. I swear to God if it wasn't for Dale he'd have killed me and left me in the bushes. He goes from camp to camp." This made me nervous. I rubbed my arms and looked at her. The fear in her eyes was real. "He tried to fuck me one night when Dale was getting beer. He came in our tent and told me to take my pants off and I laughed in his face. I was trying to act like I thought he was kidding. Then he held my arms and tried to kiss me. I can still smell his breath, it smelled like drunken dog shit. I didn't know how to fight and then I heard Dale outside the tent calling my name. Brian told me to be quiet but I yelled for Dale. He came in and threw him out of the tent. All the guys in the camp told Brian to get the fuck out. He said he was going to kill me and kick Dale's ass." Brian continued to lurk around the homeless camp like stench on spoiled milk. The seven or eight men and women felt terrorized by this man. Later he showed up in a crack haze, yelling and screaming and he went after Jenny, smacking her across the face before Dale used a splintered two-by-four to pummel him. Only then did he disappear.

When the homeless outreach workers of Columbus put their resources towards finding housing for the camp, Jenny and Dale insisted on being housed together. They were given a small one-bedroom apartment, a mile from the nearest bus stop. There were gun holes in the walls, and roaches openly defied any person who chose to sit on the threadbare couch. They had no food stamps, income, or phone. They would get up every morning and walk the three miles to the freeway where they would hold a sign asking for money. They did this trek daily, even with severe alcohol and mental health issues, their clothes ruined by months of homelessness, both were unemployable.

Jenny would pack a lunch and the two of them would take a break from flying the sign to sit in the woods having a picnic and passing the time telling stories, listening to music on a boombox they had found dumpster diving, and trying not to drink too much. "The drivers don't wanna give you any money if they smell alcohol," Jenny explained. "Plus, it's so hot out there most days, you get too dehydrated. You kind of just have to hold out."

They would average about $11 a day, more when she could hold the sign but her legs were increasingly failing her.

Holding the sign ran the risk of being issued a ticket that they would never be able to pay and soon a warrant would be issued for their arrest. But they needed the money to buy food and, more importantly, alcohol. Jenny had severe seizures if she went too long without it, sometimes requiring hospitalization.

They loved to travel the eight miles to the OSU campus so Jenny could watch The Ohio State Marching Band before football games—something that didn't cost money and they thoroughly enjoyed. Just being on High Street provided her with some sense of belonging. In spite of her apartment being in Columbus, it was a long way from her former life.

The apartment was a basement dwelling. One of the local dope-boys kicked a window in, mistaking their apartment for the one behind them. "Open up you chickenshit motherfucker! Gimme my fuckin' money, bitch! We gonna pop you, motherfucker! You can't hide from us, we know you in there!" Dale was indeed hiding in the closet. Jenny was getting 40-ouncers at the carry-out. The young men dispersed as she walked up. She stared at the broken window. "What the fuck?" she muttered to herself. "You got a problem with somethin', bitch?" she heard behind her. "Nope." Jenny and Dale put plywood up over the broken window. The men never bothered them again, but Jenny said they beat the shit out of the guy next to them and soon there was an eviction notice on his door.

A stray cat came and went. So did many of the "tramps" as Jenny called her homeless friends, when the weather turned sour or the cops cracked down. When we'd lived together, it was not uncommon for me to come home and find some barfly, whose fingernails told of homelessness, on our couch with a plate full of food and one of my Milwaukee's Best ensconced in his hand. Even now that Jenny and Dale had so little, she was still taking in strays and feeding them from whatever little they had. When I visited, I'd wear my work badge, and the otherwise menacing group of black teenage boys conferring in the parking lot at all hours would acknowledge me with a nod. Even drug dealers have a soft spot for social workers. It allowed me relatively safe access to the most dangerous of places.

Jenny was frail, her clothes hanging off her—a skeleton propped up by slivers of skin. With a life fraught with reckless behavior, Dale increasingly lost the use of his mind, his organs, and his limbs. Jenny asked me one day, "Hey, do you know anyone who needs Depends? They just dropped off Dale's supply, and they must have fucked up because they brought so many they are literally stacked to the ceiling. They kept bringing them in. I was like, hold on, he can't even shit this much for the rest of his life."

Dale went into a nursing home. Shortly thereafter, Jenny became unable to stand, and was taken to the same nursing home. Their rooms were around the corner from one another. Jenny's mood brightened, she had made the staff adore her as well as the sad-sack residents who she would wheel by and devastate with her wit. Off of alcohol for nearly three months, her mind was quick, although she never regained use of her legs. Meanwhile, Dale sank deeper into a swamp of death. Most days, he was unable to feed himself, but when Jenny wheeled in he would flash a crooked smile as his cloudy eyes flickered with the spark of recognition. Then it would vanish as quickly as it came.

Jenny was discharged from the nursing home, and Dale passed away silently and alone that September, not even Jenny by his side. She was unable to get transportation, yet another aspect of abject poverty. "I can't take another death," she said to me. "What the fuck will I do?"

"Survive Jenny, that's what you'll do."

A deep breath, followed by an exhale. "I know. That's what ol' Jenny does. At least I got a lot of Depends if I need them." Always laughing, even in a room with death.

There was no service for Dale. His family, from whom he had been estranged since he went to prison in the early 1990s, did not want to have a funeral, or even drive from West Virginia to see his body interned in an indigent's grave.

1991.

Jenny continued yelling pronouncements through the screen door of the misery that awaited me if I left her. It was October. The ground was muddy, wet leaves had already started rotting into the soil. The large black walnut tree cast even darker shadows than the cloud-filled night, and scattered its leaves onto the yard, solemn as it waited for the snow to cover its limbs. As I trudged across the lawn, small pockets of inky blackness would swallow me whole for an instant—a reverse strobe-light—as I bounded away from the insults. A part of me yearned to turn around, as the words nicked my insides like a penknife. One section of my being wholeheartedly believed her: that in the end, defective was what I was, there was no escape. Another part did not believe her and knew continuing the way we had been was doomed. Alcohol had risen around our ankles and although I was only 22, life had become quicksand, the vomit-looking quicksand in 1960s B-movies.

A slight breeze swept from the west with a snap of cold attached just to make sure that a person felt small against Mother Nature. Against the backdrop of the stone church that bordered the yard, I glanced up, and a few tears trickled down my face. I said a prayer to a God that I wasn't really sure about and climbed into the car. I spent that first night in Athens. The hour and a half drive provided calm in which to think. It solidified what was, so far in my life, the most terrifying decision I had ever made. It felt as if I'd been trapped in a melodramatic scene from a shitty movie when all that I wanted was a slapstick comedy. I drove back to work at Used Kids early Monday morning. The start of a pinball existence that would ricochet my life from bed to bed and bar to bar for a decade.

Jenny's last words to me at the time were: "You have no friends, they're all mine. And you will never get laid again." I was nervous, aware of my once again awkward and clumsy body, of wire framed glasses that had been bent and bruised by too many late-night stumbles and having Jenny toss them across the room just to see me scurrying after them. "Goddamnit Jenny," I'd cry out, "these are my only fucking glasses. I can't fucking see without them."

"Ahh, but you are adorable when you're looking for them, Nerdla."

Somehow that broken man attracted Sharon from New York, she of steely beauty and quiet, mysterious manners. She of friendship with Sonic Youth and having lived with J Mascis of Dinosaur Jr.

J Mascis had almost single-handedly given definition to my existence with his blazing guitar solo on "Freak Scene." I could go no further than handholding with Sharon at first. Sex was out of the question —the fear of emotional disappointment loomed large.

J was coming to Columbus to visit Sharon and to see Soundgarden at the large boxy concert venue the Newport. I had seen Soundgarden at Stache's the year before and was nonplussed by them. They sounded like a lumbering Led Zeppelin with yowling vocals and nary a semblance of a melody the entire evening. Still, I was excited to meet J and to see my new girlfriend. I drank a great deal of coffee and a shot of Jim Beam on the way to meet up with them. As I left Bernie's in the cool autumn sun, smiling to myself, a small group of teenagers approached me. "Hey, look at Urkle!" one of them yelled to his friends and punched me full on in the mouth. Spitting half a tooth into my hand, knowing the hopes of impressing Sharon and J had disappeared with the teenager's perfectly placed fist, I grabbed him and wrestled him to the ground, my glasses hurtling in the other direction. The skirmish ballooned with his posse of friends kicking me while he scrambled in my clutches. Passersby pulled them away and yelled for someone to call the police. I sat on the ground, heat rising into my ears, heart beating fast and for a moment I was back in high school—the nerd. I went looking for my glasses. They were gone. One of the ruffians must have taken them. I sat with one less tooth, blind on the High Street sidewalk, and that's how my girl and my hero found me.

The next morning, I went to Lenscrafters and bought a new pair of glasses with all the money I had, $90. I picked some Buddy Holly type frames from the bottom of their sale drawer that I assumed would hold up well during drunken evenings and the dangers of the bar room.

I managed to cut way back on my drinking during my relationship with Sharon. She was even more emotionally unavailable than I was, and her company mostly left me satisfied; the coldness was something I felt used to. Like being in a cloud. I didn't need booze.

Jenny was dumbstruck that her predictions about me being unable to survive without her didn't come true, and I had even fallen in love. She decided we had to inform each other of our plans so we could avoid running into each other. "Bela, I can't see you. Maybe someday I can, but you just hurt me too much." I could almost feel the wetness of her tears through the phone.

"Don't say that Jenny, I want to see you. I still need you in my life."

"No. Not while you are fucking some other girl."

Exasperated, I said, "What the fuck are you talking about? You're with guys all the time."

Her voice was cold and sharp. "You know it's different with me; I can't be alone. Ever. I fuck them for a reason. You're OK to be alone, you deserve it." She hung up.

Confused, annoyed, I said, "Goddammit, Jenny," into the dead phone.

Yet we continued to circle each other, trading insults and blame for the misery of our lives, neither taking a modicum of responsibility for our own sadness, until usually I would crack under her spell and apologize. Other times we would have that inevitable ruinous ex-sex, where we humped our bodies together for a brief period to help squelch the past or the present or whatever longing needed squelching. This was always followed by a promise that we were not going to get back together again and I left her house as soon as it was appropriate to do so. Navigating our lives was hard enough, there was no sense that these episodes constituted unfaithfulness on either of our parts. Still we were like Kryptonite to each other, and the insults that lingered kept coming. It was inevitable that Jenny and Sharon would meet and late that fall we ran into one another. Drinking in Sharon for the first time, Jenny asked her, "Is he as shitty in bed with you as he was with me?" Not running into each other was starting to sound like a better idea.

One night Sharon and I stopped at Stache's to grab a beer. The industrial band Head of David were performing. They were dreadful. Sharon grabbed my arm and asked if a woman sitting up front was Jenny. I leaned over and looked. No, this woman looked almost Asian with black smooth hair. Then she turned around and it *was* Jenny, wearing a wig. She scowled at me. Shaken, we left.

Sharon begged me to end all correspondence with Jenny, and to stop allowing tales of her to dominate my conversation: her music, her laughter, her way of life. Jenny asked me to come back to her, said she would change and even slow down her drinking. I told her I was committed to Sharon. "That bitch," Jenny said. "If you keep seeing her, you cannot be my friend." In bed, I told Sharon what happened. She told me how happy she was and we made love.

Two weeks later, my girlfriend of the last year and a half dumped me unceremoniously, for her boss at Ameriflora. An international flower show. All I wanted to do was crawl back in my bed and cry. That's when I took the aspirin milkshake. When I called Jenny and told her what happened, she was hesitant. She said, "I told you so. But you are my friend and I'll help you." She came by, but would only wave to me outside my window. She wasn't ready to see me yet; we could only talk on the phone. Jenny felt threatened by the secrets we held together, the truths we experienced and the hopes that had burned away like a poorly rolled cigarette. It was the same for me. What an awful realization that something in and of the other that helped create who you were, who is part of the very essence of *you*, at the same time created so much pain.

1986.

The great American fascination of the automobile fell upon deaf ears to most of us, unless it was tied up in a song (aka, "Born to Run"), books (*On the Road*) or film (as a metaphor for freedom). The insular world that we inhabited was confined to walking distances or to the touring van. In rural Ohio, a car is a necessity, where the space between spaces is miles, not city blocks.

In high school, we drove when we could. Upon reaching the age of 16, procuring a car was the highest priority no matter how poor the family was. A car provided escape, from the boredom of the humid summer days that cracked upon the sweaty backs of angst-ridden teenage boys, from the isolation of playing Atari video games while Pink Floyd sang about adolescent rebellion, and from the pangs of burgeoning sexuality that caused near madness. Our family of four lived solely off of our stepfather Bob's paycheck, which hovered around $12,000 per year. Zoltan was given a car by a friend and when he was deployed to Germany I got his pale gray Mustang that hadn't run right ever since he tried to plow through a creek (with me in the passenger seat). The car got stuck in the mud and slowly filled with creek water. Smoke billowed out above the cool water that rose above the bumper. I crawled in and yanked out the Radio Shack tape player. The player somehow formed a perfect union with the engine—as one pressed the gas pedal, the whining of the engine would play through the speakers. "Bela, get the hell out of there! The car might blow up!" yelled Z from the bank of Mud Creek.

"It can't blow up," I screamed to him as I wrestled with wires. "It's submerged in water!"

Eventually a kind farmer pulled the car out with a tractor and after a few days of it airing out, it ran again…but never quite like the $400 car it was. More like a $350 car.

My next car was a 1967 Dodge Valiant, bought for $500 from Matt Newman, guitarist for High Sheriff Ricky Barnes. Ricky was the first band in Columbus to start playing old country standards among a handful of at times brilliant originals. Ricky influenced the Gibson Brothers, Hank McCoy, and others. Matt was moving to California to seek more lucrative professional possibilities than playing for a handful of regulars at Stache's while wearing thrift-store western attire.

The Valiant's warming system worked solely on the passenger side, and left a small patch of ice on the floor when parked overnight during the winter. My first drive to New York was in the Valiant. I went to see Sharon, who lived with the beat poet Herbert Huncke. Herbert had the same apartment he'd lived in since the mid-'70s. He was on methadone daily and would rise early, write, and walk the five blocks or so to the clinic. Sharon said he'd venture out with a young Puerto Rican man who she wasn't sure was Herbert's boyfriend or not. I made that first trip with Jack Taylor (Richie Violet), who was going to see his friends in New York, bands from the lower-East Side who had released their fair share of scuzzy rock music— Judah Bauer from The Blues Explosion, and members from Railroad Jerk and the Unsane. He was close to Sharon and would razz her in front of me about our relationship.

The drive was good for both Richie and me; he was trying to stay clean, and while we did not discuss his heroin habit, we bonded over *Exile on Main Street*, The Blues Explosion, A Tribe Called Quest, Big Daddy Kane and our love of country music. He was funny and poked fun at me for my unabashed love of alcohol, which he derided as "Unnecessary. You don't need it to laugh, do you?" As we pulled into view of the Manhattan skyline, the tape deck blasting the Silos, my heart beat faster. 'Good Lord,' I thought, 'it's the biggest fucking thing I've ever seen.' We went through the Holland Tunnel, and came out upon a sea of graffiti and garbage piled high. I became lost in a storm of streets as I tried to navigate traffic and Richie pointed where to turn. Soon we were driving towards Alphabet City where Sharon and Herbert lived.

The apartment was between Avenues C and D on 8th, just below the sidewalk. It was filled with books, magazines, and old furniture. Sharon blushed when she saw

Sharon Anderson and Richie "Jack Taylor" Violet

me. We kissed and she introduced me to Herbert, who was small and hunched over. He shook my hand: his grip was strong and his hand seemed to be constructed of leather—rough and covered with the experience of hustling and scrapping. He had bright blue eyes and a shock of gray hair that sprouted from the top of his head. He did not appear to be in his eighties. "Bela!" he cried. "Glad to meet you! Sharon has told me all about you. Bela like Bartok, right? She tells me you love to read. I'm curious to find out what you like to read. Did you know that I'm a writer?" I knew who he was. I was not the outrageous fan of the Beats (whom he'd coined) like so many in the underground scene, but I enjoyed Beat poetry and the movement itself. Huncke was a major influence on both Burroughs and Ginsberg and was portrayed in both *Junky* by Burroughs and in Kerouac's *On the Road*.

I felt at home in New York. This partly came from having ingested music from New York since the age of 15. The Ramones, Lou Reed, Garland Jeffreys, and east coast hip-hip. The grime of the lower east side was burned into my consciousness, and as I walked the streets, the business of the sidewalks were already tattooed on my synapses. Sharon liked driving in the Valiant, the tape player hissed when the engine was revved, and she would scoot up next to me, her arm tucked under mine, fastening into me. I felt total love. I made her mix tapes and painted her pictures of whatever was on my mind. I told her I wanted to see the house where Langston Hughes lived, as I had been reading and listening to much of his poetry and his Simple stories, "That's in Harlem, and it's a long train ride" she laughed.

"Can't we just drive my car?"

"No, are you crazy? You don't just drive to Harlem from the Lower East Side. People don't drive in New York!" she laughed some more.

New York was built of asphalt and steel, with bustling that mimicked the opening scene of *Cagney & Lacey*, or of Dustin Hoffman and Jon Voight huddled next to one another, rather than clumps of dry cornstalks, gravel roads and flat ranch houses. I had never heard music as grotesquely inviting as *Street Hassle* growing up in the Midwest. It would be a few years before the frantic noise of Pere Ubu and the Dead Boys, Cleveland punk bands, would echo the realistic poetry of Lou and other New Yorkers.

I would make the nine-hour trek many times to various rock and roll shows at Under ACME, CBGB's, and the Knitting Factory, all of whom were open enough to book Columbus bands. One such trip was when Gaunt played with Prisonshake and a few other Ohio bands at CBGB's, whose restroom was designed after the open sewer systems of Calcutta. I drove on my own and got to the club early, mid-afternoon. Gaunt was already there. It smelled like any other bar: of bleach and stale beer. I ordered a Budweiser and was alarmed at the $7 cost. How in the hell anybody could afford to drink in New York was beyond me. Jerry grabbed me in the dressing room. "Dude, don't drink here," he said, and steered me by my shoulder out of the bar. We strolled across the street to a small carryout, complete with guy-with-unwashed-clothes-and-defeated-look sprawled out on the sidewalk, brown paper bag clutched firmly in his hand, his head wedged between the brick wall and a metal garbage can. One half-expected Oscar the Grouch's head to pop out, perhaps with a needle hanging out of Oscar's neck. Jerry led me straight to the good stuff, which was 24-ounce bottles of Crazy Horse, a malt liquor that had recently been discontinued in Columbus. Next to that were rows of green-bottled Ballantine, another malt liquor that was guaranteed to fuck you up. They were $2.50 each and I bought one of each. "Where the hell do we drink it?" I asked. Jerry scoffed at me. "On the street, you dumbshit! They don't fuckin' care, it's fuckin' New York!" He cackled.

New York made me feel big, as if the soles of my feet made an indentation into the sidewalks. There was an energy that fed into the boyhood dreams of a Midwest outcast that it was possible to shake the inner turmoil and isolation by smelling the smells, tasting the food, blending into the scenery of the city. Feeling small in the tiny town of Catawba propelled the perception of being gigantically alive in the city. I made friends in the city through the record shop; indie-rock was a very small world and it was common to have coffee, lunch, or drinks with many of the folks who the store did business with.

Some ten or 12 years after that first trip to New York, I stopped in the city with my wife, who had some business to do there. Many of the old haunts I had known were now left to the faded pages of punk rock books and time-stained flyers of music collectors. CBGB's, Under ACME and Brownie's had been shuttered. The move out of lower Manhattan had already begun, with the bearded and ironic hipsters moving into Brooklyn where rents were still low enough. The dive bar that our friend Paul Lukas had taken us to a few years prior in Red Hook had now become a destination point. We stayed with our friend Matt Majesky, a man of unblemished taste in books and music, who suffered no fools and had a stinging sense of humor. While my wife attended her conference, I headed to the lower east side, this time not in search of a bar but a 12-step meeting. I grabbed a small cup of coffee, holding the tiny Styrofoam cup in my hand I took a seat in the third row. I glanced around the small basement room crowded with 16 or 17 plastic chairs. A few people ducked in and out. One man with black greasy hair clinging to his forehead jumped down the three stairs that emptied into the room. Looking around nervously, he clasped his hands together. Tattoos covered his forearms, a biographical inking for all the world to see, as if his arms were issuing a challenge for anyone who looked in his direction. An image of Lucifer snaked up one arm amidst flames, nude women, and a pair of dice. It was if he ate an entire tattoo magazine and they magically appeared on his skin. He bounced on the balls of his feet, shook his head and bounded back up the stairs. The air was charged, as if someone had taken the tops of the electrical sockets and the air was being pumped full of invisible sparks. To my rear a man with a dark suit and a briefcase sat back, whistling softly. A John Denver song? I looked back, he appeared tired, fatigued, glancing at his watch. Nobody was relaxed. In the front of the room, two men whispered to one another, and one pointed to me. Raising my eyebrows, I asked if they needed something. "Well yes, we do. I think you have the most sobriety in the room and we need someone to qualify for us." Luckily, after absorbing many Lawrence Block books about an alcoholic private detective named Matthew Scudder, I knew that qualifying on the East Coast meant giving a lead. That is, I had to tell my story. I had only nine or ten months sober but I had been instructed by my own sponsor that when AA asks something of you, you are compelled to give back. I accepted.

I gave my brief story which was in its infancy, but perhaps that is what made an impression on the handful of members in the small group. My life had changed dramatically over the past nine months or so, things appeared brighter and a calmness had started to fall around many of the racing thoughts I had. The worry was still there, but it was tempered, and the urge to tamp down the worry, to treat it by some unhealthy behavior had been quieted, muffled. Here I was in the middle of the East Village, an area that I had only experienced under the sway and domination of alcohol, addressing a meeting of alcoholics trying to stay sober, one day at a time.

1970S-90S.

The walk to the record store was a mile and a half. When drunk it was three miles depending on the amount of zigzagging my body chose. Usually I was ten minutes late to work. If by chance I arrived early, a ribbon of superiority over my less responsible coworkers hung over my head, but that did not happen very often.

I had my first drink at four years old. My Hungarian grandmother would serve us tiny glasses of port wine mixed with sugar, and every grandchild who wanted a small beer would get one at her dinner table, along with as many sips of Cuba Libre we could charm out of her with our drunken smiles. At times my older sister passed on her beer and my brother and I would argue over who would get it. Usually my uncle would split it for us. Nobody was allowed to touch their drink before the dinner prayer was said. Inevitably I would find something to giggle about and my father would ply his fingers deep into my wrist. Twisting my hand back, rubbing the red swelling from his grip, my eyes would well until finally the amen was spoken and Zoltan and I would lift the glasses to our mouths and drain them, then pound them back on the table. The adults would laugh and fill them up again.

Drinking was always present at our rambunctious family get-togethers where three different languages split the air like an ax through rotted wood. The chaos percolating in those family gatherings was as familiar as the smell of a mother's perfume, a cacophony powered by rum, Rolling Rock, and port wine. My grandmother's house was busy even when nobody was there. The house shook with memories, the walls a shrine of family photos and my grandfather's paintings smothering every surface. Hundreds of plants were stacked high over shelves, floor to ceiling, with vines running over it all.

The drunken stories of my dear uncles Pablo and Peter were propulsive in fueling a sense of adventure. The lives they lived were epic and even today some elderly grandfather or grandmother will approach me and ask, "Koe-Krompecher? Wow, I haven't heard that name in a while, are you related to..." I interject: "Peter and Pablo?" Their eyes sparkle and a mischievous smile crawls across their face. "They were some crazy guys, so much fun. I'd tell you but you probably shouldn't know." Oh, I knew. These yarns were slyly dug into my consciousness as we ate egg and chicken soup, Hungarian paprikash, mashed potatoes with sour cream. and a dessert made with copious amounts of rum. One Christmas party when Zoltan and I got drunk as fuck was particularly crazy. My father got into a fistfight with his younger brother outside in the cold. I remember vividly the spots of blood in the snow. My father left hastily that night and Zoltan and I stayed at my uncle's.

When I was seven or eight my brother and I were at a gathering of Venezuelans held at a party hall somewhere in Columbus. It was loud. I was talking-yelling with a Vietnam veteran who showed us the bullet that was still suck in his knee. He let me put my hands on top of the knee, and move my finger over the bump of the bullet, like a roly-poly bug of violence. Later that night there was dancing, swells of Latin-Americans gyrating and twirling. In the middle was a tiny elderly man leading the throng of partygoers, shimmying and swaying his hips, a smile as large as a Volkswagen Beetle stuck on his face. Wide-eyed, Zoltan and I soaked it in, stealing sips of beer and daring ourselves to venture into other hallways and empty rooms. Finally, very late, we were sitting in the hallway, exhausted, our backs to the wall, when the double doors from the dance-hall burst open. The elderly man staggered, put both hands on his knees, wobbled some more and started running towards us. He was at least 20 feet away and then suddenly as he ran he vomited with such force that his dentures rocketed from his mouth and flew down the hallway. As if in slow motion, the fake teeth skidded past me in a flood of pink puke, coming to a stop between my brother and me. I eyed those teeth for a good long while as the grandfather was escorted to the restroom. Eventually a gray-haired woman came with a brown napkin and picked up the poor man's teeth. She looked over at me as she bent down, disgust on her face as she shook her head slowly at having to retrieve her husband's teeth.

At 14, I was a goofy, nerdy smartass stuck in the middle of cornfields, pickup trucks, John Deere hats and coveralls—an intense, scary version of Hee-Haw to my adolescent mind. I got officially wasted for the first time at Jeanette George's barn party. All of a sudden the farm boys found that the dopey kid with the weird name seemed kinda cool as one-liners poured out of my mouth as if directed by some God of sitcoms. Girls smiled slyly at me. Soon I found some good friends—Chris Beister, Mark Geiger, and Jeff Entler—who loved music as I did. We'd drink beer on the weekend as we mocked everybody in our school and tried to shake the awkwardness we all felt.

I quickly learned that a morning hangover could be assuaged by a flush of black coffee followed by Diet Coke, mixed with John Cale, Nick Drake, or Gene Clark. At night, I would drink several large glasses of water or juice before splashing head first into bed, my body giving off tiny invisible electrical sparks as alcohol pushed my internal energy into all directions, thoughts a whirlpool of outsized focus, splattering out of my mind as I crashed into the sheets. A mushroom cloud erupting in my wake, pity to the person who shared my bed. Other times I would eat several slices of bread or even better, a pizza that I would snuggle up with under the blanket as if the mozzarella cheese and tomato sauce were a stuffed animal, waking up to find my face greased with cold pizza, occasionally in a pool of urine if I had slumbered too deeply.

My grandmother was massively overweight. When my Grandmother and Grandfather fled Hungary in World War II, she left behind a life of easy luxury sprinkled with opulence to that of refugees. They went days without eating. She breastfed all of her boys for several years as they went from one refugee camp to another until finally sailing to Venezuela on a barge. This was the only food the young boys had, my grandfather weighed all of 100 pounds when they arrived, he was near death from starvation. She owned only two dresses during this time. So, when the blessings came of fast food and bargain wares in cheap department stores such as Gold Circle, Harts and K-Mart, Grandmother was taken. She fell in love with disposable food and goods. A good part of her old age was spent cultivating eating and filling her subconscious fear of ever going hungry again with Cheez-doodles, Little Debbie snack cakes, and Kentucky Fried Chicken, sucking off every piece of meat from every single chicken bone. One time at an all-you-can-eat Ponderosa I witnessed her stabbing my uncle Peter in the backside of his hand as he tried to steal a spoonful of mayonnaise and cheese from her bowl of uh, mayonnaise and cheese. "Goddamnit Mommy!" he yelled, rubbing the back of his hand where four fork teeth indentations were created. "Dat is my cheese and mayonnaise!" she growled.

Eventually the consumption stretched her body to its breaking point—first one, then another hip collapsed under the sheer weight of her never feeling satisfied.

At family dinners she made curisert, a Hungarian dish of paprika and mayonnaise and cream cheese, duck, mashed potatoes and for dessert what can only be described as Vanilla Wafers and Rum soup. "Beelaaa, pleese put more r-r-r-um in it," she instructed, her tongue rolling out the R's as if she were a tiger.

"Grandma, there is a ton of rum in this already. The cookies are dissolving."

She limped over, eyeing the bowl of a half box of cookies and an entire package of whipped cream and most of a bottle of rum. "Beela, don't be stupid, please. Just put more cookies in and some cream, then add rum." She spooned some out, sticking it into her mouth, looked skyward and declared: "More rum!"

My sister walked by, scrunched her face together and asked, "What is that?" She smelled it. "Don't you dare feed that to my daughters."

After dinner, Grandmother insisted her two young granddaughters be served, "Thee children *must* have dessert!" I ladled it into their cut-glass bowls and overheard my sister hiss at her daughters, "Don't you dare eat that."

1989.

My grandmother, with two canes and sparkling eyes, opened the door. "Come in children, please. I am so happy to see you Geen-if-fer, Bela now go fix some drrrrinkss." I made my way to the kitchen feeling the comfort of her air conditioning against the summer heat in Ohio as thick and sticky as tar-paper. "Bela, you must wash your hands first! I know what you men do with your hands and it's dis-gusting!" Jenny gave grandma hug. They immediately started yammering about the hundreds of plants that my grandmother had in her house. They covered everything, the stacks of mail, the paintings and photos on the walls, windowsills, draping down from the cabinets and refrigerator. "Grandma," Jenny was saying, "I need to tell you about the garden I planted in our attic, its amazing." My grandmother let out a laugh. "You built a garden in your attic? Dat is amazing! You are so crrrazy, Jenny!"

Grandmother ordered a pizza from Pizzeria Uno, a large with everything and we had a few drinks. I was instructed to go fetch the artificial Christmas tree. "Bela, it is under the stairs in de bazement, but be careful: you are such a clumsy man and Pablo bought me that treeee. So be verrry careful. Don't touch anything else vile you are down der." The old woman was petrified that people were going through her belongings and swiping a notepad, a pencil, or jewelry. She was a hoarder, with stacks of papers, egg cartons, small cut out pictures of animals, flowers and cartoon characters slipped between bills and letters. She coveted perpetually. Anything. Her living room consisted of paths through piles of magazines, stuffed animals, and Kleenex boxes forming miniature mountains, with Cheeto tubs and Triscuit boxes strewn along the paths to offer fortitude to the weary traveler. The basement was stacked high with boxes, plastic laundry baskets bursting at the edges with more paper, photos and empty canisters of peanut jars, puffed cheese balls, fabric, unopened packages of sheets. To find anything was a chore. After three minutes of searching for the tree, I heard the old woman holler with suspicion in her voice, "Bela, vat are you doing down der? Hurry up!" Finally, I eyed the tree, it had been moved and was stacked under an old ironing board, several winter coats and a yellow rubber clothes basket filled with empty plastic bags and an artificial fern. "I found the tree, it wasn't under stairs!" I yelled up the stairs. "You must have moved it last time you were here because it was der when I took some chicken to the freezer" she scolded me.

We set the tree up, pushing aside her warped dining room table that she'd bought at a fraction of the original cost at Lazarus because, well, it was warped. I began unpacking boxes upon boxes of Christmas ornaments, many of them carried within the confines of a bruised and dented leather crate by foot, truck, and train from Budapest to Lake Balaton into the mountains of Austria, then lugged onto a freighter chugging across the Atlantic to Caracas and, finally, to Columbus. These were the precious ones, the ones my grandmother would hold in her hand as if they were made of baby skin, softly eyeing them, her wide blue eyes sparkling as if made of candlelight. Grandmother then barked orders to me from her plush La-Z-Boy as to where each ornament belonged. It seemed like there were thousands of them. Jenny sat next to her talking about plants and food and gossiping. "Beeeelaa, nooooo!" Grandmother would interrupt. "Look, my finger, put that little green Santa on dat branch. No, not dat one, *dat* one!" She turned back to Jenny. "Jenn-i-fer, how could you love such a stoo-pid man? OK, yes dat is ver you put it, verrry good, Bela. You know in Hungary, we celebrated Christmas in the right way, it was none of the dumb sings you have here."

Later I came to understand the magic of things holding memories. I quit promoting shows by the late '90s, when my alcoholism and depression had grown to such stature that going to shows would just be an interruption of my drinking. The garage is stacked high with boxes of show flyers and memorabilia. They are in no order, just piled up on one another haphazardly. Zines such as *Spank*, *Wiglet*, and *Feminist Baseball* sit gathering dust. But when I open a box and hold a flyer from 1993—"The Ex w/ Tom Cora, V-3, and

Guided By Voices" painted by hand on newspapers, accompanied by a small drawing of my dog wearing a baseball cap, drinking and smoking a cigarette at the bar, I remember: *These things were real. They happened.*

1990-98.

Jim Shepard was a short man, who wore his mat of greasy black hair as if it were a prop from a Harry Crews short story. He walked with a slight lean as if the weight of the world pulled him forward, waiting to smother him in its gravitational pull. Jim's gait was slow and deliberate, much like his deep voice; when he managed to utter words they bellowed out in an almost Spock-like fashion, sometimes followed by a short machine laugh that went "huh-hup-hup." His jokes seemed to be of the inside variety—way inside joke. Jim kept things very close to his vest, resulting in his humorous comments causing only himself to laugh. He was constantly unshaven but never bearded; it was as if he had gotten a George Michael shaving kit from the liquor store. He was an eternally ruffled sort, who spoke in a deep mumble as if he were sending himself coded messages. Jim wore his clothes as if they were an afterthought, articles for warmth, nothing else. He carried himself as if he were Harvey Pekar, with distrust of the modern world and its complexities a point of contention. Even though I spent hours on barstools next to Jim drinking vast amounts of alcohol, I never really knew him. Then again, I'm not sure if I've ever really known anybody.

Jim worked for a local jukebox repair shop and would drop into Used Kids during his lunch break to flip through records and chat or huddle with Mike "Rep" Hummel next door at the Used Kids Annex and fuck with his tapes and bang out music. His band Vertical Slit was a quiet yet solid underground force in Columbus. His songs revolved around science fiction, social commentary, and the pursuit of a connection that I think he never gained with the exception of his music. Perhaps his greatest line was "negotiate nothing, tear it all down."

V-3 came about after the breakup of Vertical Slit. It was an unsightly band, made up of Jim's paranoid, dark, blue-collar mystique, drummer Rudy, of small dimension, and Nudge Squidfish, a jovial, wide-eyed gentleman prone to talking about UFOs and conspiracy theories. Live they were a freakish sight straight out of community access television, but they carried a powerful force with Jim's melodic art-ish squall that was one part early Fall, another part Joy Division and the rest filled out with landlocked Florida bizarreness (his homeland) and Midwestern sludge.

Jim was funny, at least I figured he was from his almost inaudible comments that would slip out of his mouth like a small bump in the road. For a moment when he suddenly spoke after so much silence, you would think that a ghost had passed through the room; you would think you heard him and then you'd think you didn't. One steamy summer day, Jim and I were at Used Kids while Pere Ubu blared in the background. "Hey Jim," I said, "I really love that Vertical Slit record. Maybe you wanna do a V-3 single on Anyway or something?"

Nodding to himself as his thoughts pulsated to the music, Jim said, "Pere Ubu, huh. You like them? You know V-3 covers 'Final Solution'? You should check us out."

Did he not hear me? "Yeah, I love you guys. Maybe we can do a single?"

Nodding more, eyes kept low, he muttered something about "Pollard's music and Ron's as well, sure."

Used Kids at various times employed a number of part-time employees who were a regular whos-who of the High Street music scene, one of these being Jim Weber of The New Bomb Turks. One afternoon when Jim Weber and I were working, Jim Shepard walked in. "I got a great tape for your single," he said to me. "We just played CBGB's with the Turks, and Eric Davidson, the singer of the Turks, did 'Final Solution' with us." It was as if Jim wasn't even there. "You know, the Turks are kinda taking off right now?" Anyway had already had a hand in putting out a single and an LP with them, as Shepard knew! As strangely as he'd entered, Shepard left, and Jim and I listened to the cassette. It reminded me of times in high school when I would wait for my favorite song to be played on the radio and I would hold the small

TJSA-Bob Petric, Nora Malone, Ron House, Keith Baker

shoe-box-shaped cassette recorder up to the speaker and manage to get 3/4 of whatever song WTUE was playing. The sound was muffled, as if whoever taped it had stuffed the cassette with five pounds of mashed potatoes. Jim looked at me. "You can't put that out." The next time Shepard came in, he brought me a radio-only single of George Jones's "Yabba Dabba Doo (The King Is Gone)" 45, complete with a picture sleeve that featured George, Fred Flintstone and Elvis Presley. He pointed and giggle-grunted, "Check it out, George getting drunk with Fred Flintstone." I paid him ten bucks for the single and asked if he could provide me with some different songs, the rest of the tape he had given me was bits and pieces of songs and sound collages. I explained that being a song purist, I wanted something more akin to his "Inside Outpost" or "Another Exterminator." Although he appeared taken aback, he came in a week later with the songs "American Face" and "Son of Sam Donaldson." The single did OK.

Jim Shepard of V-3

On certain Monday evenings, Jerry and I would stroll down to Larry's to be disappointed by poetry night. We took offense to collegiate artist types butting in on our drinking time. On many of these Mondays both Jim and Mike would be there, spontaneously spouting off their poetry. Jim's was science fiction gutter-found prose influenced by Phillip K. Dick and William Burroughs. Jerry and I were impressed, but too chicken-shit to express our own poetry in such a stark setting. Jerry would couch his in between blasting guitars and punk-rock beats and my own would lay dormant in dog-eared notebooks where they still sit, 20 years later.

It wasn't long before Jim and Jenny forged a strong friendship over a shared fondness for slurping a few drinks before the sun set. They would meet at either Walt's or Bourbon Street passing the afternoon hours in a connected shadow world lit by bar lights and their own brilliant creativity. They started recording together, mostly her adding keyboards and trumpet to some of his tracks. It would appear that musically Jim and Jenny had little in common, as many of her pop songs were constructed out of a love of The Beach Boys and the bounce of early '80s college rock, whereas Jim's music was as serious as death. But they bonded over a sense of melody and a meeting of the bohemian lifestyle, meaning creativity, late nights, cheap rent, and the cultivation of laughter.

Jim marveled at Bob Pollard of GBV's ability to pluck melodies out of the air and told Bob he "was a vampire on Titus, sucking songs out of the earth." Titus was the street that Bob lived on at the time. The next Guided by Voices album was named *Vampire on Titus*. Bob Pollard showed some of the manic frenzy Jerry had, but with a hint of autistic brilliance about him, too. He was funny, gentle, and extremely eager. Bob and the rest of Guided by Voices made one or two visits a month to Columbus from Dayton, usually to record music with Mike Rep or play shows, and to drink beer with Ron, Jim, Jerry and myself. We talked music and sports mostly, because in Ohio there is really nothing else that matters. The weather is always gray, the economy is grayer, and politics is just something to shake one's head at. They drank like we did, which meant a vast amount. The drinking didn't appear to impair their lives as nurses, teachers and artists just as it didn't appear to adversely affect our lives as record-store dudes and musicians.

In Columbus, the finest bands of the '90s had been guinea pigs in the major label experiment: Scrawl, The Thomas Jefferson Slave Apartments, Watershed, and, of course, Gaunt. They had all been scooped up and quickly spit out after failing to immediately make a commercial success. V-3 was signed to American imprint Onion records. Johan Kugelberg had left Matador Records to take a job working directly under Rick Rubin and was given his own vanity label, which he titled Onion, a tasty yet smelly vegetable. He managed to sneak in four excellent releases before the label realized his venture would not bring in any money. These were: The Thomas Jefferson Slave Apartments *Bait and Switch*, The Monks self-titled re-issue, *Nix Naught Nothing* by The Stiffs, Inc (whose uncanny New York streetwise-art-punk would predate the Strokes by several years) and V-3's *Photograph Burns*. Even by our standards the signing of Jim Shepard to American was stupefying, basically because Jim's music was both standoffish and abrasive, a challenge of sorts to the listener just like the man himself. Still, *Photograph Burns* was tighter than the muddled pastiche of sounds that Jim had thus far caught on a rusted hook from the inside of his clever mind, a mind that held secrets that in retrospect must have been as dark and scarred as Jim looked, head drooping down as he leaned against a wall. His songs were a play-by-play of the decaying of the American dream, filled with bleak observations that celebrated the depressive thoughts of a man who never quite fit in, songs titled "Hating Me, Hating You" and "End of the Bar." The highlight was "Bristol Girl," a lonely ode to a variety of women, an inverse of "California Girls." It stung with the slow-burning sound of 4 AM emptiness, with Jim's deep sing-song carving out lyrics: "Bristol girl always giving you crap about this and that, London girl always giving you crap about this and that, find another human willing to put up with you." You don't know if he's singing about the woman, or more likely, himself. The record wasn't selling, as the pop-punk shit-explosion of Blink 182 and Wax was taking over. Johan lost his job and V-3 got dropped.

Shortly thereafter I saw Jim huddled next to the video trivia game console on the end of the bar at Bourbon Street during an absolutely depressing bout of karaoke. His eyes were flat and deep enough in his skull that they could be mined. He had a jar of beer sitting in front of him. I asked if he were ok and he said he was fine. He was as vacant as a vacuum. A few days after that at Used Kids, Ron hung up the phone and said, "Jim Shepard hung himself last night." Jim's funeral was the first of several in a few years' time for a small but close-knit scene of outsiders, artists and music fans. A collection of dazed and shaken ex-girlfriends, musicians, barkeeps, and family gathered around a photo of a smiling (!) Jim and talked, trying to avoid touching upon various hidden parts of ourselves that we dare not stir up.

2010.

Jenny she was asked to perform at Comfest, an annual event held in Columbus attended by thousands. Although she put forth a brave effort, it was difficult for her to get back into performing shape. She was recently off the streets and her apartment was smack dab in the middle of a rogues' gallery of gang warfare and crack cocaine dealing, plus she was a couple miles from the bus line. Her biggest supporter, Sean Woosley, who had made a small career of his own making prickly-pop in the vein of Bob Pollard and Elvis Costello, worked hard to get the band together, but the practices were difficult. Jenny had not played piano since living in the music building and her drinking was constant, all day and all night long. She was continuously drunk with the only interruptions being her stays in the hospital.

Jenny performed in the late afternoon. I wasn't there but heard that her once deeply emotional voice rang hollow like a raggedy flag beaten into submission, and that at the end she fell down. This was her first time in front of a Columbus audience in ten long years, and afterwards a mean-spirited emcee poked more holes into her effort by clumsily deriding her as she was carried off the back of the stage. These legs that once bounded across fields of corn and soybeans in western Ohio as she flourished on the high school cross country team. Legs that had walked through rain soaked and sun baked parking lots on the Ohio State campus as she practiced hour after hour to get down the routines for the Best Damn Marching Band In The Land. She was crestfallen and humiliated. "Bela, I couldn't feel my fucking legs—they just quit working. I was scared. And then Paul, who used to be so nice to me, made fun of me in front of everybody. That was really shitty. I'm not going to play again. I can't go through the disappointment."

She was in the ICU for nearly a month before it was discovered that she had a heart condition similar to her mother's, and that's what caused her legs to fail. It went undetected for years by physicians who were too concerned with her drinking and seizures to check for anything else. They would simply get her stabilized and then discharge her. The concern was her drinking and everything else came after it— the slow decline of the use of her legs, her inability to hold down food for vast periods of time, and the voices in her head. "They don't listen to me, its always the drinking", she murmured from her hospital bed, "the doctors sound like you with the stopping the drinking, but I'm telling you something is wrong with my legs and they never give me my Seroquel or Depakote, they shake their heads and tell me to quit. Why don't you go to AA they ask me, I'm like, I fucking went to AA and guess what, it didn't work so shut up. Will you talk to them again, they listen to you." Inevitably I would then play my social worker card and explain some of her background and sometimes she would get her medication and sometimes not. She would look small in the bed, her face pained and stiff, wrists as thin as reeds and skin as fragile as rice paper. Sometimes she would be discharged to a skilled nursing facility, the smell of shit and piss from the rooms didn't bother her. Here, in these long slick linoleum hallways she would roll her wheelchair around and make friends with everybody. The time away from alcohol and preying men did her good, the color would return to her face and the laughter would roll out of her mouth like a series of avalanches. But at some point, a man would show up, it could be Dale, or later her abusive husband Johnny or even her brother Tony who struggled with many of the same issues his sister had, and they would sneak a bottle in, hidden in long coats or baggy pants. As they inched next to her bed or scooted her chair to the garden, out would come the bottle, and soon she would be discharged. It would never stick. She would return home, whatever progress was made to strengthen her legs would tumble away as if her muscles were constructed of cracked elastic, those once sturdy legs that carried her across hills, farms and of course down the sidewalks of High Street, were just a memory.

I flashed back to an afternoon, circa 1996, when I stepped into the sunlit afternoon from a damp underground bar and saw Jenny replete in gray sweatpants, running bra and white T-shirt, running down High Street. "Jenny," I shouted as she galloped past, "what are you doing?" She turned, blew out hot breath, and said, "Shit, I got to get into shape. I thought I'd start running again. What are you doing?" Glancing down High Street, I answered, "Oh, I just went on my beer break. Larry's isn't open yet so I went to Bernie's. I was on my way back to work, but I have time for another one if you want?" Jenny looked down at her brand-new running shoes, glowing white and unblemished from any dirt, fresh out of the box. "Sure. I can always run later."

1999.

At times the haunting of Jerry's depression would sink him to tears or to futile anger at anyone around him. When I saw one of these moods coming on, I would disperse a handful of Black Labels around the chunky wooden booths at Larry's and cajole him: "Aw Jerry, relax, come on. Everybody is having a good time." He would then slide away, camping in his upstairs apartment surrounded by his best friends—his record collection and a 12-pack. Jenny, on the other hand, approached her alcoholism with glee: "I'm a fucking alcoholic, so fucking what?" And she would down another whiskey. Later, as a resident of Jackson County Hospital in Miami, when the apparitions that would sporadically spring from her mind grew too dangerous and the tremors would grind her to the floor, she confessed, "I'm so fucking scared of being alone, Bela." Her intensity almost breaking the solid heavy plastic of my phone, she sounded like she was pleading. "I don't know how not to drink; it's the ONLY THING THAT HAS EVER WORKED."

For myself, while the level of distrust in life was steadily rising, I had found subtle ways to manage my drinking: by only going out several times a week, not doing shots, not having too much in the house and making an effort to be home more. I started running in earnest. I would try to run off a hangover, which was starting to hurt more than it used to. Going to the gym helped. But these were just a temporary management of symptoms. The problem itself was steadily growing. I saw a therapist for five sessions, but I felt threatened by her questioning the one thing that had worked for me. Soon I would return nightly to the places where I found comfort. Barstools are made of wood for a reason, as the heavy slabs of wood convey a sense of martyrdom. Crucified on a barstool while the world passes slowly by outside. The safety of a glass was subtle, but the anxiety was turning into something else, something dark and difficult to quiet. At times, sipping a water and Maker's Mark while the sunlight danced a quiet two-step with the bar light and flickering television of Larry's, remorse would crawl up inside from glass to guts to brain. Jerry would join at times. We would nurse our drinks, wondering just where the hell everybody was. At times I felt like Jesus tacked up on the cross, sweating blood into my drink, twisting on the swiveling seat—moving but not going anywhere but down, winding my way into a hole.

2000.

Gaunt got dropped from Warner Brothers. Unlike many of the other bands we knew who had briefly, miraculously, made it onto a major only to get dropped, Jerry wasn't OK with going back to the way it was. He had never wanted to stay in the indie world. For a kid growing up in Parma, Ohio listening to Kiss records over and over, being on a major label was analogous to having the blessing of a father who had never been there. The local "modern rock" radio station, CD101, only played Gaunt and the New Bomb Turks when they were on major labels, ignoring their combustible earlier indie records. The station never played many of the other superb true independent bands such as Jenny Mae, Moviola, or Greenhorn. One afternoon in 1998, I ventured into Discount Records, a store I used to manage, to purchase copies of *Spin* and *Paper Magazine*, both of which had reviews of the new Jenny Mae single. The young man behind the counter wore a soul patch, a ring of bracelets, a chain of necklaces, and a primitive tattoo crisscrossing his well-manicured arms. "Wow, somehow you get your bands in all these magazines," he remarked. "You must have some secret 'cause we can't even get the local paper to write about us."

Feeling peevish, I mumbled, "I don't know. The bands work hard, and are good, so...."

"They can't work harder than my band does. I listened to her record, I don't know what the big deal is."

"Thanks, have a great day," I said and walked out thinking the obvious, "maybe your band just sucks and you're a dick."

Although Gaunt had a briefcase full of positive press clippings, had toured Europe, done multiple cross-country U.S. tours, and had four full-length records out, none of these managed to put any money in anybody's pocket. And the constant touring (and behavior) left Jerry's job at Used Kids tenuous. Jerry loved the record store. He needed it. The record store were the nails that held our collective clubhouse together, something more tangible than just the sound of three chords and Rolling Rock. And now he was losing that, too.

Wearing a white polka-dotted short-sleeve buttoned up shirt with a stretched-out collar, faded black jeans, and Chuck Taylors, Jerry walked into the store during my shift, went to the dollar bin and flipped through the records, pausing to eye me while he lit a cigarette. He asked me if I wanted to take a walk. "Hold on," I said, "let me get this stack out and we can go." The spring sunshine danced through the cast-iron barred windows, making my job of looking through a new haul of used vinyl more difficult as the sheen from the rays made every blemish on the wax more pronounced. A stack of crappy '70s and '80s rock records sat next to me. I was almost blindly putting the waxy stickers in the right corner of each record jacket and making them a dollar. I was in the midst of some poorly executed self-control with my alcohol consumption—a large black coffee from Buckeye Donuts sat next to me—but we decided to go to Larry's. Lamont "Bim" Thomas was manning the turntable. He was infatuated with the Cheater Slicks' "Forgive Thee" and the entire Unsane catalog the latter which could empty the store faster than a fire at a movie-house. "I got this, go see your man," Bim said.

"Cool, thanks, Bim." Jerry and I headed up the stairs onto the hot sidewalk of High Street. A bevy of cars with competing radios blasted the music of spring around us, heavy bass songs mimicking the thrust of passion. It was the soundtrack to a panoramic view of the Midwest's largest campus in full seasonal bloom: young women with shorts hugging tight to polished thighs, skateboarders weaving through couples holding hands, frat-boy-baseball-hat-on-backwards crews crowding the sidewalks with broad shoulders that underscored their entitled attitudes, art school students wearing torn tee-shirts and wary smiles, and older professors hustling from their offices and coffee shops. We escaped the heat and the light and the busy people by ducking into the cool darkness of Larry's where we ordered a couple of beers.

We had grown apart the past couple of years, the cord of our friendship had frayed while we chased different interests. Jerry hadn't confided with me in some time, thinking

love, death & photosynthesis

my closeness to my future wife was a betrayal to my safety and a threat to our friendship. Jerry had constantly chided me for falling in love as easy as a leaf falling from a tree. "Love is for suckers," he would giggle at me, taking long pulls from his cigarette. But he wasn't laughing anymore. Jerry's muse Anna had moved away, though I wasn't sure what that meant to him, as he was quiet about the loves of his life. One thing was sure: Isolation, already a problem, had gripped him hard. Peeling the label off my beer, forming a minor art project with the gluey underside of the bottle's logo, I waited to listen to what Jerry had to say. He looked at me, took a pull of his beer. "I can't quit drinking" was all he said.

"What do mean?" I asked. I didn't know why anyone would want to stop. Slow down maybe. But stop?

Jerry looked straight ahead and said, "Now, that I've had this one, I'll be here, BW-3, and in my room all night. Drinking." He said he had gotten hooked on 5 o'clock trivia at BW-3; the hot wings franchise served enormous glasses of beer at happy hour. A couple of them were comparable to a six-pack. He said this combined with living above Larry's and High Street had him out all the time. He was scared. "Bela, I can't fucking stop." His look of frustration with his obsession stunned me. I had no idea what to say. I asked if he tried cutting down and he said he'd try but something always came up, someone was in town or someone asked him to go for a drink. This I could relate to. Being known as a drinker, it was easy to be found by some other lonely soul looking to share an hour as the sun hid from the stars. What was once a soft elixir to keep anxiety at bay was now a necessary component for just living life on a daily basis. It was as if he had been bitten by Dracula and was only now coming to the realization that he was turning into the undead. "I don't know, man, I'm just kinda going crazy. I sleep half the day, I drink all night. Honestly, I need to get a fucking job. I wish I could have my hours back at Used Kids."

I had mentioned this to Dan and Ron. Dan was against it as Jerry had become even more undependable. I couldn't say that to Jerry, though. Sensitivity hounded Jerry. He could recoil at the smallest slight and push back with a switchblade of words that would slice a hole into the nearest victim. Depression works in odd ways, and when married to mood swings, no matter how mild the upswing or downswing, it can make for haphazard interactions leaving all parties bewildered. Humor helps, diffusing the inner tension as well as allowing others to see the humanity of the inner battle of the self-deprecating thoughts that move through the brain, a slow lava of despair that clogs all perception. Depending on how we read it, a gaze could send us to heavenly heights or to the utter rejection of the cheese-stands-alone. We both loved based on the idea of romance, implanted in us through Russian literature and the transporting sounds of a crackling record. There was no division between lust and love. A tangled yarn of emotions dictated evenings, words, dreams. The list of lovers unrolled through my mind on a daily basis: four Jennifers, Sharon, Nora, Robin, Dawn, Sara, a couple of Beths, and the list went on. Yet the feeling of total acceptance was something I never experienced, a small piece kept dormant somewhere in the recesses of my brain, hidden next to frayed Spider-Man comic books, Lincoln Logs, and the babysitter who would take my clothes off when I was in third grade. My childhood falls between the cracks in my mind—memories are there, but not. What is real and what isn't? I don't know.

Jerry furrowed his brow. His pointy incisors sucked against his lips, and his hands shook. Small trembles that I was very familiar with after my own bouts of heavy drinking. At first when I encountered these tremors, I laughed it off. I joked that I was turning into so many of the people I admired. The tremors came and went. Jerry spilled his beer; it splattered onto his already grimy jeans. He rubbed it into the black crusty cloth. Maybe a genie would appear and lift the dark curtain of depression from him. "Jesus, look at me. I can't quit shaking. It's every fucking morning. I don't know what's happening to me. I can't leave my apartment."

"I don't know, Jerry," I said tentatively. "You know I have my own history of depression, and I'm not drinking as much as I used to. Have you really thought about cutting back?"

"All the time. But I don't really know how to stop. Ron had a kid, he never goes out, you never go out. Brett fucked my girlfriend. I don't even want to play my guitar." He wiped his pant leg again. Jerry's lower lip fluttered and he wept for a few moments. I was flabbergasted. He only cried when he was very drunk.

"What about college," I asked. "Have you thought about that?"

Jerry shook his head. "Nah. I went to Kent for a while, it's not for me. Bunch of phonies. Maybe I'll go to culinary school." Jerry had always professed he was a good cook although the bare cabinets in his darkened apartment told another tale. It was doubtful he owned a spatula let alone pots and pans.

There was a long pause, the familiar smell of stale beer and cigarette smoke rising between us. "I gotta go, Jerry, Bim is there by himself. I'll hang out later if you want, I just need to let Merijn know that I'm going out."

"Thanks, buddy."

There were no hugs, no handshakes, just a few words between us. But we understood.

1977.

By the time 4th grade arrived, I was attending my sixth school. I was in a state of constant motion sickness when it came to school.

The East Elementary gym teacher, Mr. Swartz, was an intense man. He wore tight athletic shorts in all weather and was prone to barking out instructions as if all the children were standing 40 yards away and not the five feet from him that we were, and at times he would splice in two-in-one insults. "Jimbo, you are kind of wussying out there now, you're going to let Eric run right by you? Eric's not even that fast."

Being a small kid, I was often overlooked, but I also had a competitive spirit and was fast and agile. We were playing tee-ball, and as I stood on third base, Mr. Swartz bellowed that this was the final play in what looked like it would be a tie game. When the ball was struck I ran home, determined to prove him wrong and I slid into home plate, striking my knee into the tee-ball stand. The base shattered and my knee bled. My classmates huddled around me as I fought off tears and heard the teacher tell them, "Let him be, he's being a little pussy." From the ground, my cheeks covered in the fine powdered dirt of the batter's box and fingers bloodied by my knee, I yelled out, "Shut up!" Suddenly, my small body was flung against the chain-link fence, my head cracking on the steel railing, bouncing off. Mr. Swartz grabbed me by my collar. "You little punk, you broke my tee ball plate. And who taught you to talk like that?" He tossed me to the ground, scooped me back up and pushed me as I limped. "Pick it up!" he barked.

Going years without a diagnosis, living with ADHD is at sometimes thrilling and at other times a jumbled mess of panic and feelings of inadequacy.

Mr. Davis was my math teacher in 8th grade. I learned nothing in the class except that I sucked at math (besides ADHD, I have numeric dyslexia). By being perfectly silent, I had managed to not once be a target for his brutal teaching methods, which relied heavily on a wooden paddle. His personal life must have been one of misery. As students would enter his classroom, the large man would peer at each one, dark eyes half shut scanning every child up and down. He was looking for fear, and he always found it.

It was the second to last class on the last day of school. A bated sigh of relief hung over the hallways and classrooms from 400 students. Usually, I sat towards the back of the classroom, huddling behind the bigger boys. Alas, all the chairs were taken when I danced into the room. Just under two hours to go and we had the 8th grade dance that evening. I had a date with a very pretty brunette girl. As I skidded towards the lone remaining seat, I apologized to Mr. Davis for being a few minutes late.

"You're still late BKK, and if it wasn't the last day of school, that would earn you a detention. Now just sit there and shut up until the end of the period."

"But Mr. Davis, I was with Ms. Houska helping set up the dance."

"I said SHUT UP and put your head down!"

Placing my head down and looking sideways, I saw my friend Danny Abdala make wide eyes, warning me that this was no time to act up. Smiling, I pointed my finger at Danny, like a gun and pulled the trigger. Suddenly I was lifted out my chair, in one fell swoop Mr. Davis flipped me into the air, all 90 pounds of me. Once I hit the floor, he kicked me towards the corner. "I told you not to move, not to talk, not to do anything! Now get up and stand in the corner!" Hunkering in the corner, fat tears crawling down my soft boyish face, I eyed the window. It was halfway open. The soft green grass beckoned. *It's what maybe six feet to the ground? I can jump out and run to mom's office, he would never catch me.* Bees flew from soft white flowers while the wind made tempting waves upon the green carpet. Cars drove by, and college students walked the sidewalk. I suddenly yearned to be old like them, to be strong, to be big enough to fight back. When the bell rang, I hurried towards the exit. I felt sick. Behind me I heard my name, "Bela, Bela, wait up!" It was my brother. "We gotta call mom. If you leave then nothing will get done."

Zoltan called our mother from the payphone in the cafeteria doorway. A few moments later, he hung up. "She's on her way."

There is nothing like seeing a mother come to the rescue. Her short red hair and confident walk comforted me somewhat, but it wasn't until she pulled me in tight to her waist and kissed the top of my mussed hair that I let myself feel again. More drops escaped my eyes as I described what happened, "We are going to talk to Mr. Smith about this." Mr. Smith, was the principal, a short stocky man with a full Grizzly Adams gray beard. His daughter was in my grade and they went to the same church as us. Entering the office, my mother asked to see him and he ushered us in.

"Why didn't you come straight to me?" he asked.

"I was scared. I wanted to go home." I meekly replied. But really, what was the use? The school did nothing when Mr. Davis manhandled my brother the year before and broke the arm of another kid.

"I want an investigation Donald!" My mother was angry. "I'm taking Bela home now. We can talk next week."

The short fat man held his hands together, parsing his words carefully. "Susan, if Bela leaves now he will only be counted a half day and he can't attend the dance tonight." He stared across the desk at me. "That is the rule of the school and I can't override it."

With a small voice I pleaded with my mother. "That's not fair. He beat me up, and now I have to stay. I already have my ticket to the dance and I'm taking Colleen."

"Sorry, rules are rules," Mr. Smith repeated.

In the end, full of weary fear and stress, I stayed so I could go that night to the final dance of the year. Despite my mother and stepfather being friendly with the principal through the Methodist church, there would be no investigation. The abuse was too deeply embedded in the system to allow any of it to be brought out into the light for fear the whole thing would collapse. At the dance, my classmates hovered with trepidation, as if the violence inflicted on me that afternoon might rub off on them. No one could save anyone. Less than two weeks later we moved from Athens to Catawba, Ohio.

Having children brings the world into a perspective that could never have been imagined. It's as if a person lived their entire life living underwater in the dark, and suddenly they are thrust above the waves into the shimmering sun, pulled from a cold and blurry life into one of brilliant colors. One may not know one has been drowning until they can suck in the air. When Bruno runs across the soccer field, a determined look across his face, his blond curls dangling past his shoulders, it's as if I was there with him, living a childhood I never had. The joy that dances from his cheeks is as infectious as lightning streaking across the dark summer sky, brilliant flickers of white energy that boom across the landscape.

1979/2002.

It was a comfort to hear my father laugh at Archie Bunker while I pretended to be asleep. He had a deep yawp that cut through the fear that would grip me whenever I lay down. Life was a daily trial, as the mornings in classrooms were spent braving anxiety that undiagnosed ADHD caused, only to adjust on the playground then back into the classroom as my mind wandered, stumbled, and got me in trouble. After school was a time of great relief, building rocket ships, tanks, and caves from the prickly branches of various bushes in the neighborhood, exploring abandoned houses, and playing pick-up football. At night, anticipation of tomorrow filled me with stark, cold fear. Sometimes my brother allowed me to crawl into bed with him. Other times he would order me to "grow-up, you're going to have to learn to sleep at night on your own someday." (It took me nearly 35 years to learn that lesson.)

On brotherless nights I would curl up on the living room hardwood floor and hold the yellow blanket with the frayed corners to my cheek, the uniquely soothing touch of that blanket combined with my father's familiar laugh was comfort for a lonely scared kid. I would soon fall asleep, waking to my father's heavy breaths as he cradled me in his arms and carried me up the stairs. Rubbing my eyes, I'd watch him exit my room, back to his own that was littered with dog-eared paperbacks that appeared to crawl in slow movements over his room, as if they were bulky insects exploring the world outside of their rocky abodes.

My father was a lonely man, an immigrant not just in one country but many. He fled Budapest at the age of four to Austria and six years later to Caracas, Venezuela. Having to assimilate into three cultures in ten years, he was neither here nor there, physically or mentally. His two younger brothers identified as Latin while my father was always groping for a sense of identity.

After divorcing my mother—I watched him through the rear window as we three drove away, tears streaming down his cheeks—he became a monk, spending his days in the quiet, ivy-covered brick buildings of the Benedictine monastery St. Vincent in Latrobe, Pennsylvania. We would visit him, a broad smile expanding across his face, making his black moustache dance a jig across his upper lip. In his brown robes and sandals, he appeared, finally, at peace. When he left the cloistered life, something happened, and that peace turned to mistrust and, finally, shouting and violence.

My mother had remarried several times by the time I turned 12. I attended a church camp where the instructor believed that Satan was walking the streets, and could, quite easily, find a place to dwell inside of little boys and girls. "*The Exorcist* is a true story," she explained over a plate of Nestle Tollhouse cookies. "If you don't pray and keep guard, you, too, can get possessed by the devil himself. He finds his way into your heart and mind through television, movies, and, of course, rock and roll." If I had hairs on the inside of my body, they would have stood straight on end, and dug into my soul. I wanted to rid myself of her words. I asked my mother if *The Exorcist* were true, could people be possessed? "No honey, it is a movie," she said while driving, AM radio blasting out soft rock hits. Perhaps the devil resided too in the easygoing tunes of David Gates and Bread, and had brainwashed my mother through them?

Going straight to the authority on all things God, I asked my father the next time I visited him and my new stepmother. Sipping a glass of burgundy wine, his eyes peering through gold wire-framed glasses, he answered, "Of course *The Exorcist* is true. You must always be on guard of the devil." He swallowed a hearty piece of beef and stabbed a tomato. "The devil could be anywhere, in a store, on the street or even a restaurant. He will be charming and seem nice at first." He took another gulp from his glass and looked over at his wife. Her lip quivered slightly. "Bela, your father is right. He can come at any time. That is why you must pray and go to church. You might see him at the playground

love, death & photosynthesis

or a party—most likely he will be a gay man." A gay man?! Turning off my ears at that point I was ready to pack up my things and go back to my mother's. "I have to go, I have homework." My stepmother's face grew darker, more serious. My very soul was at stake. This made no sense, but the fear had been planted. That summer was a time of constant worry, especially at night when even soft brushes of wind could startle me at my deepest core. And my father, who had once been a source of comfort, had become harder and harder to relate to. His constant paranoia about evil stood in pointed contrast to both my memories of him and to the stories I had been reading of Christ.

He was seething in the front seat, his eyes burning through the rearview mirror while his hands clutched the steering wheel. He drove wildly, his foot pressing the accelerator as if it were possible to outrun his disappointment in me. The tires squealed around the corner, while the car twisted into the street. His mouth was turned down, his lips were sealed. Frightened, I pretended I was small and melted into the corner of the seat. Trying to talk, he only pushed air out. It was loud like a bear smelling its prey. He was choking with anger while his eyes bulged, shaking his head to rid himself of the simmering fury he was barely holding in check. My eyes burned, tears were welling, but I didn't want him to see me cry, curled up against the backseat door, the hot vinyl seats warming my ankles as I pulled my feet under me. I was making myself as small as possible. There were at least two stoplights he ran. I looked away from his staring eyes and looked outside the window. I thought, *If everyone knew what he was really like they would all hate him as much as I hate him now.* We came to a stop and as he turned around and looked at me he erupted, "Goddamnit! How dare you say anything back to me! You have embarrassed me in front of my future bride!" I shrunk some more, his words soaking into me, I was folding in half. My fear enraged him further. He leaned over the backseat and swung his right hand at me. It was an awkward motion as his violent hand had to navigate the headrest, but he still got my side, the soft fleshy part below the ribs. It was a full-handed slap and it stung, but I was determined not to let him win. My mouth remained shut. Not satisfied, he swatted again, this time making full contact on the side of my head, which caused me to catch both the metal part of the car door and the window. My ear was ringing, but I said nothing and stared at him. A car behind us honked. He glared, turned around and started driving. *I hate you,* I thought. It was hard to reconcile this man with my father, the one who took us boating on Dow Lake, who painted watercolors with us and told the lamest jokes ever, or the man who once clutched me so hard while dropping me off at the airport I thought there could never be anyone who loved me more.

I was itching on the inside. My guts wanted to crawl out of me as I sat at my wooden desk, the one my Uncle Pablo had refinished in college and given to me. I was scrolling through her emails, looking for any clues that would help lay the blame for my deteriorating life on someone other than myself. Outside, the sun was out. It was always out in Gainesville—it never turned off. Spanish moss dripped off the trees in our front yard, golfers reared their arms back and swatted at tiny white balls while just a hundred feet away from the golf course, I sat at my desk watching my life wind away one click at a time. The dogs were at my feet, hiding from the heat underneath the desk. I could hear their panting, tongues flopped on the floor, legs stretched out. The air conditioner kicked on, but it didn't make that much of a dent in the humidity. Just soft whiffs of cold air rising out of the vents to be swallowed in gulps by the Gainesville humidity. The room was stacked with records and vintage clothes, shelves of vinyl guarded me, as they had since the third grade. They had given me solace when nothing else did, but now I was annoyed by them. They sat unplayed while I resented them. Everything had gone to shit. The hole I was sinking in was my own, the alcohol I had poured into it only caused it to cave in more. The sides were slippery and I could not claw my way out. The hairs on my neck stood on end, and I read them—the notes she and he had exchanged and I felt myself crumble, although it was an odd feeling, as if I had torched my own house and blamed the matches. My father had told me in one of his sour lectures that I was birthed into betrayal, that there was no one I could trust but him. He had been forsaken by my mother, and later, by my sister. His lectures were cruel. The wall he tried to build around me was one of his own bitterness. I tried to resist his words at the time, but the memories of deception by those I loved the most now rushed me, shaking me from the inside out. My mother had left me, Jenny had never been honest, then Sharon, and now Merijn. Standing up, I turned towards the tall record shelf behind me and threw it forward and hundreds of records fell to the floor. Screaming, I pulled another one down, then another. I went into the next room, scraped my arm along the dining room table; everything was swept off in one motion. Glass shattered and slid over the hardwood floors; there were shards everywhere. Grabbing handfuls of CD's, I threw them onto the floor. It wasn't enough. I punched pictures on the wall, slicing open my knuckles. I was enraged. The dogs had run into the bedroom.

Her office was only a mile away. I walked in on her speaking with a student. I looked closely at the photographs on her office wall. Some were from her lover. I nearly vomited.

love, death & photosynthesis

"I read them! I read them all!"

"Don't leave, you always leave," she whimpered. I stopped only long enough to vomit on the side of the road.

Tell her. This was running through my mind. *Come clean.* I didn't trust myself. I had not been faithful for years. Another, slyer thought peeked through. *This is your way back to Ohio. You can blame her for everything.*

Throwing a few belongings and some beer into my car, I started driving north. I could make it there by last call if I didn't stop. Or I could stop, get a hotel room, and end my life. I drove fast, my foot pressing the small car to go faster than it should have as I bent its small frame through traffic along I-75. After driving roughly 40 miles, I pulled off and checked into a Motel 6 with a moldy faded sign.

"The cheapest room you have," I said to the clerk. It was only 3 PM.

"How many nights are you staying?"

"Just tonight."

She had been calling over and over. I sat on the edge of the bed, drinking warm beer after warm beer, staring at my phone. I called her back.

"I'm so sorry," she said in a rush. "I thought you left me after 9/11. I begged you to come and be with me. I'm your wife. You were supposed to be with me and I was so scared. You never came. I assumed you didn't love me. Please come home. You destroyed everything."

I didn't know if she meant "everything" or just the house. I was wondering where I could buy a gun. It couldn't be hard in northern Florida. My next thought went to the poor person who would discover my brains splattered across the bed and wall. I wouldn't want to put that on anyone.

"Where are you?" Her voice was soft, tender and worried.

"It doesn't matter. Somewhere. I'm so mad." I took another drink, the beer felt like a hand in my mouth, it was hard to swallow. The thought of a gun kept sweeping up, becoming more of a reality.

"Please come home. I'm scared. I wish you were here." Her tears were reaching through the telephone.

"I don't know. I'm stuck. Should I go back to Ohio? I hate everything." There were no tears in me, just bullets of regret and rancor.

"We can work things out, I love you. I've only wanted you to be with me. You're always far away. Where are you?"

Where are you. Where are you. Where are you.

"I have no idea. I really don't. I want to die. This much I know." My eyes were tired, my shoulders felt heavy, achy.

"I thought you would say that. I need you here. Don't go back to Ohio. You should be with me. I can help you."

"No. I don't think so, Goddamnit! What the fuck is wrong with you?"

"Please don't yell. Please just come home"

"There is no fucking home to go to. Fuck, fuck, fuck, fuck. You can keep the fucking dogs. Fuck."

The gun felt closer. I pictured the metal in my mouth. Cold and hard. I could taste it. I had only held a gun a few times in my life. "I'm scared," I said.

"Just come home."

I hung up, and threw the hotel phone against the wall, cracking the receiver.

On the drive back, the rage was still there, but it was tempered by sadness. That blunted its force. It felt emotionally like I was punching mud. There was blood on my pants and shirt, on the stick-shift of the car. Shame encased me. I felt broken into tiny fragments, like I was constructed of shards of glass and they were stabbing everything I touched and everything inside me. When I walked through the front door, I saw that she had cleaned up. There was no evidence except holes in the doors. She was in my office, putting the records away, carefully, one by one. She hugged me, held me tighter than my father did all those years ago, and I felt nothing. Her shoulders shook with pain, her warm tears bled into my chest. "I am so sorry Bela, I am so sorry." I could not return her hug. I was empty.

"I was also unfaithful," I said woodenly. "I can't let you take the blame—you're right, I didn't come when you asked. I'm just scared. I. Am. Just. Scared."

1997.

The party was in the back of a large brick building that housed the excellent Monkey's Retreat, a bookstore that stocked *HATE* by Peter Bagge, titles by Daniel Clowes, *Re-Search*, and a plethora of other underground books, comics, and zines. Monkey's was run by two Brooklyn transplants, Rosie and Daryl, whose thick New York accents made them almost as exotic as the reading materials on their shelves. The party was bustling. The New Bomb Turks were filming a video for their next record on the large indie record label Epitaph. Against a backdrop of streamers, confetti, and other party-like fair, people swayed and yammered. In the back of the room, on frayed couches, a group of us drank from a keg and the small metal flask I had brought filled with Maker's Mark. My fairly new girlfriend had stayed home, studying for her last semester of classes before graduation, already tiring of the episodic binge drinking that would hurtle her man into a series of blind nights.

I held court with Jerry, we felt splendid as we made the women around us laugh. While cameras rolled, with the prompting of Jerry, I shed my clothing and then walked to the other side of the room and calmly filled our plastic cups from the keg. Soon even this grew tiresome, and as I put my clothes back on and wound my way through the crowd, a small feeling of anxiety climbed up my shoulders. I went outside where a group of smokers gathered, cracking jokes and discussing music, books, and the general gossip of High Street. The video shoot had ended and Bill and Jim from The New Bomb Turks were laughing. Jenny pulled on my shoulder as we four gabbed in a small circle. "Hey, Jim Shepard is really fucked up," Jenny said. "Maybe he needs to go home?" We all looked at Jim. He was leaning against the brick wall, next to the spray-painted words "Art Force One," his head slunk down so his chin rested on his chest, as if his neck was a broken hinge. His eyes were closed. "Is he ok?" Bill asked. It was as if we were looking at the video of the slow-motion crash of the skier from the Wide World of Sports. Jim lifted his head, saw us and made his way lumberingly over. He crookedly walked into a young, well-groomed man who looked more out of place because he tried too hard to look in-place. Jim accidentally crashing into him toppled the beer from the man's hand. Jim obliviously kept walking, and the fellow grabbed Jim's shoulder and threw him to the ground and jumped on top of him. Jim hugged the man tight and bellowed, "Jesus, stop! I'm just a lonely alcoholic! Leave me alone! Stop!" His voice was as crumpled as his body, broken and bruised. But the young man wouldn't stop seeking his vengeance for getting bumped.

Without thinking, I dropped my beer, flicked my dark plastic glasses to Jenny, and pulled the man up off of Jim. My fists dotted his head and chest and the fight was over in the time it took the plastic beer cup to roll across the gravel driveway. "Help!" cried a muffled voice below me. Jim Weber pulled me off the guy and I heard Jenny say, "There's Bela, fighting again. He has such a temper." Eric Davidson's girlfriend walked up to me, blood splattered over my homemade silk-screened T-shirt that read "Blood Family," and said, "Jesus, Bela. You just beat the shit out of my hairdresser." Someone handed me a beer.

Jim Shepard gathered himself up, his clothes spackled with tiny bits of gravel and beer. "Uh, thanks Bela. I don't know what that guy's problem is."

When I got home, my girlfriend looked at me aghast, "What happened? Were you in a car accident? Oh my God, you are bleeding so much!"

"I'm OK. It's not my blood; I was in a fight."

"What do you mean, a fight?" Her eyes were aglow with surprise.

"Yeah, sometimes I fight." I said, slipping past her.

"You do?" she said as if she'd just discovered I was secretly an alien.

"Yeah, sometimes."

From the other room I heard her say, "What the fuck?"

The house was filled with broken stuff. A hole here, a chipped telephone there, a smashed plate in the garbage can. There were plates thrown or tables toppled in fits of explosive rage, cars covered with dents. There were times I went to the hospital because I hit a wall, or put my arm through a door, learned behavior from the earliest times in my life. All the physical things were filled with scars of rage, busted from frustration, and an anger that arose from I had no idea where. It would erupt, flail about, and disappear as quickly as it came. This is why we can't have nice things.

1985.

The end of the summer was fast approaching, and rural Ohio felt as if it were burning one corn stalk at a time. Tractors hummed across the valley from our house and grasshoppers jumped hither dither while the laundry blew rhythmically across the backyard on a clothesline, a ballet of fabric and wind that was being replicated countywide. Rick's brown sedan crackled onto the driveway, Jimi Hendrix blaring. "You gonna be OK, man?" he asked. Then: "Do you think your mom can give me $20 to get back to Athens?" He had driven two hours to Catawba to get me home. School was starting in a few days and I didn't have a ride back. I'd asked my brother to pick me up, but he said he couldn't because he had football practice and told me that Mom wasn't coming to get me, either. I'd stayed till the last minute in Athens, working cleaning chickens at Casa Que Pasa, drinking beer, on the search for teenage sex. Rick had agreed to take me under the condition that he be given gas money to get back home, as he had to work that night.

My mother walked out to the car. No hello, no welcome home, just: "Bela, come here, I need to speak with you."

"OK, but we need to give Rick $20 for gas."

"You didn't discuss that with me. Come inside and we'll talk about it." She glared at me.

"You could have come home a month ago, and now you want me to pay for your friend's gas?"

"Uh, yeah. He drove 125 miles to get me home because you wouldn't come and get me."

She turned to yell behind her. "Bob! Come here please." Bob, her husband the minister, came out of his office. He looked like Andy Griffith, wearing a blue sweater over a buttoned up shirt and carrying his wooden pipe in the middle of August. *Why the fuck is he wearing a sweater?* He didn't address me or say hello or anything, only looked at my mother. "Yes?"

"Do you have $20 to pay Bela's friend for gas?"

"I suppose. But didn't you tell him he'd have to pay his own way home?"

"Jesus," I spit out. "You didn't have to spend a dime on me this summer because I worked and stayed with Erica! Just fucking give him the $20 to get home."

"Don't you talk to your mother that way!"

Taking the money from Bob's hand, my mother went outside and handed it to Rick while Bob and I went at it in the living room.

"Well, that was fucking embarrassing," I spat out. "Guy drives halfway across the state to get your son who you haven't seen all summer and you don't want to pay him. Not even a fucking how do you do?" I had grown up that summer, both physically and emotionally, breaking out of the isolated pimply shell. I had found my rebellion in the back kitchen of Casa, on darkened train tracks drinking whiskey mixed with grape Kool-Aid, and in various record stores and uptown college parties, the turntables cranking out the new sounds of the Replacements, R.E.M., the Smiths, and the Tom Tom Club.

"I said you don't talk to your mother that way!" Bob yelled.

I thanked him for the $20 and headed for my room, where I put in an R.E.M. tape and blared it. Pacing, with blood rising into my ears, I wanted out. Suddenly, the door flew open, revealing Bob, all 6'2" of him, standing there scowling.

"Go apologize to your mother!"

"Get out of my room. She should apologize to me!"

Bob lunged at me, got ahold of me and tossed me across the room into the wall. A small end table broke under my legs. I was still only 125 pounds or so, half his size, yet surprisingly I had no fear. I rushed him, arms flailing, hitting into his stomach. He gathered me up again and chucked me headlong into the wall where a chunk of plaster fell into my soft curls, my glasses falling to the floor. My mother appeared behind him, horrified. "What on earth is going on here?" "Apologize to your mother!"

"Fuck off!"

He made his way towards me again.

"Stop it! Stop it!" my mother wailed, stepping between us.

1992.

All these tiny labels put effort into bringing the music that connected us. Tim Adams was a big factor in promoting music from New Zealand, not only by carrying Flying Nun records but also putting out records by Graeme Jefferies, the Cannanes and This Kind of Punishment. He also was an early proponent of the Shrimper label from California, getting the bands Mountain Goats, Refrigerator, and Nothing Painted Blue into indie stores. Robert Griffin championed a little-known band from Dayton called Guided by Voices, investing his own meager earnings into the band. Every town had its indie music hero.

Walking into the store late one morning, I found that Ron had already priced our Scat order, a small stack of records, CDs, and fanzines, and was just waiting for me to put them away. "You know, Ron," I said, "we might sell some of these quicker if you just put them away yourself before I got here." Without looking up from his paper, Ron said, "Nah, that's your job." There was a pecking order in the store, or at least in Ron's mind. A cover of The Rolling Stones' "She Was Hot" was on the turntable. "Who's that?" I asked.

"Karl Hendricks. It's the only song on this record I don't like." Ron shuffled to the stereo, speaking to me with his back turned, "The Stones haven't made a listenable record since 1972, and that song is off *Undercover*, which was released in 1983, so ergo it's not a good song. But the rest of *Buick Electra* is great. It might be the best record of the year." I peered at the jacket of Karl Hendrick's debut album, featuring a black and white cartoon by Daniel Clowes of a band driving down Main Street America. "Robert Griffin recommended it," Ron added. "I should have ordered more." Robert was a member of Cleveland's Prisonshake and ran Scat records.

By the end of the afternoon, I had tracked down Karl's phone number and called him at his home in Pittsburgh. Within a few months, The Karl Hendricks Rock Band was booked for a show with Gaunt that went mainly unattended. Karl met me at Used Kids mid-afternoon. He didn't match what I had pictured: a greasy-haired blue-collar worker gone off-grid from Pittsburgh. Instead, he was a tall, boyish man with a buzz cut and glasses. He held out his hand. "Hi, I'm Karl Hendricks. The rest of the band are trying to park the van." I was asking him if he wanted a beer when Jerry walked up, cigarette dangling on the end of his cracked lips as if it were gathering the courage to jump from his mouth. "Hey, who's this?" Jerry asked, nodding to Karl. Never one to make best first impressions, Jerry grabbed a stack of records to put away without waiting for an answer, turned and walked away. "This is Karl Hendricks," I said, and Jerry stopped mid tracks and put the records back down. "Oh man, I love your record, do you wanna a beer?" We record store guys had a very limited vocabulary in social settings. "I was just telling Bela that I should wait until the band gets here." Jerry handed him one anyway. "My band is playing with you tonight. I'm going to do my solo thing first, The Cocaine Sniffing Triumphs." This was the first I had heard Jerry give his solo project a name. "Like the Jonathan Richman line?" Karl asked. "Exactly," nodded Jerry, spilling ashes on the floor.

Karl appeared normal, almost boy-scout-ish, always polite with a veneer of humility that was as authentic as the personal songs he wrote. *Buick Electra* is a stunningly beautiful record about self-doubt and love that tends to hang around people in their early twenties like a long dress, always a little in the way. Karl was as wry as any Midwesterner could be, with titles such as "I Think I Forgot Something...My Pants" and "The Smile That Made You Give Up." He wrote about the clumsy awkwardness of love, with the sense of always feeling alone at the party.

Life sometimes is akin to living inside a large revolving door, one where only the visitors get to exit, a person shares a space with them and then they are gone, as the door sucks another person on the next go round. At a time, the door moved faster, building points of contact into a continuum that spans a lifetime. Passion trumped everything else, negating a person's upbringing, beliefs and future, foisting many of us together into a world built on a love of music that transformed the feeling inside into real meaning. Sound bubbles burst the pangs of isolation, one note at a time, exploding in our ears. For three minutes everything melted together, but then the music would stop. We would shuffle to the bar, repeating the stories of the day, filling the space with words or silence depending on the level of anxiety a person felt until the next perfect song was played.

1994.

Mike "Rep" Hummel was one of the first people along High Street to record his own music and then press it to vinyl. His *Rocket To Nowhere* (Moxie) came out in 1977, a blistering speaker-blower of a song that captured the sonic waves burping out of Cleveland but infused with Mike's love of the arty flamboyant sounds of the Alex Harvey, early Alice Cooper, and Lou Reed. He was a shaggy figure who would drop by the store, carrying loads of white record boxes between the furnace of the back room and his car, and later that night it wasn't uncommon to see him manning the pool table at Larry's, a large leather hat and long leather coat casting a shadow over the table, a large glass of whiskey nearby. He was usually with Jim Shepard or Ron, and it was not uncommon to find them by the back door of Larry's smoking a joint and talking in hushed tones, probably exactly like they did in high school. Dan had a contentious relationship with Mike at that time, and if there were any mistakes in the auctions or record show sales, he would berate Ron, "Well, he's *your* best friend," as if Mike was responsible for every fuck-up that went on in a store full of fuck-ups.

For Jerry and me, Mike was initially somewhat of a mysterious shadow, he would slip into the store with his boxes and huddle in the back with Dan and later return with a manila envelope holding the winners of that month's auction. Still later, we would spy him and Shepard at Larry's poetry night, constantly shushing us as various nervous types wearing berets, scarves, and inky mascara stood before a bar full of people reading poems and prose from tattered notebooks. "Jesus," Jerry would say, "I forgot it was poetry night. Let's to go BW's. At least we can drink in peace there and play trivia."

By 1994, we had opened up the Used Kids Annex, which was the "collector's" side, although the philosophy of the establishment was to never have collector prices. Of course, later, as the burned timbers of the music industry crashed around our bewildered, frightened heads, we had no choice but to embrace eBay and other money-making venues. But the early '90s were the salad days of music buying, the party before the dawn.

The Annex was run by a gentle soul, Dave "Captain" Diemer, a large man who had a striking resemblance to Richard Brautigan. Cap at one time worked at Moles Record Exchange with Dan Dow and later ran Capital City Records, the collector's offshoot of Singing Dog Records. Dan loved Cap with all of his heart and soul, and Captain was as kindhearted as he was large, a tall man with a bushy white mustache. He lived a life that captured the essence of the '60s but was cynical enough to embrace the sounds of punk rock and heavy metal. He loved the sweet melancholy sounds of Phil Ochs as well as the death sirens of "War Pigs," of which he could air drum every fill. Captain had the most stable family life of any of us: an affectionate wife and a young son, all living in a small tiny farmhouse in rural Delaware County. Captain was the wise man in our world, an island of calm in the neurotic and chaotic days of our lives. He was always lending a bent ear to our tales. Mornings when I would bring him a large coffee with cream from Buckeye Donuts, he would beat me to my own punch by leaning against me, slowly shaking his head and muttering, "I got so fucking drunk last night." A respectful imitation of myself, as I never knew Captain to drink.

Mike was hired to work part-time in the Annex. One tipoff that Mike had arrived was the musky scent of marijuana that would seep through the back-room wall. Mike would flip the "Back in Five Minutes" sign up and go to the back of the Annex and fire up, and then, like a high-school kid trying to cover up his tracks, he would gargle with Scope and light incense to cover the smell. With his shaggy hair and white teeth he was handsome enough to have been a model for *Creem* and *Playgirl*. It was easy for us to find fault with Mike, as in our curmudgeonly twenties, we tended to dismiss a great deal, and Mike was prone to listen to the Doors with the same ease that one of us would the Stooges or MC5. What we didn't fully realize was Mike came of age when rock and roll turned

Mike Rep was transfixed with Ohio lore and more specifically the history of Native American spiritual sites. The importance of locale was steadfast in Mike's world. A walking internet of facts about the region, Mike was the first person who told me about the Mothman.

The ancient history of Ohio goes back thousands of years to the earthworks of Fort Ancient. The curling 1,300 foot Serpent Mound dates possibly as far back as 400 BC. Other earthworks dot southern and central Ohio. In a sad commentary on 20th century capitalism, one in Newark has a private golf course sitting on top of it. One can imagine the ghosts of Native Americans dodging errant golf shots whilst crying paranormal tears. Serpent Mound is one of the great American treasures, as mystical as Stonehenge but with nary a speck of explanation about the builders. Nevertheless, the fascination with Serpent Mound has been relegated to mostly outliers in Ohio: pagans, Native American groups, and those who tend to lose themselves in dog-eared books, long hikes, and the passing of pipes. And Mike Rep.

"I'm working on a project that is pretty interesting," Mike would say to me and Jerry. "When you close up shop come over and give it as listen." When we'd stop in at the Annex, all the lights would be out except the dangling white Christmas lights that hung from the low ceiling, and Mike would blare whatever he was working on. It could have been Guided by Voices' *Propeller*, Prisonshake's *Roaring Third*, or the Strapping Fieldhands' *In the Pineys*. Whatever it was, it was always ear-splittingly loud. The smell of marijuana drenched the air like a green wave of humidity, a smell that stuck in your nostrils like cat hair on a sweater.

This night, Mike was mixing something different—a bouncing effect-laden song. It sounded as if the vocals were being channeled through a wading pool of ectoplasm, shimmering over fuzzy guitars and a choir singing, "There's aliens in our midst." I stopped dead in my tracks. I assumed it was V-3, but its lighthearted nature, the glint in the song's eye, supplied a carefree bizarreness that Jim Shepard would have been too self-conscious to lay down on tape. "Who is this?" I asked. Smiling broadly, Mike replied, "It's the Quotas. It's a Twinkeyz cover." Not knowing who the Twinkeyz were but assuming I should, I mumbled something like, "This is a great cover."

The next time I worked with Mike he handed me a Maxell cassette with his chicken-scratch pointy scrawl. "This is everything we've been recording," he said. The tape might as well have been stuck in the Pioneer tape deck in my '82 Ford Mustang. I listened to it nonstop over the next month. The songs covered the gamut of sounds that spanned suddenly more dangerous, when the infuse of psychedelics, marijuana and Quaaludes were stuffed into tight jean pockets to be consumed in Detroit-made cars as long as speedboats, while the click-click-click of eight-track players boomed out the sounds of "L.A. Woman." Ron House once remarked that he had felt as if one had to make a choice in high school between Alice Cooper or the New York Dolls, and Mike Rep defied both sides and proudly chose both. We all realized that, like Jim Shepard, Mike had been making a mix of punk-infused art rock since high school. For the first Datapanik single, the label head asked The Boys From Nowhere, themselves an algorithm of punk and '70s hard rock, to cover Mike Rep and the Quotas' "Rocket To Nowhere." The b-side featured future Greenhorn brothers, the Spurgeons, blasting through Peter Laughner's "Dear Richard." "Rocket To Nowhere" is now a highly sought-after single, an almost sinister and gleeful three minute announcement of boastful destruction.

One day as I brought over a stack of records to the Annex, Mike was busy pricing 45s in his shaky chicken-scrawl and singing loudly along to Phil Ochs. In his smooth tenor Mike sang along: "I'd like a one-way ticket home, ticket home." Records can be a silent code, opening the possibilities of connection like nothing else. My own fascination with folk music and singer-songwriters started early with an affinity for Richard Thompson, who I saw open for R.E.M. when I was 17. I had already been fed an endless supply of Woody Guthrie, Pete Seeger, and Leadbelly as a child. Discovering used record stores along High Street when I was 18 was akin to getting into a doctorate program at an Ivy League school; swallowing the songs of Tim Hardin, Townes Van Zandt, Butch Hancock, Gene Clark, and, of course, Phil Ochs had an incredible impact on me. Finding others who held some of these now neglected songwriters close to their hearts made me feel good. The songs and artists were small fireflies of light in a life drenched in darkness. In the '80s and early '90s most of these acts were still obscure. Ron, Dan, Captain, Mike, and I had all seen Townes Van Zandt at a small nightclub/eatery called The Dell in the early '90s—there were only 11 people there. Townes got so drunk during his brief intermission he ended the second part of the show basically telling stories while strumming laconically on his guitar.

Phil Ochs, who grew up in Columbus and used to drink at Larry's, was a man who appeared to hold his principals above all else. His sensitivity to the world around him would eventually lead to his death by suicide. When Mike sang along to "One Way Ticket Home," I stopped in my tracks, and although we had known each other for several years, at was if we were just meeting, in a new much deeper way.

Mike Rep: (l-r) Bill Randt, Mike "Rep" Hummel

Mike's broad fondness of music. From Roky Erickson to the Phil Ochs-cum-ragtime "America's Newest Hero" and the experimental Flying Saucer Attack-inspired "One Thirty Five." Speaking with Mike over beers one night at Larry's, I said, "Maybe I can put the tape out?" Soon enough, Gary Held from Revolver listened to it and loved it. He and Mike had spent some time together when Gary visited. Perhaps they had even visited Serpent Mound together? After a few months of waiting for the cover, itself another in a long-line of bizarre record cover art from Mike, *A Tree Stump Named Desire* was ready to come out on CD. Mike wanted it to come out on LP, but due to the length, a proper single LP pressing did not work. Although it was cut to lacquer twice, Mike was never happy with how it sounded, so there are only a handful of test pressings of the record in existence.

1987- 1990.

In Ohio the weather would change like the moods of a drunken stepfather, at one point frigid and chilling and the next heaving warm air. Walking down High Street in the spring feels like liberation. The bleak chilly overhead carpet of clouds slip into their summer hibernation, and the bluest sky awakens while people peel away the dreariness of winter by wearing cutoff shorts and t-shirts, and glide down the sidewalks on skateboards that were shuttered for the winter months. Along the Olentangy River, small pockets of fabric appear amidst the overnight greenery of woods that line a 15-mile bike path. It is here that many of the homeless camps sprout just like the green buds and purple flowers that awaken in the spring. A stroll through the various parks along the way brings many passersby next to men with rumpled clothes, whose breath wheezes alcohol and whose shoes are cracked and frayed from years of pounding asphalt.

At some point, usually in the middle of summer within the woods of the bike path the heavy humidity of Ohio is fertile ground for millions of mosquitoes to breed. It is not uncommon for a person to resemble a welted corkboard of mosquito bites after strolling through the trees and bushes. The homeless carve out tiny homes within the thicket of bushes and the muddy shoreline, homes big enough for a body and not much more.

bela koe-krompecher

Some consist of walls of pallets, thin slabs of sheet metal and discarded plastic, while others may be as simple as a one-person tent or sadly, a sleeping bag and backpack. Bikers, joggers, and mothers pushing baby strollers may well be unaware that within the small bushes of the path they are traveling down, a person may be sleeping, brushing their teeth, taking a shit, or drinking a 40-ounce bottle of malt liquor.

We moved apartments as if we were hunter-gatherers; a new one nearly every year—from one broken-down, roach filled apartment to another. As if one patchwork wall with faded paint was a step up from another one. As we carried boxes of books and records, Hefty trash bags bulging with clothes from dilapidated cars to the newest old apartment, a small pillow of pride would burst out from our shoes with every step towards the new home. Each place birthed new experiences and stories, the tales piling on top of another. Our existence and lifestyles invited characters who could have sprouted from thin paper-back novels—Dan The Man From Cleveland, Barefoot Jeff, Crazy Jim, and more—each with a distinctive odd trait about them. One got drunk and pooped in the heating vent. Another was a compulsive liar who kept asking me to have threesomes. So, we were happy when we got Dan Miller, who took great pride in his occupation as a carpenter. Dan worked hard, harder than I ever had and he enjoyed coming home caked in mud and pride and would drink a six pack and laugh along with the laugh-track of the television. He would open a can of Campbell's Beef Soup with his key ring and eat the soup cold. Then he would pass out. He was never the cleanest man and it wasn't uncommon for him to wear part of the mountain of clothing I had at the corner of my room after his clothes had become too immobile from grime. One time he came home from work, my eyes grew wide when I eyed his shirt. I glanced toward Jenny, "Look what Dan's wearing." Her mouth dropped, and she excused herself from the living room. I quickly followed her into the bedroom where we both slowly dived into a mass on the floor. We were laughing so hard we weren't making any noise. "Oh fuck, we have to tell him" she gasped. Just then Dan appeared at the doorway. "Tell me what?" "It's about that shirt you're wearing." Dan, looking apologetic said "Hey, you said I could wear your clothes if I needed." I took a deep breath. "Dan, hate to break this to you but you're wearing our cum rag." Dan's face twisted into a slow-motion earthquake, his eyes literally filled with tears, "Oh fuck!!!???" he yelled, this too was also oddly in slow motion. It came out as "O-o-o-o-h-h-h-h-r-a-a-a-g-g-g-g-h-h-h f-f-u-u-a-u-g-h-h-k-k-k-k!!!?" As a question. His disbelief at the realization that he had been wearing this article of spent love for an entire day was too much for him. He attacked the shirt from every angle, wanting to tear it off but not wanting to touch it at all, it was if he were smothered in centipedes. Frustration was flying off him as if he were a living algebra problem. We laughed harder, there was nothing we could do. Finally he wrenched the shirt free, making animalistic noises. "You guys are assholes," he declared and stalked out of the room. We laughed for a good two weeks on that one. Dan gave us the silent treatment for at least that long.

Another Dan we let crash occasionally was a street musician named Dan Stock; he was from Cleveland and roughly 15 years older than us. Dan had matted dark black hair, a scar that ran up the side of his face and an immortal cigarette dangling from his mouth. He would sit on the corner of 11th and High and play shitty covers of Pink Floyd and Eric Clapton songs.

One day we walked into the living room and as he put down a small mirror a large chunk of his nose fell on the table. It was as big as a marble, a big bloody gob of meat. Dan stared at us horrified, as we did him; he had a small driblet of blood coming out of his right nostril. "Holy shit, Dan!" yelled Jenny. Dan, frozen in shame nodded his head back and forth. "Dan, what the hell are you doing in our house, are you OK?" I asked. Dan then picked the bloody nose meat up and stuffed it into his pocket, as if it was a wad of gum and he was just caught at school. He said, "Wish you nice folks didn't have to see that." Jenny and I vowed to each other we would never use cocaine.

Because we were so poor, Jenny and I would for entertainment drink a 12 pack and hide behind the living room curtains and make quiet comments towards the passersby. This was not as boring as it sounds. One time we witnessed a sorority girl leave her apartment, lock her door, and fart. She reached in her purse, pulled out a small bottle of perfume and sprayed it on her ass.

Another time, a man outside our window pulled an envelope out of his pants, retrieved from it a pair of pantyhose, which he pulled down over his greasy hair and beard. He placed a large silver flashlight, the kind the police use to club someone with, on the ground in front of him he fumbled with his zipper with one hand and, with the other, threw small rocks against our window. "What the fuck is that?" I asked Jenny. "I dunno," she answered matter-of-factly. "Someone throwing rocks at the window." He then had no hands left for throwing: his right hand pointed the flashlight carefully at his midsection; his left tugged furiously at his penis. The whites of his eyes shined through the woman's undergarment mask as he worked away. He was truly a man on a mission. "I think it's one of your boyfriends," I said to Jenny. I took a sip of beer. Peering out the window, she laughed and asked, "What should we do?" "I suppose call the police," I said, and dialed 911. "So there is this guy masturbating outside our window, he has a flashlight and panty hose on his head," the operator intoned. "Sir can you describe him more accurately?" "Well," I replied, "he has a penis in one hand and the flashlight in the other. It's aimed at his penis, really illuminating what he's doing…. if you don't hurry he's going to finish up." A deep sigh on the other end then: "A squad car is on its way."

Slipping my bare feet into some shoes, I rose to go outside and wait for the police. "I don't think it's safe to go out there, Bela," Jenny said.

"What's he going to do—dick-slap me to death?"

"No, but he has a flashlight."

"Oh yeah, although he might be too tired to use it. I'll wait on the staircase just in case."

Walking half way down the metal staircase, I sat down and took a sip of my beer. The man was gone and I took in the smell of the alley, rotting food and urine hovered in the backyard, the alley and small parking lots that lined the back alley were flecked with small tiny pieces of glass, sprinkled around the black asphalt. They made it look like miniature stars were embedded in the blacktop, and when the lights of passing headlights shone upon them, they resembled rhinestones. Soon, a police cruiser pulled up, I walked down and explained to the officers what had transpired. They set out looking for a pantyhose-headed man with a penis in one hand and a flashlight in the other. Jenny came and sat down next to me—we drank some more beer, the feelings of betrayal over whatever transgression she had visited upon me earlier (probably she'd disappeared for the evening) had dissipated, replaced by a closeness brought about by the absurdity of the situation. We always had laughter to pull us towards one another while our actions pulled us apart.

1993.

The house on Patterson fit well into the changing seasons, as it was constructed of bulky brown stained wooden clapboard and had stony raised gardens. In winter it looked almost haunted and lonely, while in summer the brown stain looked like it was peeling, as if the sun was blistering every chunk of wood. But in autumn, the house was really in its element— tarnished grass, fading gray and browns, yellowed leaves bulging out of overstuffed gutters. It could be a postcard for the feeling of loss and the comfort of coats that October seems to bring. Things shuddered and burped along with the days and nights, as every package that was received in the mail at Used Kids came bearing gifts of sound, and the mailbox on Patterson always seemed to contain some letter requesting music from Columbus. Time appeared as still as a television that was always on but never watched. There, but nobody paid heed to it.

I had fallen hard for the sound of the Grifters, a band from Memphis that had somehow annihilated sound and built it back up into blasts of melodic music that could at once be disquieting and soothing. I had received their first full-length, "So Happy Together" from Scat Records while working at Used Kids one morning, by the third song I was on

Grifters: (l-r) Stan Galimore, Scott Taylor, Tripp Lampkins, David Shouse

the phone with Robert Griffin, seeing if he could get me in contact with them. By the end of the afternoon I had booked them a show at Stache's with Moviola and Gaunt.

Onstage, the Grifters were a shuddering, calculated belching wreckage of sound, at once sounding like a cloud of distorted guitars straining to stay out of tune, and a spurt of electric coughing, the audio version of a half back darting from the pile into open space. They would bend onto a melody that would be as breathtaking as diving into a warm pool of water. They were in a sense the counterbalance to Guided by Voices. But while Guided by Voices injected a heavy dose of smiling hope into their minute and a half epics, the Grifters were more concerned with the disappointment that tragedy brings, a sorrowful blend of noise and crankiness.

Bob Pollard and the rest of GBV were making monthly visits to Columbus, usually to work on their next record with Mike Rep and drink beer with Ron House, Jim

love, death & photosynthesis

Guided by Voices: (l-r) Bob Pollard, Tobin Sprout, Jerry Wick (behind the beer bottle), Bela Koe-Krompecher

Shepard, Jerry and myself. Shuffling into the store in the late afternoon, fresh from the hour drive from Dayton, the timing would coincide with the five o'clock God-given right to a beer. Huddled in the booths of Larry's we would talk music, it was always music, and the kinship we formed was glued together by records. Bob was as vigilante about listening to music as he was in creating it. Soon they would start playing regularly at Bernie's and Stache's as well as partnering with Anyway for a series of 7" singles, all the while the passion for music was all encompassing.

One afternoon Bob asked me if I was familiar with "Odyssey and Oracle", by the Zombies, "Yeah, I love it, it's kinda like *Odessa* by the Bee Ges, in fact it's my girlfriend's favorite record." "Do you have a copy?" "Yeah, it's not on CD yet, in fact there is only a crappy best of the Zombies on CD, I actually think I have a first pressing as well as a Rhino re-issue, you can have the reissue or I'll trade you something for the original." Bob offered to trade his copy of "Slay Tracks" the first single by Pavement, for which I gladly accepted. We also talked about new bands we liked, especially the Grifters, whose tarnished, feedback laden sound had made an impression on Bob. "That's what I'm trying to do, get that sound... but maybe my songs are too poppy" he wondered aloud. "Oh, you have to see them live, they pull all that noise off in person, and it's like watching a choreographed car wreck." "Lemme know when they play next and I'll make sure GBV plays with them."

Roughly a month or so later, I booked another Grifters show at Stache's. By now, Jerry had become a fan, mostly on the basis of their single, "She Blows Blasts of Static"— a song of epic noisy wreckage that pulled the listener in and then pummeled him with leathery hooks before offering release— so Gaunt was on the bill. I phoned Bob who said that because it was on a weeknight, not everyone could get off of work, but he would come up anyway. During the show, Bob, Jerry, and I were just to the left of the stage as the Grifters plied their splintered sound in front of thirty or so souls, and Bob turned to us and yelled, "The three best bands ever: The Beatles, The Grifters, and Sparks!" Jerry and I would repeat this often to one another, nodding our head with laughter at our own inside joke. "The Beatles, the Grifters, and Sparks!" Indeed.

2016.

I walked the circular hallway of Ohio State University Hospital East, counting room numbers until I found Jenny's. Jenny's mother came up and hugged me, I looked down at Jenny who was crumpled up in her bed, her unused legs jutting out from the bottom of crisp white sheets. She looked small, as if the past years of her life had not only sucked the life out of her but in doing so, made her limbs and torso shrivel. One arm was crossed over her chest and the other lay limp next to the remote control. It appeared as if she had tumbled down a canyon. Her head lay at the bottom of the raised part of the bed, her neck twisted downwards. She was yellow, with a faint hint of green in her cheeks and neck. In her nose was a feeding tube, her eyes were closed.

"Jenny, Jenny…." I waited. "Jenny, it's Bela."

Her eyes flickered. Her mother spoke softly to her, calling her the pet name she had for her. "Nordy… Jennifer… Bela's here."

I leaned in and said into her ear, "Jenny, hey, its me."

Her eyes opened and she peered sideways. She made some grumbling noises through cracked lips, bits of dried blood caked at the corners.

"Do you hear me OK?"

A soft nod and a stab at words, "Urghhh...Berla."

I walked to the other side of the bed and asked her mother, "Has she been like this all week?"

"Well, yeah, mostly. Although the other day she was lucid and talking away, chattering about how she wants to move and how alone she is...but later she just sort of drifted into this."

Angling in again towards her ear, I said, "Jenny, I was just talking about some of the crazy stuff that we used to do. Bruno's really interested in all those stories."

A hint of a smile cracked her yellowed face, just a smidgen. Her memory was still intact but the mechanisms to communicate were fragile and dissipating, as if her body was made of smoke. She was melting by degrees, soon there was no doubt she would only exist as a memory.

1991.

When the gray sky spits the first cold rain of the fall, and the wind touches through skin into a body's bones, I am always transformed backwards, to 1991 or so. Maybe 1992, at this point these are just numbers, signposts on a backward highway that really leads to the abyss, fading into the vanishing point on our own inner canvasses. The memory is New Year's Day, the night before I spent with another woman named Jennifer, and her friend Haynes. A farmhouse on the edge of Athens County, the house straddled a hill, with a small winding road around the farm. An old fence faded from years of neglect was broken in spots, the wood an almost gray-black as the white paint had long been burnt out by time, a small pond with a dilapidated dock half submerged in the brown water gave one the thought of a once active time. It was not used anymore, the land gone fallow with weeds sprouting around abandoned tires, an old truck sat bare in tall grass that was holding tight to the carcass as if the metal hulk was a savoir in a sea of desperation. The night before we had listened to music on a small boombox, shuffling cassettes as the mood suggested, "Nevermind" had come out in the fall, and I was infatuated with "Loveless" by My Bloody Valentine and Superchunk's "No Pocky for Kitty" and as the new year turned over, I put on "Flyin' Shoes" by Townes van

Zandt whom the women had never heard. As we listened and relistened, I succumbed to the pressure of the wine bottle, trying to stay sober was turning into an exercise in futility. At one point, I realized that I felt no spark-I felt incapable of love in any sense. We made love that night, with me knowing this would be the last time and as we spoke in hushed tones afterwards, she confessed her love for me and my reply was silence, my skin getting hot as I knew I was incapable of the same. The next morning, I arose early, made coffee on the stove for all of us and ventured outside. It was New Year's Day and everything was fragile as I ventured across the road to a field that slopped down into a small thatch of woods. It was cold, with dried corn stalks crunching and snapping under leather boots, barren trees looking painted on against the forever gray sky. There was nothing there but thoughts and the wind, kept at bay by a thin brown jacket. A revelation happened as I walked along the woods, listening to the crunch of my boots, that in the end I was destined to be alone regardless of what I had in my life, whether it was a bottle, a friend, or a lover. The thought wasn't frightening, it was as if the riddle that had been clawing in the back of my mind had suddenly been solved—and it was ok.

1984.

It could not have been easy helping to stepparent two opinionated teen-age boys who had been moved around like swallows, migrating from season to season, year to year. We were baggage, plunked down in different schools every year, unpacking ourselves only to have to toss everything back into our emotional suitcases after the school year until finally I said "fuck-it", and decided I would interact with the world on my own terms. Using wit and humor with a very liberal background I challenged the norms of my small town school, speaking out when the football coach used the racist terms in my sophomore biology class-resulting in a trip to the office where the principal asked me point blank, "Why do you have a problem with the word n——?" At home my mother encouraged us to speak out, at one point she made her way to the very same principal's office to challenge him on referring to the wrestling team as a bunch of "pussies." After my freshman year, I quit going to church, another stain I had inadvertently flung on my stepfather Bob Brushwood's aspiring career as a minister. Zoltan had it easier, being much more affable than myself, as well as bigger and handsome with a talent to blend in with the jocks and rednecks; he played football, wrestled, and was homecoming king, while I planted verbal spitballs on my perceived enemies and pined for escape. But both my brother and I were headstrong, well read, and not frightened to speak our minds. I resented my parents for plopping me down in the middle of nowhere, thick with oppression and injustice.

Bob would drink Natural Light, not much—maybe a few every night, but he was prone to darkness and the darkness lay upon him like a coat some weeks. After a year, our mother left, moving to Columbus and later to London, Ohio. Bob and my mother were different people, pulled together by who knows what, but we bore the brunt of their mistake. While Bob tried to step into the role of a father, it was a difficult task. As was his attempt to father the community. He laced his sermons with stories of compassion and acceptance; he tried to balance the need to be accepting with his flock's ingrained suspicion of anything that was different. In the end, it was for naught. His depression gripped him like vines and pulled him into his darkness. Art helped. He went back to his first love, ceramics and drawing, making countless small bowls and religious drawings that soon covered our tables, mantle, and desks.

When my mother left him, Bob struggled to maintain a home with a disinterested teenager who had found his own escape in underground music and books. Bob was a ghost in a house filled with unrealized memories that never had the chance to hatch, smothered by a marriage that had no air to breathe. Bob went to the state hospital in the fall of 1985. He stayed there on and off through the spring. At AA, he met a woman. He would bring her home or stay at her house. A small birdlike lady who did not have the education he or my mother had. Nevertheless she was kind and tried to make small talk with me and Jenny. In between disappearances, Bob was there, making dinner for my brother and I, driving us to wrestling practice, sitting through long tournaments and overlooking the drinking that went on over the weekend. He was encouraging of our passion for literature, and finally over the summer of 1986, right after my high school graduation, Bob left the church and moved in with my grandmother as he returned to school to get his Ohio teaching certificate. At the same time, I dropped out of college, and faced with the choice of living with my mother, going to a shelter, living with my grandmother and Bob, or moving in with Jenny in her dorm room, I chose the latter for two months before I could get my own apartment.

Bob worked in Columbus public schools until he reached retirement. We stayed in periodic contact. The weight of adolescence was a lodestone on my relationship with him; I distanced myself from much of my family. Bob had suffered many losses in his life: two of his children passed, one from a drug overdose and another from cancer, and his own childhood was difficult, filled with brutal abuse he told me about over coffee one day. Finally, after many years of silence he reached out to me via email. He had moved to North Carolina where he built a house with his own hands in the woods and made art. We spoke over the phone once, discussing his depression and he offered apologies for those years we were together. I told him it was all OK. Then there was nothing.

The number I had for him was disconnected. I assumed he had died, but a google search revealed nothing. What does a person do when a past they have little connection to ends? There is a space, like the space between words on paper. A space waiting for meaning that never comes.

The leaves are turning, millions every night go from green to red or orange some even straight to brown. Instant ghosts, dropping and floating their slow-motion dance to the ground. Autumn weather is unpredictable, where one day the sun brings the humidity down like a moist blanket, and the next the October wind bites the bare legs that were fooled into wearing shorts the day before. On Friday nights, marching bands stand in lines, blowing on cold fingers, cracking jokes to split the awkwardness of teenage sexuality in half, they bleat out pop hits, odes to the gridiron, and dream of life after high school. Meanwhile young men slip on shoulder pads, long socks, form fitting pants with laces to make them secure and slap each other in locker rooms, waiting to smack another kid across the grass as bright lights illuminate the field. Onions are diced carefully, to be added to simmering pots of chili. Young women take to stores of all types, Macy's, boutiques, thrift stores, buying sweaters, scarves, leggings, all for the coming months. We all do our nesting in certain ways.

Jenny used to decorate the apartment with whatever season or holiday it was, at Halloween she would tack up pictures of jack-o-lanterns and sinister witches and tape up the crinkly fallen leaves. It was not uncommon to come home in the early evening and be welcomed with a spinning Halloween record on the stereo blaring the spooky sounds of Halloween.

Insomnia has settled in my bed, a thin invisible itch that pesters while trying to drift off to sleep, and when slumber finally arrives, the itch comes back and I am shaken awake only to face the dread of not being able to sleep. In some ways, due to the long-term nature of Jenny's death, the grief process had happened by degrees over the years. Alcoholism and mental illness carved out small parts of me with every crisis, every worry placed one on top of another as if made of a million tongue depressors stacked up over a twenty year period. Her life spread out over the years like a sinkhole, swallowing everybody who ever loved her, and if the hole could talk it would have been screaming louder with every inch it widened. She had become invisible in her own life, an apparition at the end where those of us who could still muster the energy to care for her, would huddle together outside of hospital rooms or over the phone and repeat the same script we had honed for years. "If only she got away from _____(insert any man she was currently living with), she could quit drinking", "if only she'd quit drinking, then she could be herself again", "if she could just stay in the nursing home, she could walk again" or "I can't understand why she drinks like she does if she knows she's going to die." Although she had always drank, the only sober times she experienced was when she was in the hospital, jail or nursing homes—the reality of her mind was too much to handle without numbing it. Towards the end, these conversations came with the resignation someone feels after their football team went down by four touchdowns with seven minutes left. It was all over, but the time was still ticking off the clock.

2017.

"She's back in the hospital, she went last night" Jenny's sister Rachel was on the phone.

"I just saw her there last week, she looked good, she was lucid-talking about trying to record with Sean and Mike Travis." I ran my hand through my hair.

"That's what thought, but you know the doctors told her she couldn't drink again, not a drop and apparently when she got home that fucker Johnny went right down the street and got her a 12-pack"

"Death by 12-Pack" I thought to myself, that could be a headstone for her.

"I'll go tonight, I'm at work now but I'll run over. Maybe I can talk to the social worker and see if she can go straight to an assisted living facility." This was something that had worked in years past but she only liked one of them, the one where Dale died, but she was kicked out for drinking; I wasn't sure if they would let her back. I had worked with the lead social worker in the past and sent her an email, just trying to get an idea if it was possible. She emailed me back and said that depending on the discharge date she would try to accommodate Jenny. "Bela, she is really a neat woman, but she can't drink in here. She is so helpful with all the other residents, telling them stories, she wheeled around all the rooms checking on everybody. Let me see what I can do. Ask OSU to reach out to me."

That evening after dinner I got ready to leave, "Dad, can I go with you? I want to see Jenny" asked Saskia, who was twelve years old. "Honey, it's late" I said looking across the living room at my wife for support. "I don't care if she goes" was the answer I got. Pulling into the parking lot of the hospital, my phone rang. "Hey, its Rachel, I'm almost there. A nurse called my mom and said she should fly up from Florida, she's coming tomorrow." As we waited for Rachel to arrive, Saskia hung close. "Dad, do you think Jenny is going to die?" Pondering her question I was blunt, "Maybe, I don't know—she is a strong woman. She was joking last week when I saw her…she goes to the hospital a lot. I don't know."

As we were led into Jenny's room, Saskia clutched my hand. Jenny's face was bloated from her liver shutting down, she was not just jaundiced, she was yellow, a pale yellow that covered her face like a curtain. Her lips were swollen, cracked and bleeding. One of the results of liver failure is that the body can't clot so Jenny's lips were parched and brittle, she had been bleeding from her lips for over a day. She looked a far cry from the woman who had wooed everybody who came into contact with her. Her eyes were closed when I held her hand, "Hi Jenny its me, Bela, and Saskia is with me" The whirring of her breathing machine in the background, her hand tightened around mine. Rachel approached her, "Hey sis, it's Roach, mom is coming up tomorrow to see you, hang in there." "Merijn sends her love… we all love you, Jenny." I tucked her hand under the blanket. While we filed out of the room a nurse approached us, "She's actually breathing better than she was this morning and she was talking this afternoon, I think she is just tired. Most likely she will be out of the ICU tomorrow if her breathing continues. I wouldn't worry too much." In the car Saskia asked, "Dad, she's gonna die right?" The key turned in the ignition, "I don't know, but I think, yeah, probably."

Jenny died the next day. Her mother was able to make it in from Florida and her family was with her. I was teaching a class on the history and philosophy of alcohol and drug treatment at The Ohio State University when Sean Woosley called me, '"Bela, you should come right now because she may not make it another hour." Jenny died shortly after I arrived at the hospital.

"Why are you so angry?" She'd asked me that repeatedly over the years. Perhaps it was some of the unease that grew up around me when I was near her, the frustration of witnessing a slow motion house fire, and every time you go to hook up the hose it's an inch short. This was not going to end well. I would feel a flickering of hope that would offset the pervasive creepy feeling, such as when she would go to the liquor store at 5 PM instead of 11 AM, but the victories were merely small retreats.

Never-spoken experiences drove her, memories that visited her when she was alone with the voices in her head. No wonder she gravitated towards anyone who could make her feel not so alone, even those who betrayed her with fists, insults, and forcing themselves on her. Sometimes the demons in front of us are safer than the ones in our minds.

She cackled when she laughed. And she made everyone around her laugh. She could lift a room up and transport it to a place of bliss with just one line, an aside that would cause tears of laughter to cascade down the cheeks of anyone within earshot. A few of us played off one another, a small circle of suffering outsiders who kept our sanity by laughter and by pushing the envelope. And, of course, by the music that poured out of her.

Attuned to the pain around her, Jenny comforted me. She held my head when I wept as a teenager, when the world broke apart within me. She would wipe my tears and sing to me, just her voice and her hands upon my cheek. "Edelwiess," "Greensleeves," and "Grow Old Along with Me." She could trill her voice like a 1930s Hollywood singer or turn it into a broken Billie Holiday, depending on what she felt was needed. Later, when she started writing her own music, she would pull lines from my notebooks of poetry to fit her melodies, singing songs to others from lines that were written for her, or later, for my current lover.

Over the years the relationship changed: where once she comforted me, I became the caretaker, trying to save a sinking boat in the middle of the Pacific. Creaky calls in the middle of the night, helping her get services, loaning her money that she would try in vain to pay back but of course never could, She pled with me to help change a system that is so selfish and cruel it smashes the poor underneath it with the quiet approval of an upper crust that is exactly that, crust. She is the main reason I work with the poor, the addicted, and the mentally ill. She gave me a sense of purpose to challenge the levers of power to quit stomping on the disenfranchised.

At one time, I thought I could not breathe without her; later I helped her breathe, and now there is no breath at all. I will miss you in everything I do Jenny.

2018.

The boy sits on the couch, the one with the split seam bandaged with a gray throw blanket to hide the years of use, rubbing his head with his fingers colored black, red, and green from scribbling in notebooks. These are the scars of a Saturday afternoon. He's watching TV, the sounds of the pre-recorded laughter from an unfunny television show bleeds through the music I'm listening to. But, its ok, I don't mind these interferences any more, the music will always be there and besides I've listened to this record about a million times—I know every note although I don't really know any notes. 1,000,001. Outside, beyond the houses across the street a brown-gray tree reaches into the clouds, gray marrying gray while the chill in the air makes itself comfortable for the next few months, it will overstay its welcome again this year. No doubt about that. Looking up at me for reassurance, a sliver of a smile slips out when I smile back, giving him a thumbs up. He returns to his toy, a flat white piece of technology that literally puts the universe at his fingertips, sliding his nimble fingers across the screen he can pull up live satellite images of Jupiter or watch the ten worst skateboard accidents of the previous year. Fetching coffee from the kitchen, a glance through the window reminds me that the fence outside needs replacing, the wood buckling and bowing after years of soaking

Jenny Mae in 2015.

love, death & photosynthesis

in the sun and absorbing winters filled with snow and sub-zero temperatures. To be a wooden fence in Ohio is a lonely life.

There are moments when a person feels nothing, no thought, no worry, no anticipation, no anxiety, no pleasure—nothing— just the softness of the occasion. These come in bouncy crashes, as if they were encased in feathers, in the middle of chaos comes a blunted bomb of nothingness. When they are noticed, it feels like the unraveling of a secret, and then it dissipates as soon as the mind notices it. I think then about how this never happened for you. This quietness. You were a shaking rattle— it felt like you were ten feet high and twenty feet long, lungs pushing out words as if you would have choked on them otherwise, waving above the world—the energy shooting like sparks from your electric body, and from your mind that never switched off.

He gets up, goes to the kitchen, I hear the refrigerator door open, and the sound of the milk carton on the table, the clinking of glasses and his sing-song voice, mumbling over the words of a pop song that you would have taught yourself to play. He sits at the table, sketchbook in hand and draws, the noise from his toy is not a song, and it forms a peculiar dance of sound as it seeps into my headphones. Eyeing him, I think backwards, flipping through memories being unpeeled in microseconds, and then I get stuck in the middle of them. It is then that I wish you were here, that you would tell me what memory it was that I was trying to recall about you, if you were a ghost you could try to point the way in the silent haze of whatever world ghosts hover in. In the end this would annoy you, not being able to talk, to only float about in the background. There was this one time, when you were sleeping in our garage, after I had laid down a rule that was as foolish as telling the sea not to be salty, that said you could not drink if you were to stay in our garage. As if this gesture alone would give you the motivation to finally, once-and-for-all, quit drinking. It was hot, the house was roasting, cooking in its own peeling paint and 19th Century wood, and I noticed the front and back doors were open—you had used the kitchen or bathroom or both, in hindsight it didn't matter but in the moment it did and the anger that grew as suddenly as a flash-fire engulfed me. You were on the floor upstairs in the garage, with the old green portable CD player, flecked with white paint and dust, listening to The Whiles. The same song over and over, turning your head, you looked at me, "Bela, you have got to hear this song—it's amazing. I can't stop listening to it. Its genius."

She started the song, "Emily", again.

"God-damnit, Jenny!"

With eyes half open, "Just listen."

"I know the song, I put it out, Jesus fucking Christ. Jenny."

"Shhhhhh." Putting a hand in the air, one finger extended. The international sign of "hold your horses."

And I waited. I listened. And when it got to the chorus, when three voices blended into one, "There's no way to say…..goodbye, bye, bye, bye, lalalalala"

For a few beats in time, there was no anger. There was just being lost in that chorus.

"This song is perfect, fucking fuck." She took a drink from a large plastic bottle, vodka and juice. The pint was on a box of old photos and notebooks.

"You left the front and back door open. What the fuck, and you're drinking."

Not only were her words slurring, it appeared as if her entire essence was slurring, her shoulders, her eyes and her mouth, "of course I'm driinnkkkingg…what the fuck doo you actually think I do? I drink. When will you get used to it?"

Of course I drink. Some words go together as if they were birthed at the same time, Siamese words. Ofcourseidrink. "You can't stay here if you're drinking, I can't have it. I can't have it around me." When panicked and disappointed, words come out in force, with the energy of frustration and feelings that have laid themselves off to the side. It wasn't the drinking just now, it was the prospect of sending her back out to the street, even if it was the same street we had walked and slobbered down for years. It was still a concrete canvas for both wonder and danger, that could open up its cement jaws and grab a person and chew them up by slow degrees. That was where the anger came from. "You have to leave."

"Fine, I'll come see you when I feel like it."

She grabbed a handful of her clothes, and stuffed them into a brown bag, in the corner was her trumpet, and an old electronic keyboard that she had been playing earlier in the day. She gestured to it, "I was writing a song earlier," she pushed some shirts into the bag, "I'm going to try to get the boys back together and start making a record." Bewilderment sat in the corner, it's oafish face looking skyward, I looked at it and it looked back and we shrugged our shoulders. Taking a sip from her red cup, she waltzed past me. "Where will you go?" As you bounded out the door, "What do you care, Bela? I have places I can go." And you disappeared.

I sit at traffic lights, and there are those moments that come up, when work isn't crowding me, or the kids aren't worrying me, when there is nothing, and you fold back the curtain of my mind. "Peekaboo." You appear.

epi logue

There are cut flowers in vases, long stemmed orchids that sit on new furniture, white and purple flowers contrasting with the dark walnut, old pictures hang on new-to-me walls while formerly boxed books line the shelves. The light is different as the house faces south and the morning sun breaks through grimy windows, waking me up. Many of the windows still don't have curtains, they sit in the closet, carefully folded up, waiting to be hung. The sounds of the floor are different, each floorboard creaks in a distinct fashion. They groan and ache with wear, each step bringing forth a small bleat of age. The wooden planks have been neglected, and there is nary a thing I can do. It's a rental.

On one side of the dining room is a wall of records, nearly six feet long by six feet high, a literal sculpture of loneliness. The opposite wall carries the same, but instead of vinyl records, there are rows and rows—thousands— of compact discs. Just in case the records aren't enough to placate the darkness.

Music has always been the one reliable salve for any sort of existential dilemma, it worked at the age of fourteen the same as it does at fifty, even if the shimmy across the floor isn't as dramatic as it was in 1982. There is a new stereo cabinet, it is walnut as well, a dark wood grain with glass doors that open up wide, a line of lights run under the top that make the wood, and thus the music, sparkle a little bit more than it should.

I go to the grocery store, mostly at night, wheeling the metal cart through empty aisles thinking of all the choices of food that I would never eat. In fact much of the food I buy will get tossed out in a few weeks anyway. What can one person do with ten bananas? Learning to buy just two is something that hasn't happened yet, every time I pull two from a bunch I feel like I'm breaking up a family, ripping somebody off. They all go brown soon enough.

There is a park down the street, one we went to often with the dog. The sprite white thing would gallop across the fields, stopping to smell and pee on patches of grass that only a dog would understand the deeper meaning of. It's just grass to me. The dogs in the park circle each other, crouching down on their hind legs, attuned to one's another's submissiveness. I have her over as well, maybe once or twice a week. The first few times she peed on the floor, no doubt trying to cover the stench of the cats that used to live in the apartment. Layers of cat piss and unwashed floors gave the place a distinct odor, but after what seemed like a billion times mopping and cleaning the vents out, it's now developing its own smell, mostly of coffee and flowers. The kids can walk to the park, having to be mindful of some of the homeless who make small camps in the woods, but tend to be harmless. Their lives are a daily battle of getting warm and walking to the nearby pantry to get fed, obtaining clean socks, and somehow feeling like they are a part of society. A part of *something*.

That's what's so hard to find. Connection. The strands of love seem brittle, they get pulled too much one way, and then get wrapped around one another in the most difficult of all manners, twisted and frustrated—they can break, or just get to the breaking point. Expectations, some spoken, most not, line the path of life like thick roots just barely above the surface, small traps that trip and grab from underneath. At night, when the music is drifting from the other room, it could be Mahler or some other composer, the living room feels slowly lived in while the insides collapse, dying in short breaths. Living room indeed.

A giant hole sits in the middle of something that isn't really there. There are some people who skate along the edges, eyes open wide, laughing with glee, and all the while it pulls them in. I was attracted to this for many years, living fifteen feet from the edge, just close enough to smell the depths of nothingness, with the ability to reach out and touch the skaters and madcaps who gleaned their energy for life from this void. Jenny never lived in the world as I knew it— hers was distilled and fractured through a mind that never stopped, that hopscotched through life as her thoughts skated on the thinnest sheet of ice, ice so thin one would think she walked on water.

Recently, unpacking the past, box by box, photo by photo, flyer by flyer, cassette by cassette, I found a tape of her first homemade recordings. I had thought this was lost forever, as music gushed out of her in sporadic fits, she would record it quickly and then file it away. Her life was always scattered, fractured as much as her mind, most of her belongings fell by the wayside over the years. These were songs she recorded alone on a four track one of our roommates had, a small black machine that tended to muffle songs, transforming them into something distant and frail. They were already broken but the four-track seemed to have a "loneliness-effect" that made everything sound even farther away.

These types of recordings were the same kind that Jerry Wick played me back when I first met him. In his narrow messy bedroom, sheets upturned, Chuck Taylors under the stack of fanzines, a poster of Mudhoney tacked up on the wall. He scooted unwashed clothes into the corner as he re-claimed the space for me and Jenny to sit down. He sat on the mattress that rested cheek to cheek with his smelly carpeted floor. He may have not even played these songs for anybody else—it became apparent over the next few years that his privacy was paramount. Very few people would enter his space until he finally bought a house shortly before he passed away.

It had been nearly 30 years since she recorded it, but the other night, I finally put it in the cassette deck that I purchased with my first credit card— a Sears card that had a five-hundred-dollar credit limit. My friend Matt Majesky drove me to get it, and I had the foresight to purchase the dual deck so I could dub tape to tape. I hadn't played any cassettes in quite a while. I was a bit worried that it might eat the tape, as this has happened to me plenty of times in the past (see the Guided by Voices song, "Hardcore UFOs"). But there she was, all of nineteen or twenty, singing in what sounded like a closet, short songs about frustration, with hints of burgeoning mental illness, and echoes of the voices that were starting to appear in her head.

One song stood out to me, she called it "Looney Tunes". Her voice, desolate and small, sings, *"The girl is crazy but not for him, the girl is crazy, she's just plain crazy, I mean crazy, looney tunes"* It becomes apparent she was singing about herself. There are other clues to her mindset, clues that predict her slow demise into unsettled madness. The first song, "And I loved You" has a line about "just sitting in a bar", the next song "Thoughts Go Away" goes darker even in light of its bouncy and catchy melody, "Lying in my bed and

I want to say no" and "I'm not the kind of girl who puts up a fight". Sounds innocent enough in the context of her small Casio, but at this point in her life she had been sexually assaulted several times. Listening to these songs for the first time in thirty years, I am struck by the very deep sadness that shrouded her life. She was drenched in pain, yet she held her head high and made the world laugh. The only way to let it creep out was through the small sounds beeping from her keyboard, and words trying to string it all together.

We were kids, barely able to understand how we made it out of adolescence and high school as we tried to patch a billion tiny holes in our lives with the only things we had: laughter and drink. And every hole held a story. Sex was too dangerous, the distrust too great and the animosity too tender to move towards any kind of resolution. We flailed into one another, bumping aimlessly into everyone and everything around us. But we operated on an inner radar, a radar that responded to sounds, and communicated through songs. Songs sung on stages, songs played on turntables and on cheap noisy car cassette decks— music was our language. It still is.

acknowledgements

This book was written over a period of years, sprung from memories that tumbled out during a vacation in the Netherlands. The book idea came after the writing, mostly years afterwards and it wasn't until Jenny passed away that I received a call from Joe Stienhardt about making the writing into this book. Lisa Carver was essential for the creation and her courage, smarts, humor and tenderness were/are amazing—she is one of the funniest and most brilliant people I have ever met. The memories are memories, and in that sense, they are not always accurate, and I am sure somethings I have written about are maybe wrong in terms of dates and happenings although I have tried to be as accurate as I can be. One of the things I miss about Jenny is her memory, even in her darkest depths she was able to recall some of the tiniest details of conversations, so I could not bounce anything off her as the book came together. If I am mistaken in any of my recollections, I am sorry, but I hope the essence of the book resonates with any of the participants anyway. Anyway. —*Bela, fall of 2019*

Acknowledgements: Many thanks to the following for their words of encouragement, inspiration and belief in this book. To Jenny and Jerry whom I think about every day and have been so important to my life and those whom they touched through the sheer force of their personality and their music. To my family: Susan Hartzband, Steve Goldsberry, Zoltan and Erica. All the bands and people mentioned in the book especially the members of Gaunt, the New Bomb Turks, Moviola, TJSA, Scrawl, GBV, Chuck Cleaver, The Cheater Slicks and everyone from Used Kids. Extra thanks to Lisa Carver (whose editing was essential to putting this book together), Chris Beister, Jay Brown, Andrew Choi, Liz Clayton, GC, Dan Dougan, Ken Eppstein, Amber Feit, Erika G., Michael Galinsky, Gretchen, Tim Hinely, Kelly Hogan, Daniel Hoyt, Eli Kasan, Brian Koscho, Lizard, Paul Lukas, Matt Majesky, Joe Moore, Nick Nocera, Matt Ogborn, Joel Oliphint, Rachel Leffel Orzechowski, Henry Owings, Tim Peacock, Maggie Smith, Matt Reber, Cynthia Santiglia, Ginger Shatto, Joe Stienhart, Gilmore Tamny, Two Dollar Radio—Eric & Eliza Wook Obenauf, Brett and Hanif, Merijn van der Heijden, Vicky Wheeler, Steve Turner, Eric Zimmer and most importantly Saskia and Bruno Koe-Krompecher.

Photos: All photos used by permission from Jay Brown except the last photo of Jenny by Bela Koe-Krompecher

Cover design: Henry Owings